CTHULHU
D·A·R·K · A·G·E·S

Quod in aeternum cubet mortuum non est,
et saeculis miris actis etiam mors perierit.

*That is not dead which can eternal lie,
and with strange aeons, even death may die.*

BRP

A Basic Roleplaying
Game

H. P. Lovecraft

1890-1937

Acknowledgments

Thanks are due to my wife Lydie, Kevin Anderson, Hervé and Benjamin Boudoir, Christophe Château, Frank Heller, Andreas Melhorn, and all play-testers for reviewing *Cthulhu Dark Ages* and instigating many decisive improvements. Special thanks go to Hannes Kaiser for checking the historical consistency of *Cthulhu Dark Ages*, to Christian Bloom for his scholarly knowledge of dead languages, and to Stephen Posey for his abnormally high Cthulhu Mythos skill — we pray for his soul!

Many thanks to our many supporters out there on the web; I can't name them all for lack of space and for fear of forgetting a few (mind the wrath of Mythos cultists). Walk through the gate to the Strange Aeons mailing list hosted by Chaosium to find them all (and maybe a few detractors too). Thanks in particular to Richard Extall of Dark Moon Design for his beautiful Dark Ages investigator sheet and to Matt Wiseman of Shoggoth.net for his support.

Last but not least, I want to express my thanks and affection to my three "old" pals Eric Brisson, Philippe Vallet and Jacques Baudrier with whom it all started in the late 70's. And a sad thought for Eric Devisscher — my first player ever — who eventually lost his sanity because of real life, and with it his desire to live.

CTHULHU
D·A·R·K · A·G·E·S

Stéphane Gesbert
original text

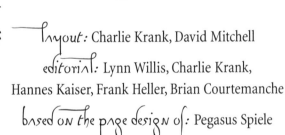

Layout: Charlie Krank, David Mitchell

editorial: Lynn Willis, Charlie Krank,
Hannes Kaiser, Frank Heller, Brian Courtemanche

based on the page design of: Pegasus Spiele

cover painting: Francois Launet

interior illustrations: Stéphane Gesbert, François Launet,
Andy Hopp, David Grilla, Meghan McLean

maps: Stéphane Gesbert & Björn Lensig • photographs: Gero "Zodiak" Pappe

handouts: Kostja Kleye

additional spell text: Lynn Willis, Brian M. Sammons, Charlie Krank

Chaosium is: Lynn Willis, Charlie Krank,
Dustin Wright, David Mitchell, Fergie
& various odd critters

Published 2004

German version by Pegasus Spiele GmbH October 2002

CHAOSIUM INC.

Table of Contents

Introduction 5

The Game System 9
  Characteristics 11
  Game System Terms 14-15
  Creating an Investigator 17
  Occupations 18
  Skills 22
  Rules 28
  Resistance Table 33
  Physical Injury 34
  Spot Rules for Injuries 36-37
  Hand-to-Hand Combat 39
  Spot Rules for Combat 40-42
  Weapons Tables 44-46
  Sanity & Insanity 47
  Costs, Equipment & Services 52

Utilities .53
  The World 53
  Cities & Trade .59
  A Quick Tour of the World 61
  Map of the World 65
  Dark Ages Glossary 66-68
  A Hundred Years & More 69-71
  Natural Disasters 71-72
  Who's Who 73

The Cthulhu Mythos 74

The Old Grimoire 77
  The Spells 82
  Limbo 91
  Books of the Mythos & More 93
  Non-Mythos Occult Books 96

Bestiary 97
  Beasts & Demons 98
  Encounter Tables 99
  Creatures of the Mythos 101
  Spirits & Limbo Creatures 114
  Deities of the Mythos 119

The Tomb (scenario) 124
  Keeper Play Aids 125
  November 1st, 998 A.D. 127
  The Civitas .131
  Hinterlands .136
  The Ambush 140
  Eye of the Storm 142
  At the Crossroads 144
  The Black Hill 146
  Statistics 157
  Player Handouts 164

Investigator Sheet 170-171

Index 172-173

Introduction

And I saw a beast rise out of the sea; and on its horns were ten diadems, and on its heads were blasphemous names.

–Revelation 13:1.

950 A.D. The Occident is torn apart: empires and kingdoms have endured two centuries of invasions, and now warlords fight over the remains like wild dogs. The clergy is weak and morally depraved, cities are depopulated, trade is stagnant and violence reigns everywhere. History is coming into the Sixth Age of mankind, the ultimate age before the end of the world.

950 A.D. The Byzantine Theodorus Philetas translates the *al-Azif* into Greek, and renames it the *Necronomicon*. It will take one century before the blasphemous tome is finally condemned, and most copies destroyed.

Cthulhu Dark Ages continues with Lovecraft's sinister tradition of men and women struggling against the dark forces of the Cthulhu Mythos. However, *Cthulhu Dark Ages* explores a "Dark Ages" era not yet spanned by Lovecraftian tales: 950–1050 A.D., nearly one thousand years before the period generally considered in *Call of Cthulhu*.

In this troubled era, in these hundred years when manuscript copies of the *Necronomicon* circulated from hand to hand, mankind almost yields to the uncaring forces of the Mythos: the dark young of Shub-Niggurath infest boundless forests, mi-go guard mountain tops, ghouls and miri nigri haunt burial grounds, and deep ones infiltrate coastal settlements. Nyarlathotep wanders about the earth in his thousand disguises. Great Cthulhu slumbers in the abyss, dreaming of the Seventh Age, when he will be unchained to rise out of the sea and walk the earth again. The last magi try powers that are not meant for humans, and are lured into Limbo, abode of Yog-Sothoth.

What This Book Covers

Cthulhu Dark Ages is a complete roleplaying game, fully compatible with the philosophy and game system of *Basic Roleplaying* and *Call of Cthulhu*. Owing to particularities of the Dark Ages, and demonstrating the flexibility of the

system, some adjustments and additions to the game have been made as described in the Game System chapter.

Cthulhu Dark Ages introduces The Old Grimoire chapter, which combines traditional elements of witchcraft and rituals from ancient religions. *Cthulhu Dark Ages* also develops the notions of Limbo (the interstices between spheres of existence) and spirits (ghosts, Old Ones) that appear in the *Cthulhu* rulebook and in Lovecraft's work. A selection of new Mythos creatures and traditional Mythos foes likely to be met during this era, as well as deities and beasts, is given in the Bestiary chapter.

A scenario near the end of this book introduces *Cthulhu Dark Ages'* grim world to players and keepers. In this tale investigators will face new unearthly enemies, and may discover scriptures more ancient than the *Necronomicon* itself.

Finally, the "Utilities" chapter is a complete guide to the 950–1050 A.D. era.

Cthulhu Dark Ages welcomes both beginning roleplayers and experienced *Call of Cthulhu* players and keepers into a world of harsh existence and ancient horrors.

Role-Playing in the Dark Ages

Cthulhu Dark Ages is historically set and presents keepers and players with a contradictory world of absolute oppression and wild impunity. In the Dark Ages almost everyone has a lord to serve, and social status largely predetermines one's fate. On the other hand, the world is rapidly changing and the changes breed more freedom than earlier or later in the Middle Ages: ambitious brigands sometimes settle down as frontier warlords, and a farmer boy named Gerbert eventually becomes Pope!

In *Cthulhu Dark Ages* the players take the part of investigators, and attempt to solve a mystery or resolve a situation in which the forces of the Mythos have affected Dark Ages life. As in other eras explored in the *Call of Cthulhu* rules, the ability to read Latin or to use a library is often worth far more than high skill with a weapon. Indeed, swords and arrows do not harm the most powerful creatures. Besides, Dark Ages societies have drastic ways of dealing with people who attract too

much attention, or present any form of threat to established customs and authority.

In the Dark Ages, social status — as represented in the game by the Status skill — reflects a person's intrinsic valor as well as personal reputation and monetary worth. In the absence of personal archives, sheer status is often accepted as a guarantee of trustworthiness. Dark Ages people spare no effort to discover the real status and wealth of a stranger.

First Encounters

A repeated challenge facing the keeper at the beginning of play is the manner in which the investigators come together. Investigators inevitably enjoy different backgrounds and occupations. Combinations of investigators of different status may be difficult to justify and maintain in a strictly medieval setting. Such interesting mixtures may very well arise in odd circumstances though, and produce exciting roleplay.

Here follow a few suggestions for first meetings (the last two in particular may bring together investigators of very different origins):

- All investigators answer an employment offer by their mutual lord, to perform some deed important to his or her cause.

- All investigators have a mutual friend, who asks them for a favor.

- All investigators are confronted with the same mystery. It may be a series of unexplained events, an obscure prophecy, or some vile intrigue.

- All investigators are present at some incident. Their common destiny is sealed when all become involved.

Here are examples of compatible occupations (see the Game System chapter for more details on occupations):

- All belong to a noble *familia* (family) or are related to it. Nobles are more or less free to do what they please, have resources and good conditions for investigative role-playing. Occupations: warrior, guard, household officer, sergeant, etc.

- All are men of the church or are related to a clerical institution or a religious order. Such investigators must observe the laws of the church, are generally well instructed and only rarely bound to servile work, and they are (presumably) devoted to the eradication of evil. Ideal occupations for investigating the horrors of the Mythos. Occupations: scholar, priest, monk/nun, cleric, mayor, etc.

- All are from the same community or are related to it. This could be a farmers' village, a fishermen's village, or a craftsmen's or a merchants' guild. Restrictions: such communities are often bound to a particular locality. Occupations: farmer, woodsman/fisherman, craftsman/shopkeeper, merchant, small trader, sailor, etc.

- All are misfits or outcasts of society. Restrictions: most of these people have to operate on the fringes of society, and possibly lack resources or status. Occupations: beggar, healer, hermit/heretic, juggler/minstrel, pilgrim, mercenary/brigand, etc.

Don't take the above classification at face value. For instance, investigators from a village community may be people with very different backgrounds: a sergeant, a priest, free and unfree farmers (including craftsmen and women, the local militia), a trader, a healer, and so forth.

Remember that the purpose of horror roleplaying is to have a good time. Rules and historical settings are just vehicles for play. Whether you stick to them or ignore them is secondary to having fun.

Rule by Fear

The oldest and strongest emotion of mankind is fear. And the oldest and strongest kind of fear is fear of the unknown.

—H. P. Lovecraft.

This famous quote from Lovecraft (the opening sentences in "Supernatural Horror in Literature") nicely sums up the reason why people play *Call of Cthulhu*: to have a good scare. Based on the premise that "the fear of any expected evil (stumbling across a half-eaten corpse in a cemetery) is worse than the evil itself (a ghoul)," here are seven ideas that can help the keeper to "rule by fear," in the Dark Ages as well as in other eras.

"Why don't you move, then? Tired? Well, don't worry, my friend, for they are coming . . . . Look, look, curse you, look! . . . It's just over your left shoulder . . . ."

—H. P. Lovecraft, "From Beyond".

CULTIVATE YOUR OWN FEARS: what books, movies, or situations really scare you? Ask yourself why and how, and whether the same situations and artifices could be used in the game.

At nightfall, * signed me to come to the deck and showed me the point of the mainmast. I believe I fell on my knees. A strange sky bent over the rumbling sea; the familiar

constellations were gone; unknown stars, arranged in new geometric patterns, shone weakly in a cosmic abyss of terrifying blackness — Jesus! I said. God! Where are we?

—Jean Ray, "The Mainz Psalter".

STOKE YOUR LOVE FOR THE UNCANNY: uncanny events (as lead-ups to horrifying ones) can be accounted for by reason, but at the same time hint at a far more terrible reality. Dim the investigators' senses, and surround them with odd occurrences and troubling coincidences.

The boughs surely moved, and there was no wind.

—H. P. Lovecraft, "The Colour Out of Space".

KNOW YOUR PLAYERS: the keeper scares players, not their investigators. Learn the players' weaknesses, their phobias (fear of heights, loud noises, pain and death, the loss of loved ones, darkness, spiders or snakes, etc.), and exploit them in the game.

The swine began growing grey and brittle and falling to pieces before they died, and their eyes and muzzles developed singular alterations.

—H.P. Lovecraft, "The Colour Out of Space".

MINIMIZE THE PLAYERS' COMFORT ZONE: help the players to forget about the real world and to identify themselves with the investigators. General keeper strategies and background information to that effect can be found in the *Call of Cthulhu* rulebook. Avoid, for instance, game jargon like "hit points." Play by candlelight in a dark room. Put investigators in situations of guilt, failure, isolation, weakness, etc.

And for seventeen years after that West would look frequently over his shoulder, and complain of fancied footsteps behind him. Now he has disappeared.

—H. P. Lovecraft, "Herbert West: Reanimator".

LEAVE THE PLAYERS IN THE DARK: the worst kind of fear is the fear imagined by the player, not the keeper. Fear resides not in the things the keeper describes to the players, but hides in what he does not. Make players hesitate about the nature of the threat: mundane or supernatural? Keep players in a perpetual state of doubt and tension. You know you're on the right track when players start imagining threats that aren't there.

Then with utter and horrifying suddenness we heard a frightful sound from below. It was from the tethered horses — they had screamed, not neighed, but screamed . . . and there was no light down there, nor the sound of any human thing, to shew why they had done so.

—H. P. Lovecraft, "The Very Old Folk".

SURPRISE PLAYERS: veteran *Call of Cthulhu* players can be a challenge for keepers. To them, deep ones, ghouls, etc., have simply become another aspect of reality. Make them wrong! Change rules, modify creatures in forbidding ways, add creepy side effects to spells, etc. Avoid standards and templates like the plague.

They had the regulation caps of a railway company, and I could not doubt but that they were conductor and motorman. Then one of them sniffed with singular sharpness, and raised his face to howl to the moon. The other dropped on all fours to run toward the car.

—H. P. Lovecraft, "The Thing in the Moonlight".

KNOW WHEN TO STOP: at times, all of the above can become too frustrating or stressful for the players. If the players feel manipulated, they will quickly lose interest in the game. Always allow for moments of rest and score settling; offer a temporary safe haven, an acceptable (yet potentially wrong) explanation for what happened, etc.

The most merciful thing in the world, I think, is the inability of the human mind to correlate all its contents. We live on a placid island of ignorance in the midst of black seas of infinity, and it was not meant that we should voyage far.

—H. P. Lovecraft, "The Call of Cthulhu".

References

Here are the main sources for *Cthulhu Dark Ages*. Many little details were gathered from a large number

of secondary references, much too long to be listed here. The keeper is invited to read some of the Lovecraftian fiction to get context for his or her *Cthulhu Dark Ages* adventures. Many of these can be found on the chaosium.com website.

Call of Cthulhu Fiction

Lovecraft, H.P. *The Dunwich Horror and Others.* Arkham House, 1985. "The Colour out of Space," "The Haunter of the Dark," "The Dunwich Horror."

Lovecraft, H.P. *At the Mountains of Madness and Other Novels.* Arkham House, 1985. "Through the Gates of the Silver Key."

Lovecraft, H.P. *Dagon and Other Macabre Tales.* Arkham House, 1987. "From Beyond," "The Hound," "The Horror at Red Hook," "Supernatural Horror in Literature."

Lovecraft, H.P., and others. *Tales of the Cthulhu Mythos.* Arkham House, 1990. Howard, Robert E., "The Black Stone"; Long, Frank Belknap, "The Hounds of Tindalos."

Campbell, R. *Cold Print.* TOR, 1987. "The Church in High Street," "The Moon-Lens."

Lovecraft, H.P. *Miscellaneous Writings.* Arkham House, 1995. "Nyarlathotep," "The Very Old Folk."

Harms, D. *The Encyclopedia Cthulhiana.* Chaosium, 2003.

Howard, Robert E., and others. *Nameless Cults.* Chaosium, 2001. "The Black Stone," "People of the Dark," "The Worms of the Earth," "The Shadow Kingdom."

General References

Panati, C. *Sacred Origins of Profound Things.* Penguin, 1996.

Encyclopaedia Brittanica. 1995.

The Holy Bible, New Revised Standard Version. Oxford, 1989.

Charles, R. H., trans. *The Book of Enoch.* SPCK, 1977.

Call of Cthulhu, The Keeper's Companion vol. 1, The Creature Companion, The Complete Dreamlands, Cthulhu by Gaslight, and *Elric!* Chaosium Inc., various dates.

Game System

Altmann, H. *Poisonous Plants and Animals.* Chatto and Windus, 1980.

Banbury, P. *Man and the Sea.* Adlard Coles, 1975.

Bestiary

Comte, F. *Dictionary of Mythology.* Wordsworth Reference, 1994.

Davidson, H. R. Ellis. *Gods and Myths of Northern Europe.* Penguin, 1990.

Lecouteux, C. *Les Nains et les Elfes au Moyen Age.* Imago, 1988.

Thomassin, S. and Marquart, J.J. *Je Découvre les Animaux Sauvages.* André Leson, 1978.

The Dark Ages

Delort, R. *La France de L'an Mil.* Seuil, 1990.

Dhont, J., revised and updated by Rouche, M. *Le Haut Moyen Age.* Bordas, 1976.

Hinz, H.M. and Wieczorek, A., editors. *Europe's Centre around A.D. 1000.* Theiss, 2000.

Man, J. *Atlas of the Year 1000.* Penguin, 1999.

Pognon, E. *La Vie Quotidienne en L'an Mille.* Hachette, 1981.

Sancha, S. *The Castle Story.* Collins, 1991.

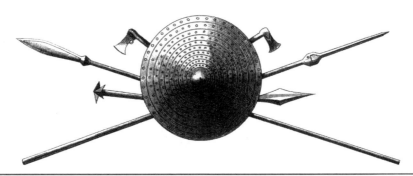

The Game System

But as it becometh disciples to obey their master, so also it becometh the master to dispose all things with prudence and justice. Therefore, let all follow the Rule as their guide in everything, and let no one rashly depart from it.
— The Holy Rule of St. Benedict (foundation of the Benedictine Order).

Cthulhu Dark Ages is an adaptation of the *Call of Cthulhu* and *Basic Roleplaying* rules, so character generation and the game system remain familiar if you have played those games. However life in the tenth or eleventh centuries is quite different from life in the nineteenth or the twentieth. This chapter discusses Dark Ages "investigators" (as the player-characters are called) their occupations and available skills, and focuses on specific rules for this era, including combat, disease and insanity.

Rolling the Dice

People new to roleplaying may never have seen dice with other than six sides. A variety of these different shapes can be found at most game stores and hobby shops. You'll need them in order to play the game as intended. Each player normally provides his own dice.

For the most part, *Call of Cthulhu* calls for three dice roll results — abbreviated as D100, D8, and D6 — to judge the success of a skill use, to indicate how many hit points were lost to a wound or fall, etc. These sorts of dice also can provide results equivalent to D20, D10, D4, D3, D2, and so on.

The letter D stands for the singular *die* or plural *dice*. The numerals after the D stands for the range of random numbers sought: D8 generates the numbers 1-8, for instance, while D100 generates the numbers 1-100.

D100 (Percentile Dice)

Percentile dice (as the abbreviation D100 means) usually consist of two 10-sided dice of different colors, rolled at the same time. Most such dice are numbered 1, 2, 3, 4, 5, 6, 7, 8, 9, 0. After rolling, read the top number on such a die to get the result.

Read the die of one color consistently as the tens-column, and the other as the ones column: thus a result of 2-3 reads as 23, a result of 0-1 reads as 1, and a result of 1-0 reads as 10. A result of 0-0 represents 100.

D8 (Eight-Sided Die)

This die has eight sides, numbered 1, 2, 3, 4, 5, 6, 7, and 8. Throw the die and read its top number as the result.

D6 (Six-Sided Die)

This sort is what people normally think of as dice. The D6 has six sides, and is numbered 1, 2, 3, 4, 5, 6. Throw the die and read its top number as the result.

D4 (Four-Sided or Eight-Sided Die)

Some versions of the D4 have four sides. There is also an eight-sided version that gives each result twice. For either version, throw the die and read the top number as the result.

Simulating Other Dice

Occasionally players may need to make D20, D10, D5, or D3 rolls. If such dice are unavailable, such results can be simulated with D100, D8, or D6 dice. D20 and D4 dice are also available and are more satisfactory to use if needed often.

- For D20, roll a ten-sided die and a six-sided die. If the D6 result is 1, 2, 3 the result is the face amount of the ten-sided die (0 counts as 10). If the D6 result is 4, 5, 6 add ten to the face amount of the ten-sided die.

- For a D10 roll, roll one of the percentile dice.

- For D5, roll a ten-sided die and divide the result by two: thus 1, 2 = 1, and 9, 0 = 5.

- For D4, roll D8 and divide the result by two: thus 1, 2 = 1, and 7, 8 = 4; or roll D6 and ignore 5, 6.

- For D3, roll D6 and divide the result by two: thus 1, 2 = 1, and 5, 6 = 3.

- For D2, roll D6 and divide the result by three: thus 1, 2, 3 = 1 and 4, 5, 6 = 2.

Different Value Dice Rolls

Sometimes a dice notation is preceded by a number. That number tells the reader that more than one die should be rolled, and that their results should be added together. For instance, 2D6 means that two six-sided dice should be rolled at the same time, and the results totaled. If you don't have enough dice to roll all at once, roll what you have for the requisite number of times and total the results.

Sometimes pluses or minuses are tacked on to die rolls. You might see 1D6+1, for instance, or 1D8-2. This means that the number following the plus sign should be added or subtracted from the result of the D6 roll. For 1D6+1, the final result must be 2, 3, 4, 5, 6, or 7.

A notation may require that different dice be rolled at one time. If a monster's claws do 1D6+1+2D4 damage, find the power of the actual attack by rolling the three requested dice, totaling your results, and then increasing the total by one. The notation +db appended to attack damage reminds the keeper to include the creature's damage bonus.

Characteristics

To create an investigator, first establish his or her *characteristics*. A characteristic is one of nine numbers which define most human characters in this game. These numbers are as basic in their way as skeleton and muscles. Usually it is better to have higher characteristics.

Characteristics rarely increase after being rolled, because investigators are created as adults. Characteristics do occasionally decrease as a consequence of magical or physical injury. Though a suggestion is included for each characteristic, the effect of 0 or 01 in a characteristic is mostly left for the keeper to describe. It should be suitable to the cause and consequence — horrible, grievous, or funny. Such a loss is always a blow to the player, too. As an identity rounds into full personality, though, every player shares in the pleasure.

APP (Appearance)

Appearance measures the investigator's relative attractiveness and friendliness. Some multiple of APP might be useful in social encounters. Initial impressions do not necessarily last. APP measures what one sees in the mirror; it can represent a quality of charisma but not personal leadership, nor does it represent the ability to problem-solve. An investigator without APP is appallingly ugly, provoking comment and shock everywhere.

Attraction (Charisma) Roll (APP x5)

The Attraction (or Charisma) roll represents a confluence of communication skills for which no game skill exists. Did he make a good impression? Did she catch everybody's attention?

CON (Constitution)

This characteristic concerns health, vigor, and vitality. It represents thresholds for resisting drowning and suffo-cation. The higher the CON, the better. Poisons and diseases may directly challenge investigator Constitutions. High-CON investigators often have higher hit points, the better to resist injury and attack. Serious physical injury or magical attack might lower CON. If Constitution reaches 0, the investigator dies.

DEX (Dexterity)

Investigators with higher Dexterity scores are quicker, nimbler, and more physically flexible. A keeper might call for a Dexterity roll in order to grab a support, to stay upright in high winds or on ice, to accomplish some delicate task, or to take something without being noticed.

In combat, the character with the highest DEX-rank attacks first. With the highest DEX-rank, a character may be able to disarm or disable a foe before the foe can attack.

DEX x2 determines the initial percentage of the investigator's Dodge skill.

An investigator without DEX is uncoordinated, unable to perform physical tasks without also receiving a successful Luck roll.

Dexterity Roll (DEX x5)

The Dexterity roll allows manipulation skills to be judged for which no game skill exists. It could decide, for instance if the investigator is able to pick that lock (Dark Ages locks are simple), or is able to grab the vine at the edge of the cliff.

EDU (Education)

Education measures the relative knowledge possessed by the investigator, as well as the number of years it took to acquire that learning. It is possible to have an education without having been taught by a tutor or scholar. An investigator would also have needed to be supported while the education occurred.

- EDU measures information, not the intelligent use of information.

- EDU partly determines how many skill points are allotted to occupations.

- EDU x5 represents the investigator's starting percentage with the Own Language skill.

Know Roll (EDU x5)

The Know roll represents what the brain has stored up. The investigator might recognize the symptoms of hoof-and-mouth disease, remember the geography of Wales, or know the number of a spider's legs. The Know roll never exceeds 100, even though a well educated investigator might have EDU 21.

INT (Intelligence)

Intelligence represents how well investigators learn, remember, and analyze, and of how aware they are of their surroundings. To help describe different circumstances, keepers use INT times various multipliers and then call for D100 rolls equal to or less than the products. INT x5 — the Idea roll — is popular. For more about it, see further below.

Difficult concepts, plans, and guesses are less likely to yield results — they get lower multipliers, down to INT x1.

An investigator without INT is a babbling, drooling idiot.

If a character's amount of Intelligence seems to contradict another characteristic, that's another chance for roleplaying: an investigator with high EDU and low INT might be a pedantic teacher, one who knows facts but not their meanings. Conversely, high INT and low EDU might illustrate ignorance in a character, but this person would not be dull-witted.

Idea Roll (INT x5)

The Idea roll represents hunches and the ability to interpret disparate evidence into something meaningful. The Idea roll is a handy way to show awareness — did the investigator observe and understand what he saw? — should he have come away with a particular feeling about a gathering or a place?

Save the Spot Hidden skill for specific clues or items not immediately noticeable. Employ the Insight skill when dealing with individuals.

POW (Power)

Power indicates force of will. The higher one's POW, the higher the aptitude for magic. Power does not quantify leadership, which is a matter for roleplaying. The amount of Power or the number of magic points (they derive from Power) measure resistance to magical or hypnotic attack, and also indicate what spells the owner can cast.

An investigator without POW is zombie-like and unable to use magic. A few spells may call for sacrifice of POW; unless stated otherwise, lost POW is lost permanently.

POW x5 is the Luck roll, about which see further below. POW x5 also equals a character's initial Sanity characteristic. The POW of most characters rarely changes; your keeper can alert you if your characteristic changes.

The number of Power points also equals the character's number of magic points. Unlike POW, magic points can be spent and regenerated.

Luck Roll (POW x5)

Luck is the ability to be in the right place at the right time. Does the investigator step on a bridge that holds, or does the bridge give way? The Luck roll is a quick way to learn the answer.

Magic Points (maximum = POW)

An investigator's maximum magic points equal his or her POW. Magic points can be spent casting spells or fighting off malign influences. They represent that personal force that resists the effect of spells. Be cautious when casting spells: spells cost magic points and that expenditure weakens the caster's magical defense. A character's spell resistance is always calculated by using *current magic points*.

Magic points naturally regenerate; all can return in 24 hours, prorate the return of partial losses. Should magic points reach zero, the investigator falls unconscious until a point regenerates.

Should POW decrease, magic points would not diminish until spent. Then they would regenerate only to the new maximum. Should POW increase, magic points would begin to increase at one point per hour until reaching the new maximum.

SAN (Sanity)

Find Sanity by multiplying POW x5. Sanity is crucial to investigators and central to the idea of this game. Elsewhere a short chapter is devoted to Sanity (pages

Game System Terms

These terms are common to the *Cthulhu Dark Ages* game system. For terms special to the Dark Ages, see the Dark Ages Glossary in the Utilities chapter, pp. 66-68.

BASE CHANCE: the percentage chance that an untrained investigator can successfully use a skill. Some skills cannot be picked up quickly by untrained characters, and thus have a 1% base chance. On the other hand almost everyone has a good chance of successfully using skills such as Climb, and so such skills have larger base chances.

CHARACTERISTIC: eight characteristics determine a player character's fundamental capacities. They are Strength, Constitution, Size, Intelligence, Power, Dexterity, Appearance, and Education. A ninth characteristic, Sanity, derives from Power.

CHECK, EXPERIENCE CHECK, SKILL CHECK: when an investigator successfully uses a skill and the keeper says something like "You get a check," then mark the box on the investigator sheet that is next to the skill. Roll for improvement when the keeper advises. Skills improve in 1D10-point increments. Improvement usually waits until the end of an adventure.

COMBAT ROUND, or ROUND: the elastic unit of game time against which character movement and skill use are compared. Actions in a round are resolved in DEX-rank order, highest to lowest.

CTHULHU: *kuh-THOO-loo in Chaosium-ese*. Cthulhu's obscene gigantic bulk lies sleeping in dread drowned R'lyeh, but is prophecied to rise again "when the stars are right". He often sends nightmarish dreams which plague sensitive dreamers. He is one of the Great Old Ones. Cthulhu's earthly cultists are many. He was created in tales by H. P. Lovecraft, and since has been present or been intimated in hundreds or thousands of stories by other authors. The Lovecraft story "The Call of Cthulhu" at the front of the *Call of Cthulhu* rules best summarizes him.

CTHULHU MYTHOS: the gods, entities, monsters, and fiendish knowledge of the greater universe. In contrast to what normal humans find comfortable to believe, the Cthulhu Mythos represents the secret horrifying truth about all things.

DAMAGE: in the game, attacks and accidents are said to *do damage* — that is, to create wounds and injuries. The game mechanics portray this by subtracting hit points from those to whom damage was done.

DAMAGE BONUS: a modifier for hand-to-hand attacks.

FAINTING: an optional symptom of temporary insanity. It's now out of style to faint, but Lovecraft's characters fainted regularly when under great mental stress. If your investigator is too tough to faint, perhaps he or she can rescue investigators who aren't.

FIRST AID: a successful roll immediately restores 1D3 hit points to a sick or injured character, but after one successful use it has no additional effect on a particular injury or sickness. See also Healing and Medicine.

FUMBLE: a D100 result of 00 is an automatic failure, usually the most catastrophic result possible in the situation.

HAND-TO-HAND: a fighting mode; a weapon attack or missile attack. Personal attacks such as Fist/Punch are also hand-to-hand attacks.

HEALING: sick and injured characters are able to heal naturally at the rate of 1D3 hit points per game week. See also First Aid and Medicine.

HIT POINTS: the average of a character's CON and SIZ. Hit points can be checked off to indicate a wound or injury. No play effect occurs for the loss of a few points. Unconsciousness arrives when 2 or fewer hit points are left. A character begins to die at 0 hit points.

HORROR: fear and repugnance intermixed, a feeling which perceives not just a threat, but a quality of intense wrongness or perversity about the threat, yielding a sense of strangeness or evil.

IMPALE: a D100 result which is one-fifth or less of a character's chance to hit with the attack. An impale represents a particularly successful attack, and consequently two damage rolls for that attack are made. Keepers also may accept the idea as inherent in a skill roll — one-fifth or less of a skill represents a fine performance, that should earn some extra reward.

INSANITY, INDEFINITE: when an investigator loses 20% or more of his or her current Sanity points within an hour of game time, the result is insanity as the keeper sees fit.

INSANITY, PERMANENT: if an investigator's current Sanity points reach zero, he or she becomes deeply insane for a period of months or years and be left to wander the earth.

INSANITY, TEMPORARY: if an investigator loses 5 or more Sanity points as the consequence of a single failed Sanity roll, he or she has suffered major grievance to the soul. The player must roll D100. If the result is equal or less than INT x5, the investigator comprehends what has been seen, and goes insane for a period of minutes or hours.

KEEPER: the person who runs the game. He or she knows the secrets of the plot, describes the situations and non-player characters, and determines what skills and rolls to apply.

MAGIC POINTS: magic points represent the fluctuating expression of characteristic Power. Magic points are inherent to humans and other intelligences. They are spent in casting, and and are the force that resists spells. Reaching 0 magic points, a character falls unconscious, and remains unconscious until one magic point regenerates. That takes an hour. Magic points regenerate at one point per game hour.

MEDICINE: European doctors of the Dark Ages can give First Aid,

Game System Terms

immediately restoring 1D3 hit points. Their hospital facilities help restore another 1D3-1 hit points. Arab doctors have better facilities and technique, and are able to restore 1D3+1 hit points per week. Finally, natural healing restores another 1D3 hit points per week. With first aid, natural healing, and an Arabian doctor and hospital, an investigator could be healed for 3D3+1 hit points during the first week of recovery. The same investigator in a Dark Ages hospital would heal for a maximum of 3D3-1 hit points. See also First Aid and Healing.

OCCCUPATION: what an investigator does for a living. An occupation never determines how a player character acts. In creating an investigator, he or she gets EDU x20 occupation points.

PARRY: against hand-to-hand attacks, a character may try one parry per round, to block or divert an intended blow. Determine success of the parry by an attack roll for the weapon. State the parry's target at the beginning of the combat round. A knowledgeable character may prefer to parry with a shield, because it offers more protection than a weapon parry.

PERCENTAGE: most die rolls in the game are D100 (percentage) rolls. Skills are expressed in percentages. Investigator skill percentages never rise above 99%. A roll of 00 is an automatic failure.

PERCENTILE: in game usage, any of 100 equal divisions that make up the whole. Percentiles may be added or subtracted from each other: thus *subtracting ten percentiles* from 60% yields 50%, while *subtracting ten percent* from 60% yields 54%.

PERSONAL ATTACK: Fist/Punch, Kick, Head Butt, or Grapple. An unarmed human can make one of these four hand-to-hand attacks per combat round.

PERSONAL INTEREST: in creating an investigator, the player can apply INT x10 skill points to any skill he or she desires.

PLAYERS: the audience-participants of the game.

RESISTANCE TABLE: a table which establishes target numbers for D100 rolls, allowing percentile rolls in order to resolve matches of one characteristic against another. See the Game System chapter.

SAN: this characteristic originally equals POW x5. Maximum SAN rarely changes, but can if POW changes.

SANITY: every character is sane, regardless of the number of Sanity points, unless 0 Sanity points has been reached, or unless the keeper has announced that a

state of temporary insanity or indefinite insanity has been reached by the character because of mental trauma. See Insanity.

SANITY POINTS: *current Sanity points* are the number of points shown in the investigator sheet Sanity points box. This number originates as equal to the SAN characteristic, but can fluctuate. *Maximum Sanity points* equal 99 minus whatever percentiles of the Cthulhu Mythos skill the investigator has. Sanity points can decrease or be increased, but they do not regenerate as do magic points and hit points.

SANITY ROLL: a D100 roll. A success is equal to or less than current Sanity points. A success may cost nominal Sanity points, or none at all. A failure always costs more, and leads toward temporary or indefinite insanity.

SCENARIO, ADVENTURE, STORY: an organized and plotted narrative devised for roleplaying, one which includes the sequence of events, character statistics, special rules and spells, and other descriptions which investigators may find useful, interesting, or evocative.

SKILL: in the game, a defined body of knowledge, technique, or physical ability, especially pertaining to investigators and the skills available to them. Many non-player characters list skills unknown to investigators — such skills are not game components, and are for keeper information only; they are unavailable to investigators.

SKILL ROLL: a D100 roll. A success is equal to or less than the character's skill percentage. A failure is higher than the character's skill percentage.

SPOT RULE: in the rules chapter or in the text of a scenario, minor rules covering special situations such as hand-to-hand combat, missile weapons, burning, drowning, etc.

SUCCESS: a successful D100 roll is a result equal to or less than the target number. A D100 result of 01 is always a success and the best result possible. See also Fumble.

UNCONSCIOUS: a character who reaches 0 magic points or who has 2 or fewer hit points left goes unconscious. So does a character who loses half or more of his hit points from a single wound or blow and whose player cannot then roll CON x5 or less on D100. Unconsciousness lasts from one combat round up to the time needed to regenerate 1 magic point or 2 hit points, as applicable. A successful First Aid or Medicine roll may return a character to consciousness.

10th Century Armor

47–51). It distinguishes between the SAN characteristic, Sanity points, and maximum Sanity. Sanity points fluctuate often in play; characteristic SAN rarely changes.

An investigator's maximum Sanity points are never more than 99. Sanity points of 99 represent the strongest possible mind, one capable of deflecting or lessening even extreme emotional shocks. On the other hand, 30 Sanity points would indicate a more fragile mind, which would be more easily driven into temporary or permanent madness. Most Mythos monsters and some natural events cost Sanity points to encounter, and some spells cost Sanity points to learn and cast.

SIZ (Size)

The characteristic SIZ averages height and weight into one number. To see over something, to squeeze through a small opening, or to judge whose head is sticking up out of the grass, use SIZ. Size also helps determine hit points and the damage bonus. One might decrease SIZ to indicate loss of a limb, but lowering DEX is more often the solution. If an investigator lost all SIZ, presumably he would disappear — to goodness knows where!

STR (Strength)

Strength measures the muscle power of an investigator. With it, judge how much they can lift, or push or pull, or how tightly they can cling to something. This characteristic is important in determining the damage investigators do in hand-to-hand combat. Reduced to Strength 0, an investigator is an invalid, unable to leave his or her bed.

Damage Bonus (STR + SIZ)

All physical beings have a damage bonus Characteristic rating. Smaller or weaker beings may not have an actual bonus, but instead have no bonus or a penalty assigned to their damage bonus rating. Nonetheless, the idea is simple: larger, stronger creatures do more physical damage than lesser, weaker brethren.

To determine a character's damage bonus, total STR and SIZ, and find that total on the Damage Bonus Table nearby. Each range of results correlates with a stated die roll. In hand-to-hand combat, add the indicated roll to all the character's blows, whether using a natural weapon such as a fist or a crafted weapon such a club or knife, and

Damage Bonus

STR + SIZ	DB
02 to 12	-1D6
13 to 16	-1D4
17 to 24	+0
25 to 32	+1D4
33 to 40	+1D6
41 to 56	+2D6
57 to 72	+3D6
73 to 88	+4D6

whether striking a foe or some object such as a door.

- For thrown objects, add half the thrower's damage bonus to the object's listed damage rating on the weapons table.

- Do not add damage bonuses to Bite attacks. The relative size and strength of the mouth is figured into the attack.

- Do not add damage bonuses to attacks which are independent of STR and SIZ, such as crossbow fire.

Hit Points (average of CON + SIZ)

All physical beings have hit points. Figure hit points by adding CON to SIZ and dividing the total by two. Round up any fraction.

When an investigator is injured or wounded, or otherwise loses hit points, use a pencil to mark off the lost hit points from the investigator sheet. Always apply the hit point loss before any loss to CON.

- Lost hit points heal naturally at 1D3 hit points per game week.

- First Aid heals 1D3 hit points immediately, but then is of no further use for that particular wound or injury.

  - A successful Medicine roll made in a hospital setting can restore 1D3-1 (Dark Ages hospital) or 1D3+1 (Arabian hospital) hit points per game week.

  - When hit points drop to two or less, characters go unconscious until regenerating enough hit points to wake.

  - If hit points reach zero or lower, the character dies unless hit points can be raised to at least +1 by the end of the following combat round.

Creating an Investigator

Investigator Creation Summary

- Allot 100 points among the eight characteristics Strength (STR), Constitution (CON), Size (SIZ), Intelligence (INT), Power (POW), Dexterity (DEX), Appearance (APP), and Education (EDU).

  The minimum assignable value for SIZ and INT is 8 (small, dull); for the other characteristics the minimum is 3 (weak, sickly, clumsy). The maximum assignable value for any characteristic is 18 (huge, brilliant, nimble, knowing). Characteristics may change during play.

  A ninth characteristic, Sanity (SAN), derives from Power x5.

- A Dexterity roll equals your DEX x5.
- An Idea roll equals your INT x5.
- A Know roll equals your EDU x5.
- A Luck roll equals your POW x5.
- A Charisma (or Attraction) roll equals your APP x5.
- Total your character's STR and SIZ, and find the investigator's damage bonus on the table nearby.
- Enter the number 99 for *99 minus Cthulhu Mythos*. If your investigator gains points in that skill, lower this number by a like amount.
- To determine *hit points*, total CON plus SIZ and divide by 2; round up any fraction.
- For *magic points*, circle that number equal to POW.
- For *Sanity points*, circle the number equal to SAN.

K eepers and players should photocopy the *Cthulhu Dark Ages* investigator sheet at the back of this book. The investigator sheet holds all the data needed for investigators to tackle mysteries.

Take a blank investigator sheet and find a pencil. You will also need dice and a scratch pad. It is often more fun to have all players create investigators together.

Name

Most people in the Dark Ages have no surname: John is just John. To further describe an investigator, or to distinguish between two with the same name, give a birthplace, as in John of Hereford, or an occupation, as in John Smith, or a distinguishing feature, as in Erik the Red.

Old French, German, or English first names are ideally suited for Dark Ages investigators, as are the more pious names from the Bible. Here are some typical examples:

Anglo-Saxon Names

MALE: Aelfhere, Aelfred, Aelfric, Aethelstan, Aethelweard, Aethelwulf, Aescwine, Birhtric, Birhtnoth, Caedmon, Centwine, Cenwulf, Cuthbert, Ealdhelm, Earcenbold, Godwine, Hildegils, Leofric, Leofwine, Odda, Offa, Ohthere, Penda, Sigebriht, Wighelm, Wigstan, Wufsige, Wulfstan, Wulfwige.

FEMALE: Aethelflaed, Aelfgyfu, Aehtelgythe, Eadgifu, Ealhraed, Hereswith, Hilda, Leofflaed, Leofware, Wihtburg.

Old French Names

MALE: Aimeri, Aimon, Aiol, Aleaume, Archembaud, Arnoul, Baudouin, Bruyant, Eustache, Fierbras, Fromondin, Galien, Gilles, Godefroi, Gui, Guibert, Guillaume, Hardouin, Jehan, Julien, Raimon, Raoul, Tancred, Thierry, Yves.

FEMALE: Adelaide, Adeline, Aiglante, Alienor, Beatrix, Beatrice, Belle, Berthe, Blonde, Catherine, Cecilia, Clarissa, Erembourg, Ermengarde, Esclarmonde, Heloise, Jehanne, Lutice, Mirabel, Nicolette, Olive, Oriabel, Passerose, Rosamonde.

Old High German Names

MALE: Adalbracht, Adalbert, Adaldac, Adelgero, Adam, Addo, Agilwulf, Aistulf, Albwin, Arnolf, Berchhold, Berengar, Bernefrid, Bernhard, Boppo, Buobo, Brun, Bruno, Chuonrad, Eberhart, Everhart, Egilulf, Egbert, Erkanbald, Erhard, Folcbert, Folcmar, Fulco,

Fulrad, Folkwin, Friderich, Gisilbert, Gislfred, Giselher, Geseprant, Godfrid, Goslin, Gozlin, Grimoald, Guntbrecht, Gundolfm Guntram, Gundelbert, Griffo, Gundpert, Gunther, Hatto, Heinrich, Herimann, Hermann, Hildulf, Ingo, Hubert, Ribald, Obert, Hugo, Lampert, Landemar, Liutger, Liudolf, Luipold, Lindwin, Liutward, Liutprant, Hlothar, Ldowich, Chlodowech, Mainard, Mainfred, Meginbert, Maginfred, Ozbert, Liutker, Frumolt, Otto, Odo, Odalrich, Ratbodo, Reginbald.

FEMALE: Adalheid, Adelaide, Adalwit, Adred, Albsinda, Bertha, Hathwiga, Hedwig, Mathilda, Mechtild, Gisla, Gisiltrude, Glismuada, Hiltiburg, Ida, Ota, Imma, Regingarda.

Birthplace & Language

Choose the investigator's kingdom of birth and language — the German empire (with four main Old High German dialects spoken: Frankish, Saxon, Bavarian, Allemanic — the term 'German' (*thiudisk*) itself is only just evolving), the kingdoms of France, Burgundy, or Italy (where Old French and Occitan dialects are spoken), the kingdom of England (Old English dialects spoken) are good starting points; see the "Languages" section on page 54 and "A Quick Tour of the World," page 61, for more details.

Sex of Your Character

Most Dark Ages societies are unfortunately very sexist. Men hold almost all positions of power, and women of low rank are usually assigned to a lifetime of menial tasks with few rights.

In order to enrich the playing experience however, we decided to stretch historical correctness and open most occupations to female player characters (avoid cleric, priest, guard, and warrior). The keeper must decide whether to consider audacious women as exceptions in a hostile male society, or to bend medieval mentality toward gentle integration.

Education

Apart from men of the church, clerics, and a few nobles, no one possesses formal education in the Dark Ages, since there is no proper schooling system outside of the monasteries. The game concepts of Education (EDU) and the Know roll measure *factual* knowledge in *Cthulhu Dark Ages:* an investigator with a high

Education may not be schooled, but still might be studious, observant, and judicious.

This definition of Education does not contradict the *Call of Cthulhu* rules — in *Cthulhu Dark Ages* the "school of life" has the same status as formal schooling.

Age & Aging

Your investigator's age is 15. For every ten years or fraction older that you make your investigator, add a point to EDU and allot 20 occupation points. Also remove your choice of 1 STR, 1 CON, 1 DEX, or 1 APP.

Occupations

Occupation defines what your player character did, what position in society did he or she fulfill, before becoming an investigator. About two dozen occupations are listed below, well-suited for producing likely investigators. Each occupation denotes applicable skills and potential savings, given in deniers. Choose an occupation.

Now multiply your character's EDU times 20: spend all those points among the eight or so skills listed for the occupation.

Now multiply your investigator's INT times 10: these are personal interest points, and can be allotted to all skills except Cthulhu Mythos.

Add these points to base chances printed on the investigator sheet, and any amounts already in the spaces to the right of the skills. Total the amounts for each skill.

Not all skills need be given points, but all points not spent are lost.

Learn more about the people and the society they in which they lived in the Utilities chapter, pages 53*ff.* Spells can be found in the Old Grimoire, pages 77*ff.* See also nearby the optional Language Bonus for three occupations.

In the Dark Ages, most people were tied to clergy or a lay lord. Whenever possible, we suggest "freeman" or

Language Bonus

If the keeper wishes, an investigator with the occupation of Cleric, Merchant, or Scholar may receive an additional 100 skill points to spend for languages.

"high-status" versions of common occupations, which give the player more autonomy.

All occupations allow at least one free choice of skill among those in the skills list and weapons tables. Remember that the Cthulhu Mythos skill cannot be chosen, only learned during play.

Money & Equipment

In the Middle Ages the question of currency is a complex one, since every governmental power mints its own coins. For the sake of playability, *Cthulhu Dark Ages* adopts a standardized monetary unit: the *silver penny* or *silver denier*. One denier represents the minimum amount necessary for one person to survive one day in a city. Of course, one can always go hungry.

All occupations endow the investigator with a certain number of deniers — representing what the character might conceivably have saved living frugally, and indicate that occupation's yearly potential. Please note that people of the time never accumulate monetary wealth, living from day-to-day, scraping by, and largely using barter in transactions.

Buy weapons, clothing and other effects fit for your investigator's occupation. Typical purchasable items can be found in the Costs, Equipment & Services table on page 52.

Magic

A few occupations (healer, hermit/heretic, and exorcist-priest) allow the investigator to select Old Grimoire spells instead of skills. Such a choice is always subject to keeper approval — count 50 skill percentiles for every *targeted* spell, and 100 skill percentiles for others (see "Casting Spells" in the Old Grimoire. Men of the church have in principle no access to magical lore, but may be granted miraculous powers by divine intervention. In a Christian context, the craving for divine powers should be regarded as a mortal sin.

Beggar

As a beggar, you devote your life to niggling food and sometimes money from passersby.

Skills: Bargain, Conceal, Fast Talk, Insight, Listen or Spot, Hidden. Three other skills are personal specialties.
Money: 1D4-1 silver deniers. **Yearly Income:** 240 deniers.

Cleric

You are the child of a rich man, or a brilliant peasant boy who caught the notice of a man of the Church. You received a formal religious education in a bishopric or a monastery. Now you are a secretary, an administrator, a jurist, or an architect at the service of a count or a bishop.

Skills: Latin, Library Use, Persuade, Own Kingdom, Status, Write Latin, (or the local chancery language). Two other skills are personal specialties (*may gain Language Bonus*).
Money: 1D3+6 x50 silver deniers. **Yearly Income:** 2400 deniers.

Craftsman or Shopkeeper

You might be a smith, a baker, or a weaver. Choose your craft. You live in a village community or in a city.

Skills: Bargain, Craft (choose one), Fast Talk, Insight, Natural World, Own Kingdom, and Status. One other skill is a personal specialty.
Money: 1D3+1 x100 silver deniers, +400 deniers in product. **Yearly Income:** 1200 deniers.

(Free) Farmer

You are the salt of the earth, a well-to-do farmer or colonist. Dark Age society depends on your crops, and you work like a horse.

Skills: Bargain, Craft (choose one), Drive Horses, Listen, Natural World, and Track. Two other skills are personal specialties.
Money: 1D100 silver deniers, +300 deniers in stored grains or in herd animals. **Yearly Income:** 600 deniers.

Guard

You work in a cathedral city for the burgrave or the bishop. In times of peace, you have little to do but practice with your weapons and keep in shape.

Skills: Fist/Punch or Head Butt or Kick or Grapple, Own Kingdom, Sneak, Spot Hidden or Listen, Status, Throw, and one weapon skill. One other skill is a personal specialty.

Money: 1D3 x100 silver deniers, plus fighting equipment as assigned by employer. **Yearly Income:** 1800 deniers.

Healer

To foreigners, you look like a villager. But villagers know better: your mentor granted you powers of the invisible world. Now villagers come to your hut for a cure or a potion, or for advice about love or birthing a child, the promise of rain and the evil eye. Be wary of the ever-suspicious village priest!

Skills: First Aid, Insight, Listen or Spot Hidden, Natural World, Occult, and Potions. Two other skills are personal specialties (spells are allowed).

Money: 1D3 x100 silver deniers. **Yearly Income:** 900 deniers.

Hermit / Heretic

You are an outcast, a drifter, a person plagued by dreams and visions. You grasp at strange clues and bewildering notions. You either hide in the woods or live in a secret community.

Skills: Hide, Insight, Listen or Spot Hidden, Natural World, Occult, and Persuade. Two other skills are personal specialties (spells are allowed).

Money: 1D6 silver deniers. **Yearly Income:** 240 deniers.

Household Officer

You serve your lord in his urban palace or his *castrum*. Select one of the following functions: steward, headman of the stables, or keeper of the order. You spend much of your day bullying lesser servants to do their work.

Skills: Craft (choose one), Conceal, Fast Talk, Insight, Listen or Spot Hidden, and Sneak. Two other skills are personal specialties.

Money: 1D3 x100 silver deniers. **Yearly Income:** 900 deniers.

Juggler / Minstrel

You're witty and articulate, dress gaily and are interesting looking, and you love to get attention. You might be adept with *chansons de geste* (see page 66) — your heroes are Roland, Charlemagne and Alexander the Great — you play a musical instrument, recite poetry and stories that everybody already knows, and are maybe proficient at tumbling, juggling, rope walking, or some other entertaining craft. You might even own a tame bear or monkey!

If possible, you enter the services of a nobleman, whose praises you sing and whose generosity you praise. In return, you hope for gifts and treasures and the security only a court can offer you.

Skills: Art (choose one), Bargain, Fast Talk, Insight, Own Kingdom, and Persuade. Two other skills are personal specialties.

Money: 1D6 x50 silver deniers. **Yearly Income:** 1500 deniers.

Mercenary / Brigand

As a mercenary you fight for the highest bidder and then scavenge battlefields for trophies. As a brigand, you may have been the victim of some natural catastrophe or some heinous injustice that changed your life forever. Now you hide deep in the woods and rob traveling monks or traders.

Skills: Fist/Punch or Head Butt or Kick or Grapple, Natural World, Navigate, Track, Sneak, Throw, and one weapon skill. One other skill is a personal specialty.

Money: 1D4+1 x50 silver deniers, plus 500 deniers for fighting equipment. **Yearly Income:** 2100 deniers.

Merchant

You are a Jew living in a port city or on the outskirts of a cathedral city. You make a living from accounts and agents. You import wine, exotic spices, and silks from

heathen countries and sell them to arrogant nobles. Not being a Christian, you are allowed to be a moneychanger and a moneylender.

Skills: Accounting, Bargain, Fast Talk, Own Kingdom, Other Kingdoms, Other Language, and Write Language. One other skill is a personal specialty (*may gain Language Bonus*).

Money: 1D4+4 x100 silver deniers, plus 700 deniers in product or outstanding loans. **Yearly Income:** 9000 deniers.

Monk / Nun

You live in a monastery, in silence and in prayer, leading a simple life. When you don't pray or sing, you perform domestic tasks, or copy arcane manuscripts from the monastery's library. As a member of your order, you are not allowed to own private property but if you leave the monastery with special permission, you can always count on the hospitality and charity of other monasteries.

Skills: Art or Craft or Science (choose one), Latin, Library Use, Listen, Occult, Sign Language, and Write Latin. One other skill is a personal specialty.

Money: Money and equipment as assigned by order. **Yearly Income:** 600 deniers.

Pilgrim

You live by the charity of other people. You accomplish a pilgrimage to a holy place such as Jerusalem, a monastery, or a cathedral city housing holy relics. You have your own reasons to be a pilgrim, maybe for the expiation of some crime, the wish to elevate your soul, or simply the desire for adventure in its noblest sense. You could be headed to Santiago de Compostela in Spain, Mount Saint Michel in France, Jerusalem, or Rome.

Skills: Bargain, Natural World, Navigate, Own Kingdom, and Sneak. Three other skills are personal specialties.

Money: 1D8 silver deniers. **Yearly Income:** 240 deniers.

Priest

You are on a mission from the church to enlighten laymen and women in the ways of God. You are an exorcist or a full-fledged priest who is bound to a parish and collects the tithe from the farmers, most of which goes to your greedy lord. Although St. Paul highly commends celibacy and it is strongly recommended, you may have a concubine and even children, though they will not inherit from you.

Skills: Fast Talk, Insight, Latin, Occult, Persuade, and Status. Two other skills are personal specialties (religiously appropriate spells are allowed).

Money: 1D8 x25 silver deniers plus holy book or bible, prayer books, other equipment as determined by denomination and parish. **Yearly Income:** 600 deniers.

Sailor

You're skilled with sails, boats, and ships, and know tides, the wind, and the stars. You have seen Hamburg, Venice, or Constantinople. Life is glorious, except for storms, pirates, and the terrors of the deep.

Skills: Climb, Fast Talk, Natural World, Navigate, Other Kingdoms, and Pilot Boat. Two other skills are personal specialties.

Money: 1D3 x100 silver deniers. **Yearly Income:** 1200 deniers.

Scholar

You belong to a monastic or cathedral school. You are the recipient and the dispenser of godly knowledge. You spend your time reading classical authors, writing manuals, and teaching. When you don't teach you're involved in political intrigues for some good cause.

Skills: Latin, Library Use, Own Kingdom, Persuade, Science (choose one), Status, and Write Latin. One other skill is a personal specialty (*may gain Language Bonus*).

Money: 1D3+1 x50 silver deniers, plus writing materials. **Yearly Income:** 1500 deniers.

Sergeant / Mayor

You are employed by a lord or a monastery to supervise the administration of the domain. Your main task is to collect tax money and dues in kind.

Skills: Bargain, Fast Talk, Insight, Sneak, Spot Hidden, Status, and one weapon skill. One other skill is a personal specialty.

Money: 1D3+4 x100 silver deniers, plus 600 deniers in livestock or horses. **Yearly Income:** 3000 deniers.

Small Trader

You own a few pack animals or a small ship. You circuit inland, up river, or along the coast for the benefit of your master. You know a lot about that route and its particular dangers.

Skills: Bargain, Drive Horses or Pilot Boat, Fast Talk, Insight, Own Kingdom, Other Language (common trading speech), and Navigate. One other skill is a personal specialty: depending on your trading route you might know Medieval Latin or Greek (Mediterranean), Flemish (around the North Sea), Low German or Old Norse (around the Baltic Sea).

Money: 1D3+1 x100 silver deniers, plus 400 deniers in product. **Yearly Income:** 3600 deniers.

(Free) Warrior

You are a proud *miles*, a professional warrior. You are a bold adventurer on his own or hired by a warlord. Your proudest possessions are a horse, a long sword, and chain mail.

Skills: Grapple, Natural World, Own Kingdom, Ride, Status, Track, and one weapon skill. One other skill is a personal specialty.

Money: 1D4+6 x50 silver deniers, plus a horse, longsword, and chainmail. **Yearly Income:** 9000 deniers.

Woodsman / Fisherman

As a woodsman you exploit the forest: you might be a hunter, a honey gatherer or a woodcutter who produces charcoal. As a fisherman you are living in a fishing community by a lake or by the sea.

Skills: Craft (choose one), Listen or Spot Hidden, Natural World, Navigate, Pilot Boat or Track, Swim or Sneak, and Throw. One other skill is a personal specialty.

Money: 1D6 x25 silver deniers. **Yearly Income:** 240 deniers.

Skills

Skills define the means for a character's participation in a roleplaying game session. There are many skills; the most commonly employed and useful are included in this game. Keepers can and sometimes should create and define additional new skills, or aspects of existing skills, to suit his or her game and the adventure of the moment.

Skill Classes

The skills described in the next section can be grouped into five classes defining similar type or effect. Diseases, drugs, or spells might affect a skill class, typically halving skill chances for a few hours.

COMMUNICATION: Art, Bargain, Fast Talk, Insight, Other/Own Language, Persuade, Status.

MANIPULATION: Art, Conceal, Craft, First Aid, Missile Weapons, Pilot Boat, Repair/Devise.

PERCEPTION: Listen, Spot Hidden, Track.

PHYSICAL MOVEMENT: Art, Climb, Dodge, Drive Horses, Fist/Punch, Grapple, Head Butt, Hide, Jump, Hand-to-Hand Weapons, Kick, Ride, Sneak, Swim, Throw.

THOUGHT: Accounting, Cthulhu Mythos, Library Use, Medicine, Natural World, Navigate, Occult, Other/Own Kingdoms, Potions, Science, spells, Write Language.

Skill Definitions

Definitions of skill necessarily summarize intent and coverage. Unforeseen circumstances provoke new uses and interpretations of skills. Discuss special applications with your keeper.

Following each skill name, the base chance for the skill is parenthesized.

Skills represent what is known to an era. Skill percentiles are not proportions of what is hypothetically knowable. If they were able to stack their respective knowledge on a table like poker chips and measure the difference, an astronomer of 60% in 2004 knows much more than one of 90% skill in 998.

A skill level of 50% is high enough to let a character eke out a living from it. If an investigator rises high in a skill, player and keeper could confer about a new profession, and increased income from it.

Accounting (10%)

Basic knowledge of arithmetic, calculus, and the ability to use an abacus to understand and manage inventories, accounts and crop registers.

Art (05%)

Specify acting, dancing, playing a musical instrument, jewelry-making, juggling, singing, sculpting, illuminating manuscripts, etc. The investigator sheet contains blank spaces for different versions of this skill.

Bargain (05%)

The skill of obtaining something for an agreeable price. The bargainer must state the price at which he wishes to purchase the item and, for each 2% of difference between that amount and the asking price, he must sub-

Skills Base Chance

Dark Ages Skill	Base %	Modern Equivalent
Accounting	10%	*Accounting*
Art	05%	*Art*
Bargain	05%	Bargain
Climb	40%	Climb
Conceal	15%	Conceal
Craft	05%	*Craft*
Cthulhu Mythos	00%	Cthulhu Mythos
Dodge	DEX x2%	Dodge
Drive Horses	20%	Drive Horses
Fast Talk	05%	Fast Talk
First Aid	30%	First Aid
Fist/Punch	50%	Fist/Punch
Grapple	25%	Grapple
Head Butt	10%	Head Butt
Hide	10%	Hide
Insight	05%	*Psychology*
Jump	25%	Jump
Kick	25%	Kick
Library Use	EDU x2%	*Library Use*
Listen	25%	Listen
Medicine	05%	*Medicine*
Natural World	10%	*Natural History*
Navigate	10%	Navigate
Occult	05%	*Occult*
Other Kingdoms	01%	*History*
Other Language	01%	*Other Language*
Own Kingdom	20%	*History*
Own Language	EDU x5%	*Own Language*
Persuade	15%	Persuade
Pilot Boat	01%	Pilot Boat
Potions	01%	*Pharmacy*
Repair/Devise	20%	*Mechanical Repair*
Ride	05%	Ride
Science	01%	*Astronomy, Physics, etc.*
Sneak	10%	Sneak
Spot Hidden	25%	Spot Hidden
Status	15%	*Credit Rating*
Swim	25%	Swim
Throw	25%	Throw
Track	10%	Track
Write Language	01%	*Own/Other Language*

Skills with different names, base chances, and scope than in modern times are italicized. Please refer to the "Skills Definitions" section and to the Weapon Tables.

tract 1 percentile from his Bargain skill. The keeper determines the bottom-line price secretly — a seller should not accept a loss. A simple bargain may be struck in a few minutes. By implication, use this skill in any situation featuring an exchange of value by matching Bargains on the Resistance Table.

Climb (DEX + STR%)

Climbing freehand requires a Climb roll every 10 to 30 vertical feet, depending on availability and firmness of handholds, wind, visibility, etc. To climb quietly, the investigator makes a single D100 roll, the result of which is matched against the investigator's percentages in both Climb and Sneak. This could represent a noisy climb, a stealthy ascent, a silent fall, or a noisy fall.

Conceal (15%)

Attempting a visual covering up, secreting, or masking of objects, perhaps with debris, cloth or other illusion-promoting materials, perhaps by making a secret panel or false compartment, etc.

Craft (05%)

The skill-holder can make and repair, or bring to market, a class of objects such as shoes, pottery, or farm food and fodder. Crafts are skills used to make practical things — armorer, boat-builder, carpenter, weaver, mason, etc., are examples of specialized crafts that may verge into arts. The investigator sheet contains blank spaces for different versions of this skill.

Cthulhu Mythos (00%)

This skill differs from the others in the game. No investigator may take points in Cthulhu Mythos either with occupation points or with skill points. Successful use of the skill does not increase the investigator's percentiles in the skill; hence no check-box on the investigator sheet.

Points in Cthulhu Mythos are gained by Mythos encounters that result in the loss of Sanity points, by optional insane insights into the true nature of the universe, and by reading forbidden books and other Mythos writings. A successful D100 roll against Cthulhu Mythos allows the investigator to identify an entity or to deduce something about its behavior.

Dodge (DEX x2%)

With it, an investigator can instinctively evade blows, thrown missiles, surprise attacks, and so forth. A character attempting Dodge in a combat round may also parry or block a blow, but not attack. If a blow or other attack can be seen, a character can try to dodge it, but an unseen attack (from the rear, by an invisible attacker, in the dark, etc.) cannot be dodged.

Drive Horses or Oxen (20%)

Usually a one-animal drawn cart, or a two-animal wagon. Includes care for the beast or beasts, harnessing, folklore about the beasts, and at least one good story. The animals never belong to the driver.

Fast Talk (05%)

Flattering words cause the target to agree with the fast-talker for a short time. Without reflecting, the target allows the trespass, hands over a fine ripe apple for nothing, believes the gossip, and so on. Given a little time to think and the benefit of a successful Idea roll, the victim comes to his senses and the Fast Talk loses all effect.

First Aid (30%)

The percentage chance of awakening an unconscious or stunned comrade, setting a broken limb, treating a burn, resuscitating a drowning victim, etc. First aid has no lasting effect on diseases or subtle physical ailments or poisonings. After one successful use, healing 1D3 hit points, it has no additional effect on a particular injury.

Fist/Punch (50%)

This might be described as a closed fist, a downward chop of the hand, a violent slap, etc. Fist/Punch can parry Kick or Head Butt. Martial arts are unknown in western Europe of this time.

Grapple (25%)

A Grapple is a special personal attack, frequently chosen in order to subdue an opponent. This attack may be parried by an opposing Grapple or other attack, but only in the first round of an attack, or before the attacking Grapple succeeds. If the attack succeeds in the first round and is not neutralized, the attacker holds the target and has several options.

- Immobilize the target by overcoming the target's STR with his or her own STR on the Resistance Table. With a success, the target is held until the Grappler attempts movement or some other ordinary action.

- Knock down the target. If used, this option automatically succeeds against a human opponent.

- Knock out the target in the first or a later round; see the Knock-Out rule.

- Disarm the target. With successful Grapples in consecutive rounds, an investigator could Grapple to prevent a hand-to-hand attack in the first round and then seize the weapon or weapon hand in the second round.

- Injure the target. The opponent must already be successfully Grappled. The Grappler must receive a second successful Grapple roll in the next round or some later round. Success costs the target 1D6 hit points plus the attacker's damage bonus. The same process may inflict more injury to the target in later rounds.

- Strangle the target. Beginning in the round in which the intention is stated, the target begins to asphyxiate as per the Drowning rules. This continues in subsequent rounds. The attacker needs no further Grapple rolls.

- In either injury-making Grapple, the victim can escape by a successful STR versus STR match on the Resistance Table.

- If there are multiple attackers, no more than two people's STRs may be combined in an injury-making Grapple.

Head Butt (10%)

A personal attack useful while brawling; apply to the belly or head. Useful in a cramped, crowded location such as a bar. A head butt attack is quick, stunning, and demoralizing. It cannot parry. At 75% or more, a character can head butt twice in the same round — make the second attack at half DEX rank.

Hide (10%)

As opposed to Conceal, Hide concerns the individual's ability to escape detection. Roll this skill during patrol, surveillance, pursuit, etc. Some cover must be present, or the skill is useless — try Sneak instead. With a successful Hide, the user chooses the best bushes, the deepest shadows, etc., in which to lurk or hide behind. If the skill user needs to move while hiding, make a fresh D100 roll at half normal Hide.

Insight (05%)

An investigator can learn about another person by observing his or her behavior, and deducing the person's motives. Insight may be countered with a successful opposing Insight roll on the Resistance Table. Skilled deceivers cannot be studied with Insight.

Jump (25%)

Using Jump, a character can leap up vertically and grab to his or her own height, or leap down a vertical distance equal to the person's own height. He or she can also jump horizontally to a distance equal to half the jumper's own height, or run and then jump horizontally to a distance of twice the jumper's own height. If falling, a successful Jump prepares for the impact by restoring up to 1D6 hit points to any lost. With Jump 60% or more, the character may routinely perform gymnastic maneuvers, walk a high rope, or other such feats.

Kick (25%)

Whether a straightforward kick to the groin or jaw, or a kick with both legs while lying on the floor, a kick is powerful enough to do injury wherever it lands. The knock-out rule does not apply to Kick. A kick may be parried. At Kick 75% or more, a second kick may be made at half the user's DEX rank.

Library Use (EDU x2%)

Allows the user to find pertinent clues and information. He or she must be able to read at least one language, and the reader must have access to a library of books. Each use of the skill represents four hours of continuous research. Most people are not educated enough to apply this skill.

Listen (25%)

Measures the ability of a character to interpret and understand dim sounds, including overheard conversations, mutterings behind closed doors, or words whispered during a noisy dance or festival. Was your investigator awakened by the snap of a twig? To use Listen to detect someone's Sneak, compare skills on the Resitance Table. The lower result wins.

Medicine (05%)

Medical science is rudimentary in the Dark Ages, especially in northern and western Europe. To exercise this skill, monks and scholars rely on profane books written a thousand years ago (Aesculapius, the church fathers, and some recent Arabic authorities like Avicenna). Common treatments for illness consist of bleeding or special diet, meant to re-establish the fragile equilibrium of fluids within the body, but usually offering patients little advantage. A successful Medicine roll restores 1D3-1 hit points per week of observation and treatment and only when the patient enjoys hospital-like conditions. Fortunately, natural healing restores another 1D3 hit points for all characters, hospitalized or not.

- Successful application of Medicine may require an additional Potions roll to prepare beneficial infusions, etc. The keeper may rule that a fumble causes a loss of 1D3 hit points as a result of bad treatment.

- In the era Arabian doctors are more skilled in Medicine, and also can successfully perform simple surgeries. A hospitalized investigator treated by an Arab physician heals at a 2D3+1 hit points per week — 1D3 for natural healing and 1D3+1 for hospital treatment and the benefits of Arabic medicine.

- Medicine also covers rudimentary surgery, but since anesthetics are unknown, treat every operation as a wound inflicted by a small or a large knife (depending on the operation). See the Weapon Tables for the damage done; a fumble doubles the damage while an impale success halves it. The keeper may rule that an amputation, like torture, calls for a Sanity roll, with a potential loss of 0/1D3 to 0/1D10 Sanity points. For more about Dark Ages medical practices, see under Technology in the Utilities chapter.

If death approaches, most people would want to see a priest to hear their last confession, since death without absolution means eternal damnation.

Natural World (10%)

Compared to Science, the focus of this skill is on personal experience and hearsay. It encompasses general knowledge concerning animals, plants, sea life, and climate in an environment familiar to the investigator. The keeper should halve this skill in unfamiliar lands. Also use this skill for knowledge and care of domestic plants and animals.

Navigate (10%)

Allows the user to find the way to a place he has been to before or has been told about — in daylight, by land or sea, in good weather. But at night, in low clouds, in fog, halve the chance for a success. Day or night in a storm by sea, the chance for a success is Navigate 05%.

Occult (05%)

This skill's purview is Old Grimoire magic, signs, and spirits, just as the Cthulhu Mythos skill concerns Mythos magic, monsters, books, etc. The user recognizes occult symbols and paraphernalia, and provides knowledge of alchemical and astrological concepts, but nothing of the Cthulhu Mythos. On a successful Occult roll, the investigator is able to recognize occult content and context. An Occult 60% or more allows individual and original solutions to problems of Occult knowledge.

Other Kingdoms (01%)

This skill shows how much the investigator knows about peoples and lands other than his own.

Other Language (01%)

This skill represents the user's chance to speak and understand a particular language. The skill includes rudimentary ability to read the language, but not to write it (see Write Language for that). Local dialects can be understood at half chance.

Own Kingdom (20%)

This represents what the investigator knows about the peoples, lands, and legends of his or her native kingdom. This information comes from gossip and broad traditions. Use this skill to identify the place and significance of a dialect.

Own Language (EDU x5%)

If the language has a written form, the skill includes a rudimentary ability to read the language, but not to write it (see Write Language for that).

Persuade (15%)

Like Fast Talk, employ Persuade without reference to truth or falsehood. Use Persuade to convince a target about a particular idea, concept, or belief. Unlike Fast Talk, the effects of Persuade linger indefinitely, until events or another Persuade roll turn the target's mind. A successful application of Persuade might take an hour to several days, depending on what's being attempted.

Pilot Boat (01%)

The character understands the behavior of small craft in wind, storms, and tides, and can read wave and wind action that suggest reefs and other hidden obstacles, changes in the weather, etc.

Potions (01%)

With this skill, the investigator can recognize, compound, and dispense the infusions, poisons, antidotes and hallucinogens of the Dark Ages. Finding ingredients may require considerable Natural World skill. Preparing a plant potion takes 1-3 days. Preparing poison for a weapon takes a day if using animal venom, and up to two weeks if using infectious agents. Beware! A fumbled infusion or antidote may be a poison.

Repair/Devise (20%)

Every investigator can fix or devise simple equipment, boats, roofs, and so forth. With Devise, an investigator can create pitfalls and other clever traps to catch animals or humans. Tools and special materials may be needed.

Ride Horse (05%)

The rider of horses can care for the animal and the riding gear. He or she can control a steed at a gallop or on difficult terrain, and can remain seated as it jumps an obstacle. Should a steed rear, stumble, or fall, the chance to stay mounted or to safely jump free equals the Ride percentage. If an investigator tumbles from a mount because the animal has failed a jump, been wounded, or because a Ride roll failed, the rider loses 1D6 hit points in the accident. However, a successful Jump roll saves 1D6 hit points.

- To effectively wield a weapon from horseback takes Ride 60% or better. Halve the weapon skills of a rider whose Ride is less than 60%.
- The skilled rider at this level is able to race cross-country and through broken terrain, and is a keen trainer and appraiser of horses.
- Until the keeper modifies them, also apply these rules to mules, donkeys, and camels.

Science (01%)

Of all the occupations, monks, clerics, and scholars (and possibly a few nobles) may be trained in one of the 'seven free arts' — the science of the Dark Ages. Specify music, astronomy, arithmetic, geometry, theology, canonic law, etc. (See Medicine under its own heading.) From the point of view of the church, these sciences exist merely to reveal the perfection of the god-given order in the world. The investigator sheet contains blank spaces for different versions of this skill.

Sneak (10%)

The art of behaving or moving circumspectly, so as not to be noticed or heard by guards, residents, passersby, etc. Proper costume is important, but so is seeming to be like everyone else, even if there are only two people in a hall. No cover is needed for Sneak, but confidence and wit are definitely called for.

Spot Hidden (25%)

The user may be able to spot a secret door or compartment, notice a hidden intruder, become aware of a bulging purse, etc. Spot Hidden cannot be used in darkness; a candle gives enough light. Points in excess of Spot Hidden 60% might

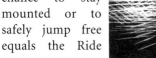

be added to Track percentiles, if the keeper thinks it appropriate.

Status (15%)

In the narrow communities of the Dark Ages, status is an index of personal reputation and rank. It may also suggest monetary worth, but the important matter is that the investigator has personal connections that give him access to important people. For example, Andreas, the bastard son of Froderik V, has little money and indifferent looks, but he cuts a mighty swathe through society because he knows many influential people. This skill can represent an investigator's chance to get a loan from a Jewish merchant, or to bluff his way past the Count's guards for a private audition. His status may ebb and flow as well because of a scandal or a heroic action. In special situations, the keeper might call for a Status roll instead of Fast Talk, Persuade, or Bargain.

Swim (25%)

The ability to float in and to self-propel through water, a vat of beer, etc. Roll Swim only in times of crisis or danger, and only when the keeper calls for the roll. Humans and horses have MOV 2 while swimming. A failed Swim roll causes an investigator to start drowning; see the spot rules for drowning. If CON and DEX are both 10 or higher, those with Swim 60% or more can also:

- Dive without harm from a height of up to the Swim skill percentage in feet, given a D100 roll equal to or less than the Swim percentage. Failing the roll, he or she loses 1D6 hit points for the awkward landing.

- Sink into water and then return to the surface for a depth up to the Swim skill percentage in yards, given a successful Swim roll.

Throw (25%)

Various items can be thrown with a variety of intentions. To hit a target with an object, to hit a target with the right part of a thrown object such as the point of a knife blade, or to encompass a target with a loop of thrown rope, use Throw.

- A small object of reasonable balance, such as a javelin or a dagger, can be accurately thrown up to three yards for each point by which the thrower's STR exceeds the object's SIZ.

- A palm-sized object designed to be thrown in play, such as a ball or a water-smoothed rock, can be hurled up to seven yards for each STR point in excess of the object's SIZ. It may

bounce on for more. Keepers must choose the suitable multiplier.

Track (10%)

With Track, an investigator can visually follow the trail of a person or animal over soft earth, through leaves, across broken ground, etc. For each day that has passed since the tracks were made, subtract twenty percentiles from the chance to track. Heavy rain washes out exposed tracks within a few hours. A being cannot be visually tracked across water or at night, except in unusual circumstances. The scent of a passing animal may cling to the protected underside of leaves, even after considerable rainfall. People of ghoulish temperament often are expert trackers, able to rely on both visual and scent trails. With Track 60% or more, Spot Hidden points in excess of 60 may in effect increment the Track skill when the trail grows difficult.

Write Language (01%)

In the Dark Ages, writing is a different skill from reading, and is taught separately. This skill gives the user the rudimentary ability to write the specified language, provided he or she has proficiency in reading it, and provided the language has a written form. In the realm of the Dark Ages, the principal languages with written forms are Arabic, Anglo-Saxon (Old English), Old French, Old German, Hebrew, Latin, Old Norse, Occitan, Slavonic, and Syriac (Greek).

Rules

Rules transform play into a game. With rules each player is treated equally and each participant has the same chance for success. In *Cthulhu Dark Ages*, the players form one side, while the keeper plays all the other characters and that of Nature herself. Rules define the limits of what the game can handle, including the sorts of characters and actions important to the game. New players understand this point acutely: their "Who shall I be?" gets to the center of roleplaying in a sentence. Every rule limits

itself because it would be foolish to use rules to describe all situations. Where rules join, common sense must smooth the seams.

Movement

Rates of movement vary by the kind of creature. Individual rates for many forms of life can be found in this book. These are the MOV (or Move) entries. All humans, for instance, move at up to eight units per combat round. Eight is the maximum sustainable rate of movement.

This number represents an average ability to move, one not pretending to represent effort in foot races, short or long. Since all people move at the same game-rate maximum, no MOV entry appears on the investigator sheet. Exact distances and rates are rarely important in the game. If the keeper wishes, each unit stretches, from a yard to several yards, depending on the situation. If distance and rate become important in the game, the keeper can provide estimates, or better yet answer the question in game terms: "You get there in one combat round". In the Dark Ages, exact measurements are rarely made or needed.

Rates of movement are proportional. Animals and supernatural creatures may be faster or slower than humans. Proportionality makes races between them simple to resolve and reasonably accurate in result. Subtract the higher from the lower to learn who opens up a lead or closes in. Thus a tiger (MOV 10) gains not less than two units per round on its human prey, or leaves human pursuers further and further behind by not less than two units per round.

Tokens or figures on a table need not represent movement. The keeper can set the scene, and statements of intent can be general. If physical position is not kept, the keeper uses Luck rolls or some other semi-random way to determine which investigator is near or far, touching or untouched, and so forth.

Handling Movement

If the movement rates differ, the gap between pursuer and pursued closes or opens by that many units per round, until capture, escape, or combat.

In a long race, the keeper also may begin to ask for CON rolls in order to find out who is exhausted first.

Between opponents of the same kind, such as humans against humans, roll CON against CON, DEX

Distance & Movement Rates

effort	rate [1]	duration [2]	rest [3]
explosive (dash)	MOV x10 yards per round	1 round	2 minutes
intense (run)	MOV x5 yards per found	CON rounds	1 hour
sustained (forced march)	MOV / 2 miles per hour	CON hours	1 day

1 - One combat round lasts a nominal game time of 12 seconds. There are 5 combat rounds in one game minute.

2 - Duration is the length of time that the effort can be sustained before experiencing fatigue.

3 - Rest is the time required to fully recover from the effort.

against DEX, Swim against Swim, etc., on the Resistance Table, as the keeper finds appropriate.

If wounded or old, an investigator may have to move more slowly, at a rate set by the keeper.

Chases and Fatigue

As noted above, to resolve chases, compare the movement rates (MOV) of pursuer and pursued. If they differ, the gap between them opens or closes to produce a resolution.

For game purposes all humans have MOV 8 and all riding horses have MOV 12. Both humans and horses have MOV 2 when swimming. Rates for other creatures occur in the *Cthulhu Dark Ages* rules.

If the effort is sustained for longer than indicated (and the needed rest is postponed), the runner tires and moves more slowly, by MOV 1 for each extended period. Complete exhaustion (the character cannot run or fight) occurs when MOV has been halved. At this point all skill rolls should be halved. To recover from exhaustion, the investigator needs 24 consecutive hours of rest, and sufficient food and water. If the investigator attempts any kind of strenuous physical activity while exhausted, a successful CON x5 roll is necessary to retain consciousness.

The above rules can be adapted to all sustained physical activities like swimming, climbing, combat (intense effort), etc.

Wilderness Survival

Humans can survive indefinitely on meager food rations, if necessary — down to one fifth of normal. With a comfortable dry shelter, and plenty of drinking water and rest, an average person can live 8-12 weeks without any food.

- For the first three days without food, the investigator operates normally.

- For the next CON days without food, physical performance is impaired, and the keeper may apply negative skill roll modifiers.

- For the final phase without food, the starving investigator is exhausted (all skill rolls halved). He or she becomes delirious and eventually dies, having lost 50% of body weight. To simulate this, the starving investigator loses 1 hit point every five days. In this period, any strenuous physical activity calls for a CON x5 roll; failing the roll costs an additional hit point.

By far the two greatest outdoor threats facing investigators are dehydration and exposure to cold.

- Lacking both water and food (all foodstuffs contain some water), lose 1 hit point per day; the keeper rules exhaustion when hit points are halved (round down any fraction).

- As with starvation, strenuous activities call for CON x5 rolls. Failing a roll, the thirsty investigator loses another hit point.

- The keeper may double the hit point loss rate in warm weather (above 70°F or 20°C) and triple it in hot weather (above 85°F or 30°C). Conversely the keeper should halve the rate in cold weather (under 60°F or 15°C).

- When exposed to cold air or cold water, the keeper requests CON x5 rolls at regular intervals (see below). Each failed CON x5 roll costs 1 hit point for hypothermia. The frequency of these rolls depends on the exposure; for frequencies see the Exposure Table.

- In water, halve the interval of the CON roll if naked, and double it if wearing insulated clothing.

- On land, divide the interval of the CON rolls by 10 if naked or wearing wet clothes. Multiply by 10 if wearing dry insulated clothing. The keeper may apply a wind-chill factor if appropriate.

- The distance an average human can hope to swim in 50°F or 10°C water is two-thirds of a mile, or about a kilometer!

Fire and Light

Candles, torches, oil lamps, and lanterns make portable light by which an investigator can read or Spot Hidden. The light they give in darkness is visible a hundred yards away.

- A candle flickers, burns for two to six hours depending on length, and is easy to blow out. A candle is only reliable if inside a lantern — a punched-metal cylinder with a rectangular opening that can be covered with a thinned plate of clear ox horn to protect the flame from blowing out.

- A torch gives a large bright flame, burns for an hour, and only hurricane force winds can blow it out. If dropped, a torch keeps burning with a successful Luck roll.

- An oil lamp is no brighter than a wax candle. An oil lamp can be quite dangerous if dropped, because of the spread of burning oil.

We assume that nearly all people of non-urban cultures know how to quickly make fire using, for instance, flint and tinder. Under adverse wind or rain, the keeper may ask for Luck rolls.

- A hand-held torch does 1D6 hit points of burn damage in each combat round that it is thrust against the target. He or she gets a Luck roll to prevent clothes and hair from catching fire. If they do catch fire, the target continues to lose 1D6 hit points per round.

- Caught in a flaming hut, on a burning ship, or engulfed in a bonfire costs the target 1D6+2 damage each round. A Luck roll is needed each round before the victim begins to asphyxiate as per drowning rules.

- Armor insulates against fire damage for 1D6 rounds. After that, the character takes normal damage.

Breaking Up the Scenery

On occasion the investigators may have to dig up a corpse, a mysterious treasure, or burrow their way out of a dark pit or prison. Keeper and players alike may find the following digging rates useful.

These nominal rates assume one average person equipped with a shovel, spade, pickax, and wheelbarrow. With more people, pro-rate the effort.

For large-scale mining or quarrying, hire additional workers to dispose of the rubble. Under adverse conditions or with improvised tools, the keeper should

Exposure Table

Temperature	Water	Air
Unbearable (<5°F or -15°C)	Not applicable	Roll every 10 game rounds
Extremely cold (<20°F or -5°C)	Not applicable	Roll every half game hour
Freezing cold (<40°F or 5°C)	Roll every 10 game rounds	Roll every 4 game hours
Cold (<60°F or 15°C)	Roll every 15 game minutes	Roll once every day

increase the effort required. Conversely and at the keeper's discretion, workers skilled in special mining techniques may process raw material at substantially higher rates than listed.

Obstacles

In other situations an investigator may be required to break through obstacles like doors or walls. For these the keeper may apply armor-like rules: each obstacle has an armor rating that absorbs damage, and a number of hit points. Use the appropriate tool or weapon skill, and determine every round if the obstacle has been damaged. Each time the damage exceeds the armor rating of the obstacle, subtract the points of damage in excess of the rating from the obstacle's hit points.

A nearby table enumerates different types of obstacles of nominal thickness.

Notes Discussing Demolition of Obstacles

- Taking down a palisade or a yards-thick castle wall may require a considerable number of rounds. The keeper is advised to use the average time to demolish instead, with suitable modifiers. In such cases special siege or demolition techniques (battering rams, fire, etc.) are probably more efficient.

- The most appropriate tool for wood is the timber ax (15% base chance, damage 2D6). For less than six-inch-thick walls, the quarry hammer works wonders (20% base chance, damage 2D6). For masonry or stone walls thicker than six inches, one needs a pickax (10% base chance, 2D6 damage).

- Lacking the tools, the keeper may allow player characters to use regular weapons such as a battle-ax or a long sword.

Digging, Quarrying

1 cubic yard of...	requires...
loose soil	1/2 game hour of sustained effort
normal soil	1 game hour of sustained effort
compact clay	2 game hours of sustained effort
limestone or sandstone	25 game hours of sustained effort
granite	40 game hours of sustained effort

Some keepers will want to rule that an inappropriate tool breaks on a roll of 99-00.

- The pickax and timber ax can impale — and get stuck — on a roll of 01 (double damage, ignore damage absorption. Skill roll to pull the tool free). All weapon/tool rolls less than one-fifth of the skill percentile are "critical" blows (double damage, damage absorption applies). Always add damage bonus.

- Reducing the hit points of a section of the obstacle to zero makes a hole wide enough (roughly half a square yard) for a SIZ 13 or less to squeeze through. "Thin" supporting structures may collapse when weakened.

Natural Obstacles

At this time in Europe, forests cover 40%-60% of the land. A party keeping to a road travels 15 miles per day with oxcarts, 20 miles on foot, and 40 miles on horseback. For off-road travel, halve the moment rate, and if traversing hills or mountains, halve the rate again. When crossing marshlands or tracts of drifted snow, quarter the movement rate.

Unless bridged or fordable, each major river takes an entire day to cross.

These movement rates can be sustained indefinitely with adequate food and drink, and nightly rest. Desperate people can move twice as fast, but need one full day (24 hours) of rest for every day of sustained effort.

Under these circumstances it seems obvious why the waterways are used much more frequently than the roads, for they provide by far the fastest and cheapest way of traveling — especially across huge distances. By daylight and under favorable conditions, a coasting ship can sail about 60 miles in 10 hours.

Game Time

Play out combats and encounters which are potentially combative in combat rounds. See the Combat section, pp. 39-47.

Man-made Obstacles

Obstacle	Armor[1]	HP[1]	Time[2]
Hut walls and door	1	5	3 combat rounds
Pinewood boards	2	10	5 combat rounds
Wattle & daub wall	2	15	10 combat rounds
Ordinary oak door	3	15	10 combat rounds
Timber stockade	3	60	10 game minutes
Foot-thick masonry wall	6	300	100 game minutes

1 – Hit points, but not armor, are proportional to thickness. Adjust as needed.

2 – Time to demolish in minutes assuming a single average person with an appropriate tool and 25% skill in its use.

Occasionally a rule deals with longer spans of time. For instance, finding information in a library might take a game day or more. Healing is always spoken of as restoring hit points in game weeks. Magic points regenerate in 24 game hours or less.

Game time is fictional: it has nothing to do with real time. Game time is variable. It passes at whatever rate the keeper says. Keepers routinely expand and contract time and space in order to maintain a lively narrative. As storytellers, that is their province. When nothing happens, the keeper may simply remark, "Days pass." He or she can make years pass in the same number of syllables.

Players rarely get more than one try at any skill roll in a reasonable amount of game time. That amount of time varies, depending on the skill and situation. Riding a horse that is galloping out of control may demand several Ride rolls in a minute or two of game time, while someone struggling to comprehend the dull and verbose *Codex Vobiscum* may get a Latin roll only every week or two.

Skill Time

The use of a skill can also mark the passing of time. Though fighting skills can be repeated round after round, a skill which summarizes a process may represent the passage of hours or days of game time.

The frequency with which a particular skill roll can be attempted correlates with the length of game time the keeper thinks adequate to the job. A Library Use roll customarily represents four hours of persistent application, while a simple job like freeing a jammed door might take a quarter of an hour of Repair/Devise. This sort of repair could be successfully performed many times in the same day.

Actions

An action that can automatically succeed in an ordinary situation will, in a crisis such as an attack, require resolution by rolling dice. Most such rolls are made with D100; percentile dice are fundamental to the game. Other sorts of dice help determine characteristics or the damage done by an attack.

Automatic Actions

Routine actions in routine circumstances always succeed. There is no need to roll dice to walk, run, talk, see, or hear, nor is there reason to roll dice for any ordinary use of a skill. But the routine may become extraordinary in a moment.

Extraordinary Circumstances

Attempting to perform ordinary actions or to use skills under dangerous conditions, under critical scrutiny, or in ways that demand concentration requires resolution with dice.

Skills such as Pilot Boat, Climb, or Sword — those inherently dramatic or dangerous — are usually rolled for whenever used.

The keeper determines when and what the needed roll is. It may be a skill roll, a characteristics roll like INT x5, or a characteristics match-up on the Resistance Table.

D100 Rolls

To determine a player character's success with a skill, the character's player usually rolls D100. The keeper rolls for non-player characters. If the result equals or is less than the investigator's percentile level, the action succeeded. Otherwise, the act failed. (Exception: a result of

The Resistance Table

Active Characteristic

Passive Characteristic

P \ A	1	2	3	4	5	6	7	8	9	10	11	12	13	14	15	16	17	18	19	20	21	22	23	24	25	26	27	28	29	30	31
1	50	55	60	65	70	75	80	85	90	95	—	—	—	—	—	—	—	—	—	—	—	—	—	—	—	—	—	—	—	—	—
2	45	50	55	60	65	70	75	80	85	90	95	—	—	—	—	—	—	—	—	—	—	—	—	—	—	—	—	—	—	—	—
3	40	45	50	55	60	65	70	75	80	85	90	95	—	—	—	—	—	—	—	—	—	—	—	—	—	—	—	—	—	—	—
4	35	40	45	50	55	60	65	70	75	80	85	90	95	—	—	—	—	—	—	—	—	—	—	—	—	—	—	—	—	—	—
5	30	35	40	45	50	55	60	65	70	75	80	85	90	95	—	—	—	—	—	—	—	—	—	—	—	—	—	—	—	—	—
6	25	30	35	40	45	50	55	60	65	70	75	80	85	90	95	—	—	—	—	—	—	—	—	—	—	—	—	—	—	—	—
7	20	25	30	35	40	45	50	55	60	65	70	75	80	85	90	95	—	—	—	—	—	—	—	—	—	—	—	—	—	—	—
8	15	20	25	30	35	40	45	50	55	60	65	70	75	80	85	90	95	—	—	—	—	—	—	—	—	—	—	—	—	—	—
9	10	15	20	25	30	35	40	45	50	55	60	65	70	75	80	85	90	95	—	—	—	—	—	—	—	—	—	—	—	—	—
10	05	10	15	20	25	30	35	40	45	50	55	60	65	70	75	80	85	90	95	—	—	—	—	—	—	—	—	—	—	—	—
11	—	05	10	15	20	25	30	35	40	45	50	55	60	65	70	75	80	85	90	95	—	—	—	—	—	—	—	—	—	—	—
12	—	—	05	10	15	20	25	30	35	40	45	50	55	60	65	70	75	80	85	90	95	—	—	—	—	—	—	—	—	—	—
13	—	—	—	05	10	15	20	25	30	35	40	45	50	55	60	65	70	75	80	85	90	95	—	—	—	—	—	—	—	—	—
14	—	—	—	—	05	10	15	20	25	30	35	40	45	50	55	60	65	70	75	80	85	90	95	—	—	—	—	—	—	—	—
15	—	—	—	—	—	05	10	15	20	25	30	35	40	45	50	55	60	65	70	75	80	85	90	95	—	—	—	—	—	—	—
16	—	—	—	—	—	—	05	10	15	20	25	30	35	40	45	50	55	60	65	70	75	80	85	90	95	—	—	—	—	—	—
17	—	—	—	—	—	—	—	05	10	15	20	25	30	35	40	45	50	55	60	65	70	75	80	85	90	95	—	—	—	—	—
18	—	—	—	—	—	—	—	—	05	10	15	20	25	30	35	40	45	50	55	60	65	70	75	80	85	90	95	—	—	—	—
19	—	—	—	—	—	—	—	—	—	05	10	15	20	25	30	35	40	45	50	55	60	65	70	75	80	85	90	95	—	—	—
20	—	—	—	—	—	—	—	—	—	—	05	10	15	20	25	30	35	40	45	50	55	60	65	70	75	80	85	90	95	—	—
21	—	—	—	—	—	—	—	—	—	—	—	05	10	15	20	25	30	35	40	45	50	55	60	65	70	75	80	85	90	95	—
22	—	—	—	—	—	—	—	—	—	—	—	—	05	10	15	20	25	30	35	40	45	50	55	60	65	70	75	80	85	90	95
23	—	—	—	—	—	—	—	—	—	—	—	—	—	05	10	15	20	25	30	35	40	45	50	55	60	65	70	75	80	85	90
24	—	—	—	—	—	—	—	—	—	—	—	—	—	—	05	10	15	20	25	30	35	40	45	50	55	60	65	70	75	80	85
25	—	—	—	—	—	—	—	—	—	—	—	—	—	—	—	05	10	15	20	25	30	35	40	45	50	55	60	65	70	75	80
26	—	—	—	—	—	—	—	—	—	—	—	—	—	—	—	—	05	10	15	20	25	30	35	40	45	50	55	60	65	70	75
27	—	—	—	—	—	—	—	—	—	—	—	—	—	—	—	—	—	05	10	15	20	25	30	35	40	45	50	55	60	65	70
28	—	—	—	—	—	—	—	—	—	—	—	—	—	—	—	—	—	—	05	10	15	20	25	30	35	40	45	50	55	60	65
29	—	—	—	—	—	—	—	—	—	—	—	—	—	—	—	—	—	—	—	05	10	15	20	25	30	35	40	45	50	55	60
30	—	—	—	—	—	—	—	—	—	—	—	—	—	—	—	—	—	—	—	—	05	10	15	20	25	30	35	40	45	50	55
31	—	—	—	—	—	—	—	—	—	—	—	—	—	—	—	—	—	—	—	—	—	05	10	15	20	25	30	35	40	45	50

(Top-right dash region: Range of Automatic Success)

(Bottom-left dash region: Range of Automatic Failure)

For success, roll 1d100 equal to or less than the indicated number

00 is always a failure.) Failing, the keeper usually rules that some time must pass before another try can be made. The keeper determines the appropriate interval.

> *Example: while sailing off Norway, Harald's knorr encounters a great whirlpool. Harald instructs the crew to free the vessel by adjusting her sail. His Pilot Boat is 60%. For Harald to succeed, his player must roll 60 or less on D100.*

Resistance Table Rolls

To pit characteristics against one another, use the Resistance Table. Find the number equal to the active or attacking characteristic at the top of a column. Then find the passive or defending characteristic number at the left of a row. The number where the column and row meet represents the highest D100 result at which the active characteristic can be a success.

The same or different characteristics can be matched on the Resistance Table. Were an investigator to try to lift a friend to safety, it might be appropriate to pit the lifter's STR against his friend's SIZ, for instance.

> *Example: Harald and an enemy wrestle to gain control of a knife. Harald has STR 17, and his player must match it against the enemy's STR 13. Tracing the intersection of the two lines on the Resistance Table, we see that Harald has a 70% chance to win the match and control the knife. His player must roll 70 or less on D100.*

Rewards of Experience

A great pleasure of roleplaying is in participating in the advancement of an investigator from humble beginnings. Increases in skills are particularly noticeable, since the more a skill is used, the better at it the investigator becomes. As investigators succeed, solve, and overcome, players remember the circumstances and savor them.

The Skill Check

Investigator sheets record skill (experience) checks. When an investigator successfully uses a skill in play, the keeper may prompt the player to check the box beside that skill on the investigator sheet. This gives the investigator a chance to learn from his or her experience.

No matter how many times a skill is used successfully in an adventure, only one check per skill is made until the keeper calls for experience roll. Then only one roll can be made per check to see if the investigator

improves. Typically these experience rolls are made concluding a scenario, or after several episodes, when the character has had opportunity to reflect on events.

When the keeper calls for experience rolls, examine the investigator sheets to see which skills have been checked as successes. For each skill check, the player rolls D100.

- If the result is higher than the current skill number, then the investigator improves in that skill: roll 1D10 and immediately add that many points to the skill.
- If the player rolls equal to or less than the investigator's skill level, then the investigator hasn't learned from the experience, and the skill amount does not change.

Repeat the procedure for all the skill checks, then erase all checks on the investigator sheet. The Cthulhu Mythos skill never receives a skill check, and no box for such a check exists on the investigator sheet. Not improving a skill has no other consequence.

Succeeding at something poorly known is hard, but if successful then the investigator learns from the experience. Conversely, being expert at something guarantees success most of the time, but that high skill leaves the investigator unlikely to learn something new from employing it. It gets progressively harder to add percentiles to a skill.

90% Skills

If in the course of play an investigator attains 90% or more ability in a skill, he or she adds 2D6 points to current Sanity points. This reward reflects the discipline and self-esteem gained in mastering a skill. The Cthulhu Mythos is an exception to this.

Physical Injury

Hit points measure the immediate health of investigators, and show the amount of injury they can absorb. Losing hit points indicates the physical harm caused by attack or accident. An attack is that sum of damage done by a single opponent in a related sequence of combat rounds. An

injury is damage taken in an accident or as a consequence of natural force, such as a hurricane.

With exceptions, physical harm is inflicted by physical cause such as falling from a height or being stabbed. An investigator's attacks are said to *do damage*; an investigator who has been attacked successfully is said to *take damage* or, more precisely, to lose hit points.

When an investigator is injured or wounded, subtract the loss from the amount currently shown on the investigator sheet. Unless the keeper decrees otherwise, or unless losing half or more of current hit points from a single attack, an injured investigator functions normally until lowered to 2 or fewer hit points. He then goes unconscious or dies, depending on the loss. This cut-off point is an abstraction: it keeps investigators in play and eases bookkeeping.

Descriptions of wounds and injuries should agree with how they were received. They should offer some drama, or details to remember. Thus a dueling investigator is not only cut, but on the left arm near the shoulder, and it bleeds profusely for a while, requiring a bandage. A character who loses 4 hit points in a fall does not merely lose hit points, but sprains his right ankle which swells purplish and painfully. A blow to the skull not only raises a lump, but one that causes dizziness for half an hour, and that may affect the character's skills.

Stun

A knock-out attack, fall, or other injury may incidentally stun an investigator for 1D6 combat rounds. Stunned, the investigator may parry or dodge, but not otherwise act, because of disorientation. The keeper indicates when a

Poison Table

Poison[1]	Dose	POT[2]	Onset	Duration	Symptoms, in time
Adder, Aspic	1 bite	8	few min	hours	Pains, anguish, collapsus, necrosis, edema.
Bees/Wasps	50 stings[3]	1	few min	2 days	Pain, shock, collapsus, lung edema.
Belladonna	1 fruit	1	few min	varies	Excitation, spasms, phobia of light, thirst.
Bittersweet	1 fruit	1	instant	varies	Sickness, diarrhea, agoraphobia, cold.
Death Cap	1 cap	10	8–16 h	2–5 days	Sickness, colic, collapsus.
Hemlock	2–3 grams	10	few min	varies	Vision loss, sickness, diarrhea, paralysis.
Yellow Scorpion	1 sting	8	few min	10 hours	Pain, anguish, lung edema.
Spurge	contact	6	instant	2–3 days	Anguish, fever, paralysis; blindness if sprayed in the eyes. Used by Spanish crossbowmen.
Wolfsbane	contact	10	10–20 min	varies	Cold sweat, pains, vomiting, colic, failure.

[1]Preparation time is 1 day for animal poisons, 1–3 days for vegetable poisons.

[2]The potency of the poison is proportional to the dose, e.g. 10 fresh belladonna fruits have a potency of 10. Prepared poisons, as opposed to fresh ones, generally work at half the listed potency.

[3]The number of stings delivered each round to a single victim depends on the size of the wasp nest or the beehive: count 25 wasp stings per round for very large wasp nests, and 50 bee stings for very large beehives.

Spot Rules for Injuries

Besides being attacked, other ways exist to be injured. All injuries cost hit points, which will regenerate over time. It is possible, though, that an injury may cost hit points as well as CON or APP; such an injury is one from which full recovery never occurs. The loss of a limb is an example.

Acid

Damage from acid is a function of molarity (the relative dilution) of the acid. For game purposes, only significant contact with the acid, such as the immersion of a hand or arm, causes injury.

- Weak acids cost 1D3-1 hit points per round.
- Strong acids cost 1D4 hit points per round.
- Very strong acids cost 1D6 hit points per round.

Drowning & Suffocation

Apply this rule to drowning or failed swimming rolls, and use the same procedure for strangulation or to dramatize the effect of a choking cloud of gas containing no oxygen.

If the investigator is unable to breathe, the player attempts a D100 roll of CON x10 or less during the first combat round. In the second round, the roll lowers to CON x9. In the third round, the roll becomes CON x8, and so on, until reaching CON x1. It stays at that multiplier thereafter.

A surprised character has not had time to prepare by inhaling, so the keeper chooses a lower multiplier with which to begin. CON x6 is often appropriate.

If a roll fails, the character has inhaled a medium which cannot be breathed or he or she has begun to suffer serious injury to the respiratory system or brain. The character loses 1D6 hit points. In each round following, the victim automatically loses another 1D6 hit points. Continue the rolls until escape, rescue, or death.

Explosion

Alchemical laboratory explosions usually combine shock, glass and ceramic fragments, and damage from smoke and fire. Calculate the effect by determining how distant the person or item is from the point of the explosion.

Should the keeper allow it, a preparation of gunpowder can be held in a small jar. It does 3D6 damage.

yards away	damage done
0	5D6 hit points
1-2	4D6
3-4	3D6
5-6	2D6
7-8	1D6
9-10	1D3

Falling

Freely dropping from a height costs 1D6 hit points per ten feet fallen, or fraction over the first ten feet. With a successful Jump roll when leaping, the investigator loses 1D6 fewer hit points. This is a bonus for being prepared.

Fire

Fires that threaten investigators must be tailored by the keeper. Fire size can vary from a torch to the burning wooden framework of a castle. As well as from direct burns, death may come from asphyxiation or inhalation of poisonous gases. Burn damage equal to or greater than half of an investigator's hit points may cost APP or CON as well.

- A hand-held flaming torch does 1D6 damage each round it is thrust against a target. The target gets a Luck roll to prevent hair and clothes from burning. If they burn, the victim loses 1D6 hit points per round without added application of the torch. Use a First Aid roll to put out the fire, or perhaps a Sanity roll to stifle both panic and flames. A fire of about 1D6 would be reasonable for a campfire, but it would have much the same characteristics.

- A bonfire does 1D6+2 damage each round. The target's hair and clothes are automatically engulfed.

- An average wooden hut in flames does 1D6+2 hit points damage each round, to each person trapped inside. A Luck roll must succeed each round for each character, or begin asphyxiation rolls, as per the spot rule for drowning.

- Larger fires are special cases, to be described individually.

Spot Rules for Injuries

Poison

Every poison has a numerical rating. The higher the rating, the more deadly and speedy the poison. A poison rating is indicated by the abbreviation POT, for potency.

Use the Resistance Table to match the poison's potency rating against the target's CON. The poison is the attacking force. If the poison overcomes the target's CON, then something bad happens. Commonly, the victim loses hit points equal to the poison's POT. If the poison fails to overcome the target's CON, the results are less serious. Perhaps half-POT in hit points are lost, or no damage at all may occur. The keeper must judge by the poison and its application.

Most poisons are slow acting, and their symptoms intensify over hours. In game terms, hit point loss due to poisoning should be applied to pro-rate the effect's duration — for instance, 1 hit point per hour during the 8 hours for the asp's bite, if the Resistance Table roll failed.

See the Poison Table on the following page: only the keeper can determine whether a dose is sufficient for death. Faster-acting poisons exhibit symptoms starting in a few minutes. Most poisons are slow, so poisoners must be subtle. The symptoms noted are only a few of those possible.

The Poison Table lists common poisons, their potency for a given dose, and their effects. Many more poisons exist, such as the African Strophantus, the Asian upas-antiar, the Slavic honey-that-drives-mad, and mineral poisons based on arsenic, mercury, or red lead (minium). The latter are easily found in the scriptoria of monasteries, since they enter the composition of inks used to illuminate manuscripts.

Ingesting the right antidote (requiring successful POT rolls to identify the poison and to prepare the antidote, respectively) will stop the poison's effects and the ongoing hit point loss.

Disease

In the Occident of 1000 A.D., illness was often interpreted as the outer sign of a sick soul or a godly punishment, and called for intensified prayers.

Under no circumstance should the keeper arbitrarily expose the player characters to infectious diseases. In the absence of proper medication all diseases are debilitating, and many are deadly enough to kill half the investigators within weeks.

A minor disease such as a bad cold or a mild flu, could be contracted after a failed CON x5 roll once exposure has been proven. It should merely cost a hit point or two over a few days. A major disease like leprosy or the Holy Fire might also attack characteristics and any associated skill class, typically halving the effective skill percentiles for the duration of the disease. Serious diseases like blood poisoning, rabies, and lockjaw should be powerful, about 1D3 hit points per day, enough to kill an average human in a week.

Note that it is possible to prepare poisons using infectious agents. Infectious poisons take 2 weeks to prepare and a successful Potions roll. They are applied onto sharp weapon edges to infect wounded victims. Failing a Luck roll *and* a CON x5 roll to avoid infection, the victim suffers blood poisoning and loses 1D3 hit points every day for a few days — keeper's discretion.

Bed rest, potions, and the Medicine skill are the best treatments against diseases. In desperate cases, only curative magic or divine intervention truly helps. See the Disease Table on page 38.

stun occurs, perhaps as a result of an impale. Being stunned may or may not include losing hit points.

Shock

If from a single wound, an investigator loses hit points equal to half or more of his or her current hit points, the player much roll the investigator's CON x5 or less on D100 or the investigator falls unconscious.

Unconsciousness

When an investigator has 1 or 2 hit points left, he or she automatically falls unconscious, and no longer actively participates in the game. Though living, he or she will not wake until hit points rise to 3 or more. The keeper may privately determine an alternative length of unconsciousness.

Time may heal the wound enough that the investigator can stagger away, or he or she may be helped by a successful First Aid roll.

Death

When an investigator's hit points drop to zero or negative, he or she dies at the end of the following combat round. During those few seconds a friend might

Disease Table

Disease [1]	Cause [2]	CON [3]	Onset	Duration	Symptoms, in time
Blood poisoning (septicemia)	unclean wound	CON x4	4–16 hours	few days	Spiking fever, chills, feeling of doom, *shock, confusion, rash, gangrene, death.*
Consumption (tuberculosis)	unclean air	CON x9	weeks–years	chronic	Sweating, fatigue, malaise, weight loss, *cough, fever, respiratory failure.*
Flux (epidemic dysentery)	unclean food/water	CON x9	days	weeks	Diarrhea, abdominal cramps, fatigue, weight loss, *fever, vomiting, death by dehydration.*
Frenzy (typhoid fever)	unclean food/drink	CON x9	1–2 weeks	4–6 weeks	Headache, fever, rash, bloody stools, *hallucinations, intestinal bleeding, death.*
Holy fire (ergotism)	unclean food	see note [4]	1–2 days	weeks	Rash, fever, *scarring, gross deformations (mainly legs, some facial), gangrene, death.*
Leprosy	leper	CON x10	6–10 years	indefinite	*Skin lesions, disfigurement, hand and feet numbness, and muscle weakness.*
Lock jaw (tetanus)	wound	CON x7	5d–15w	1–7 days	Spasms, stiffness, *seizures, fever, death.*
Pocks (smallpox)	unclean air	CON x7	10–17 days	1–2 weeks	High fever, fatigue, headache, malaise, rash, *delirium, vomiting, diarrhea, death.*
Rabies	rabid animal bite	CON x1	3–7 weeks	7 days	*Fever, hydrophobia, confusion, numbness, drooling, insanity, asphyxia, death.*
Spotted/ship fever (typhus)	cold unclean place	CON x5	10d–2w	2–3 weeks	Headache, high fever, muscle pain, chills, *stupor, delirium, rash, light phobia, death.*
Swamp fever (malaria)	swamp, river	CON x8	10d–4w	chronic	Chills, fever, headache, nausea, *bloody stools, yellow skin, convulsion, coma, death.*

[1] Disease names vary greatly with location, time, and circumstances. The modern name is given within parentheses.

[2] This is the most accurate cause of the disease that can be inferred by observant people lacking modern medical knowledge.

[3] Once exposure is proven, a failed CON roll with the specified multiplier indicates that the disease will follow its course to the end (symptoms in italics), unless the infected receives successful Medicine treatment *before* the end of the incubation period (next column). A successful CON roll means that after incurring the least severe symptoms (symptoms in Roman type), the infected victim recovers.

[4] The holy fire "disease" functions in game terms like a poison. The "disease" is caused by the ingestion of fungus-contaminated rye end products like bread and porridge, sometimes ale. The poison potency is left to the keeper's discretion: it depends on the level of rye contamination and the quantity of contaminated products ingested.

Hit Point Loss

in one hit	injury
10%	light wound or bruise.
25%	deep wound or minor fracture.
50%	serious wound or major fracture (shock) roll equal to or less than CON x5 to remain conscious.
100%	terminal wound or bone crushed: death in one round without successful First Aid or Medicine.
250%	organ or bone destroyed: instant death.

intervene. See the Healing section nearby for the potential result.

The loss of a well-loved friend is a sorrowful occasion. It calls for consolation during play, and acknowledgment and recognition when play is over.

Healing

All living creatures heal naturally. In the game, an investigator regenerates 1D3 hit points per game week until all hit points have returned. Thus it takes three to seven game weeks to replace by natural means seven hit points. First Aid and Medicine skills can speed recovery in various ways.

Possessing three or more hit points, an investigator moves and operates without penalty, except that with so few hit points even moderate injury is likely to be deadly.

What's in a Hit Point?

"**D**oes a hit point really represent something?" The Hit Point Loss table suggests that keepers twist game-speak to introduce more description to the story. There is more drama telling an investigator that an arrow pierced his lung and the wound is gushing blood, than in saying "You lost 4 hit points, 6 to go." How much more satisfying for a player to hear that his or her blow not only killed the brutish ghoul, but also wrecked its skull beyond recognition!

The fraction of hit points lost is always measured against the base amount (SIZ + CON divided by 2), not against the current number of hit points. Also mind that light weapons may actually hit several times in a single round, so that damage done in one round is distributed over several small injuries rather than a big one.

First Aid, Medicine, Natural Healing

A successful application of First Aid immediately restores 1D3 hit points lost to a single attack or injury; usually there is only one complaint.

A European hospital and doctor can heal 1D3-1 hit points weekly. An Arabian hospital and doctor can heal 1D3+1 hit points weekly.

All characters, in or out of hospital, also heal naturally at the rate of 1D3 hit points weekly.

Hit points cannot be restored past the average of SIZ + CON.

Back From Death

If, before the end of the combat round following the round in which the investigator died, a dead investigator can be treated successfully by First Aid, and if the treatment increases the dead investigator's current hit points to at least +1, then he or she was near death but not dead, and has returned to life.

Hand-to-Hand Combat

Hand-to-hand combat includes such weapons as Small Club, Fist/Punch, Large Knife, and Shortsword.

A target may lose hit points when successfully attacked. The hit points lost vary: weapons inflict different amounts of damage, and nearly all damages given provide a range of results, as can be seen on the nearby Weapon Tables.

The Combat Round

Fights occur in combat rounds, each round lasts several to a a dozen or so seconds. A combat round is a deliberately elastic unit of time in which every character wishing to act who are capable of action have the chance to complete at least one action. An investigator's equality of opportunity is much more important

Spot Rules for Combat

Armor

Some creatures have armor listed in their statistics, representing tough hide, a thick layer of muscles and fat, or an extraterrene body. Humans wear a variety of body armors, from a boiled leather vest to entire suits of plate steel. How much and what sort of damage armor stops is for ingenious investigators to learn.

Armor is not destroyed if an attack penetrates. Armor has a lot of surface area. One or two holes in armor may indicate a wound or two, or maybe not even that. The chance to penetrate armor in the same place twice is too small to consider.

To account for armor in the game, subtract the listed hit point factor from the damage actually rolled.

Sample Armor Table

armor	damage stopped
normal clothes	0 hit points
quilted leather	1 hit points
boiled leather	2 hit points
1 inch oak door	4 hit points
leather and rings armor	4 hit points
chainmail armor	6 hit points
plate armor	7 hit points
buckler shield	8 hit points
ordinary brick wall	9 hit points
Viking round shield	10 hit points
ordinary granite wall	12 hit points
kite shield	16 hit points

Dodge

Each investigator has this skill, and he or she starts with enough percentiles of it to offer some hope. Along with the Luck roll, Dodge can be the roll of last resort in a time of danger. Remember to use it.

Impales

An impale result can be achieved by pointed hand-to-hand weapons and by most missile weapons. Blunt weapons and personal attacks cannot literally impale, but good rolls for them can be rewarded.

If an attacker gets a D100 result equal to or less than one-fifth of his or her skill maximum for the attack, then an impale occurs. This means that the thrusting weapon or arrow chances to strike a vital area, driving deeply through arteries, slashing crucial tendons and muscles. Example: Harald has Bow at 20%. Dividing 20 by 5 yields 4, so if his player rolls 01, 02, 03, or 04 on D100, Harald's shot impales the target.

- Why do I want an impale? An impale does more damage. Roll for damage twice, not once, and total the results to determine impale damage. For instance, Harald's arrow does 1D8 damage, but an *impaling* arrow does 2D8 damage. In theory, in two rounds Harald could do as much as 32 points of damage.

- Some Mythos creatures are immune to impales.

- If a hand-to-hand weapon impales, it sticks in the body of the foe. In the next combat round, the attacker must pull it free by means of a D100 roll equal to or less than his skill with the weapon. An impale does no extra damage when removed.

The Parry

A parry is a defender's action to block or divert a hand-to-hand attack. Parry does not work against missile weapons. The parry skill always equals the skill percentage held by the defender in the weapon or object being used for the parry. A parry is always defensive. A parry does no damage to the attacker.

One parry per participant can be attempted during a combat round. The player states whose attack he will parry. If the defender is knocked out or stunned before the attack occurs, the parry is foregone. If the attack does not occur, the parry is foregone.

The object used the parry absorbs all damage from a parried blow. If the damage exceeds the object's hit points, the object breaks and the defender absorbs any damage exceeding the object's hit points.

- Personal attacks can parry each other.

Spot Rules for Combat

- An impaling hand-to-hand weapon can usually be parried by other hand-to-hand weapons. Personal attacks cannot parry weapon attacks without risking normal damage, but if the range is touch and the person parrying has the higher DEX, he or she could Grapple for a weapon, yielding the effect of a parry. See below.

- Most sorts of swords, maces, and other one-hand weapons can attack and parry once per combat round.

- A parry can be made with a shield instead of a sword or other weapon. Shields also offer good protection against missile fire.

- Bows and arrows, throwing spears, Frankish axes, etc., are not designed to parry attacker blows. Some are impossible to parry with, such as a sling. When a missile weapon's hit points are exceeded during a parry, the missile weapon breaks.

- Two successful Grapples can in effect parry an attack, one to establish contact and the second to grab the weapon or weapon hand.

- An investigator or other character can parry and Dodge in the same round.

- Sling stones, arrows, and crossbow quarrels cannot be parried.

Surprise Attacks

In the first round of a surprise attack, halve the DEX ranks of the defenders. Those carrying unready missile weapons would be able to prepare their weapons, but not fire them until DEX rank of round two. Those with hand-to-hand weapons ready to use can parry with them or attack at half DEX. All defenders can parry or Dodge attacks coming from the front or sides.

Dimness, Darkness, Invisibility

If something cannot be seen, there's little chance to hit it, to find it, or to notice it. If the investigators nonetheless must act in such circumstances, then the keeper lowers relevant skills by at least half in moonlight, or makes their successful use a function of some low multiplier of POW. If the intention for the darkness is that the investigators will find it difficult to act in it, then the keeper lowers skill thresholds to 01. Some tasks, such as reading a map, are plainly impossible without sight.

Knock-Out Attacks

This action aims to render a target unconscious rather than to do him or her maximum physical harm. The player or keeper should state the intention before attacking. Perform knock-out attacks only with personal attacks or with clubs and other blunt instruments. A sword butt could be used deliver a knock-out blow, but the keeper should halve the sword skill percentage in mking this clumsy version of the attack.

Roll for damage as in an ordinary attack, but match the result against the target's hit points on the Resistance Table. A success knocks the target unconscious for several minutes, and the target suffers one third of the damage originally rolled (round down fraction). If the attack succeeds but the Resistance Table roll fails, then there is no knock-out, and the target takes full rolled damage.

- Knock-out attacks work against humans, but not against most creatures of the Mythos. At the keeper's option, however, knock-outs may work against deep ones, ghouls, serpent people, and other humanoids.

A successful First Aid roll immediately wakes a victim of a knock-out attack.

Partial Concealment

A target partially concealed should not normally reduce the attacker's chance to hit with a missile weapon, or lower the observer's chance to notice the target. If the target does seem difficult to notice, allow a Spot Hidden roll or an Idea roll to locate the position.

Spot Rules for Combat

Thrown Object

If an investigator throws an object, add half of his or her damage bonus to the damage done. Also review the Throw skill.

Two Weapons

In a combat round, a hand-to-hand hilted weapon might be held in each hand, but only one attack and one parry could be made by a character in the round.

Weapon Length and Closing

This is an optional rule for the keepers who want it. On the Weapon Tables, notice that all hand-to-hand weapons include an entry for weapon length. The longer the weapon, the more likely the wielder of it is to get in the first blow in a fight, or to fend off an opponent armed with a shorter weapon and prevent him from make his own attack. On the other hand, the longer the weapon, the harder it can be to wield effectively.

- A fighter armed with a long weapon attacks first against a target using a medium or short weapon regardless of DEX rank.

- Armed with a medium or short hand-to-hand weapon, the opponent cannot attack a long weapon user until successfully dodging. The player then should state that the investigator is slipping inside the guard of the long weapon user.

- Now that the attacker is inside the guard of the long weapon user, the long weapon user cannot attack. To re-establish his distance, the long weapon user can Dodge to disengage, or drop the long weapon and pull out something shorter.

- A character attempting a Dodge in a combat round may also parry, but not attack!

- Consider Fist/Punch, Grapple, Head Butt, and Kick to be "short weapons". Wooden staffs may attack at any of the three lengths.

than that the combat round represent a precise amount of real-world time. If an inequality becomes apparent, let the keeper devise a satisfactory compromise and continue playing.

When every investigator and other character has had an opportunity to act, the combat round is over and the next can begin.

Dexterity and the Order of Attack

Who has the first opportunity to attack? In a fight, going first can be nearly as important as hitting your target once you swing. All players declare their intents and DEX ranks. The keeper determines the order of attack by ranking combatant DEX from highest to lowest. If two or more investigators have the same DEX, the lowest D100 roll goes first.

● If hand-to-hand weapons and missile weapons are being used in the same general encounter, then aimed and ready missile weapons are thrown or released in DEX order before any hand-to-hand fighting takes place. (It is relatively quicker to pull a crossbow trigger or throw a knife than to swing club or sword, hit, and then recover.)

● After all missile weapons have completed their attacks, rank the pertinent DEXes again. Include all who are performing automatically successful actions, using some version of a characteristic, using a skill, or casting a magic spell.

● In this second DEX cycle the keeper now also ranks (a) those making hand-to-hand attacks, (b) those intending to attack with missile weapons but first needing to draw or nock arrows or bolts, draw throwing knives, etc., and (c) those throwing a second stone. All these actions occur in DEX order.

Hand-to-Hand Fighting

Any hand-to-hand weapon can be used in *Cthulhu Dark Ages*. The possibilities are so numerous and often so strange that it is pointless to write them up as skills. Everyone can perform Fist/Punch, Head Butt, Kick, and Grapple. These four personal attacks are discussed in the list of skills.

Most hand-to-hand weapons can perform one attack and one parry per combat round. A particular personal attack may or may not include a parry. Knives without cross-guards cannot parry, nor can missile weapons parry.

In its attack, a hand-to-hand weapon never does damage to itself — it is designed to cut or crush hundreds or thousands of times. Add full damage bonuses

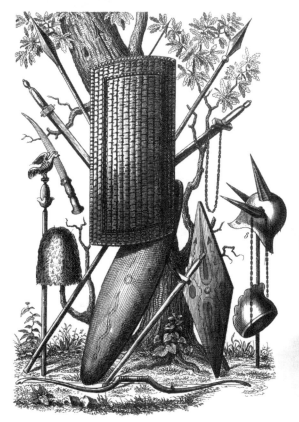

to these weapons' attacks except when thrown: thrown weapons get halved damage bonuses.

Clubs and Other Blunt Instruments

Clubs include broken branches, rocks, and fireplace pokers. No one has much interest in distinguishing them, so they all fall under the heading of "Club". Things like rocks and small clubs cannot easily be used to parry. Clubs never impale. Clubs and other blunt instruments can be used to make *knock-out attacks*.

Knives

Dirks, daggers, butcher's cleavers, and throwing knives have blades large enough to be significant weapons. An increase in skill with one increases skill in some of the others. Knives can impale.

Personal Attacks

Fist/Punch, Head Butt, Kick, and Grapple are personal attacks. These attacks can be attempted even by a person who is otherwise unarmed. All people know of these attacks, even if they are not very good at them. Each personal attack is used individually, and ability in each

Weapon Tables

Weapons listed within a gray box are considered to be similar, and a skill increase with one also increases the others.

Hand-to-Hand Weapons

Other matters being equal, the fighter with the longer weapon gets to attack first and may be able to hold a foe at bay. People below minimum STR/DEX can still fight with a weapon, but at half their effective skill. All hand-to-hand weapons get one effective attack per round.

Hand-to-Hand	base %	damage	1 or 2 hands?	HP	length	impale	parry[1]	knock-out	min STR/DEX	cost[2]
Fist/Punch	50	1D3	1H	–	Short	No	Special	Yes	–	–
Head Butt	10	1D4	0H	–	Short	No	Special	Yes	–	–
Kick	25	1D6	0H	–	Short	No	Special	Yes	–	–
Grapple	25	Special	2H	–	Short	No	Special	Yes	–	–
Ax	15	1D6	1H	15	Medium	Yes	No	Yes	9/9	80
Ax, Frankish	20	1D6+1	1H	20	Medium	Yes	No	Yes	8/8	100
Ax, Great	15	2D6	2H	25	Long	Yes	Yes	No	11/9	100
Club	25	1D6	1H	15	Medium	No	No	Yes	7/7	–
Flail	10	1D6	1H	10	Medium	No	No	No	9/7	?
Knife, Small	25	1D4	1H	10	Short	Yes	No	No	4/4	10
Knife, Large	15	1D6	1H	20	Short	Yes	No	No	4/4	15
Lance	15	1D8[3]	1H	15	Long	Yes	No	No	9/8	80
Mace	25	1D6	1H	20	Medium	No	Yes	No	7/7	60
Scimitar	15	1D8	1H	20	Medium	Yes	Yes	Yes	8/8	?
Spear, Short	15	1D6	1H	15	Long	Yes	Yes	No	7/8	40
Spear, Long	15	1D10	2H	15	Long	Yes	No	No	11/9	50
Staff	25	1D6	2H	15	Long[4]	No	No	Yes	8/6	–
Sword, Short	15	1D6	1H	20	Medium	Yes	Yes	No	5/5	150
Sword, Long	20	1D8	1H	20	Long[4]	Yes	Yes	Yes	8/7	210
Sword, Frankish	25	1D8+1	1H	25	Long[4]	Yes	Yes	Yes	7/6	?

[1] For weapons not designed to parry, accumulate damage if used to parry. If a weapon designed to parry blocks a very strong blow, the rolled damage of which exceeds the weapon's hit points, then the weapon breaks.

[2] Price in deniers. A question mark in the price box indicates a rare weapon. Price varies depending on availability and quality.

[3] Damage bonus of the horse if charging, of the investigator if standing still.

[4] Staffs and long swords may attack at any of the three lengths.

Frankish Weapons

Each Frankish weapon is the result of weeks of superior craftsmanship. The iron of the core is almost pure, while the edges contain some carbon (but not too much to enable welding). To harden the edges further, nitrogen is worked into the steel via bird excrement. Frankish swords are lighter than "regular" long swords, yet resist flexing 3 times better, *and* they are strong enough to cut through metal armor. This is represented in the game by a higher base chance (easy to handle) and a damage bonus (cuts through armor).

Unsurprisingly, Frankish weapons are much rarer and much more expensive than regular ones.

Missile Weapons

The number of attacks per round assumes careful aiming.

Missile	base %	damage[5]	base range[6]	attacks per round	HP	impale	parry	min STR/DEX	cost
Ax	05	1D6	5	1	15	Yes	No	9/11	80
Ax, Frankish	10	1D6+1	10	1	20	Yes	No	8/10	100
Bow[7]	10	1D8	60	1	10	Yes	No	9/9	60
Crossbow[7]	20	2D6	100	1/2	15	Yes	No	11/7	?
Knife, Small	10	1D4	10	1	10	Yes	No	4/4	10
Rock, Thrown	Throw	1D2	20	2	20	No	No	5/5	–
Sling	01	1D4	60	1	–	Yes	No	7/11	5
Spear, Short	15	1D6	25	1	15	Yes	No	7/8	40
Spear, Long	10	1D10	15	1	15	Yes	No	11/9	50

[5] Roll the normal damage bonus and divide the result by two. Round up fractions.

[6] Range in yards. When using missile weapons, an investigator may attempt to hit a target at up to double the base range. Halve the normal chance to hit. Double the normal chance to hit at less than DEX feet.

[7] Arrows and bolts do the damage of course, so damage bonus does not apply. An individual arrow has 1 hit point, a bolt 3.

Armor

"Rounds to put on" assumes the investigator has laid out the armor, and has practiced putting it on in the dark.

Armor & Helm	damage defl.[8]	burden	fits other SIZ?	rounds to put on	cost
Soft Leather	2	Light	±2	2	50
Cuirbouilli (boiled leather)	3	Light	no	2	100
Leather and rings	5	Light	±1	2	400
Leather and scales	6	Light	±1	4	375
Chainmail	7[9]	Moderate	±2	4	1000

[8] -1 if not wearing a helm.

[9] Deflects 4 damage from thrusting weapons (spear, bow and crossbow), and 3 from crushing weapons (Fist/Punch, Head Butt, Kick, club, flail, mace, staff, rock, sling).

Shields

Powerful blows damage shields. Each time the blow exceeds the hit point rating of the shield, the points of damage in excess of the rating lower the rating.

Shields	base %	hit points	min STR/DEX	cost*
Improvised	10	±15	7/10	–
Small	15	20	9/9	40
Medium	15	25	11/9	60
Large	15	30	12/8	80

*Listed shields are reinforced with iron. Wooden shields cost 25% of listed price, but have 10 fewer hit points.

Weapon Tables, continued

War Engines

Siege engines are bulky constructs and it can take minutes up to an hour to realign one. Therefore siege engines can only hit objects in the line of sight. The ballista shoots missiles along a more or less straight path like a crossbow, whereas the catapult and the trebuchet "lob" their payload. For these, range is a question of projectile weight: the lighter, the farther; damage remains the same.

Engine	base %[10]	damage[11]	base range[12]	time to reload	impale	crew	cost
Ballista	20	6D6 (21)	150	2 minutes	Yes	3	400
Catapult	10	30D6 (105)	100	5 minutes	No	3	900
Traction trebuchet[13]	01	4D6 (16)	75	2 rounds	No	50	300
Hybrid trebuchet[13]	05	50D6 (175)	50	10 minutes	No	10	1500

[10] Chance to hit assumes targets of SIZ 30 or more. Reduce chance to hit by 5% for every 10 SIZ below SIZ 30.

[11] The missile does the damage of course (average damage indicated within brackets), so damage bonus does not apply. The catapult launches 60–pound rocks. The traction trebuchet can lob 10–pound heavy stones. Our average hybrid trebuchet (the one detailed above) flings anything weighing up to 200 pounds! (A *large* hybrid trebuchet, not detailed above, can easily hurl a 400-pound stone, which of course does more damage.) The ballista shoots missiles resembling spear–sized bolts.

[12] Range in yards. When using war engines, the crew may attempt to hit a target at up to double the base range. Halve the normal chance to hit.

[13] Note that the trebuchet was not used in the Occident until the twelfth century. The Byzantines and the Arabs, however, had been using the engine for three centuries already.

increases individually with experience. Each personal attack is alphabetized in the skills section. Grapple especially is a complex skill and deserves close study.

- In this epoch, no systematic study of the Martial Arts exists in Europe.

- A knock-out attack can lessen the physical damage done to a target. See the spot rules for combat.

- In general, a personal attack can be parried by any hand-to-hand weapon or personal attack. Only a Grapple can parry another Grapple.

- As an option, some keepers may recognize the effect of a human Bite attack. It does no hit points of damage, but the surprise of its pain might break a human Grapple if a POW vs. POW Resistance Table roll favors the biter.

Swords and Scimitars

A variety of long-bladed chopping, slashing, and thrusting weapons exist. Most can be manipulated with one hand, but a few large swords require both hands to swing their bulk. These weapons are different enough that a skill increase with one sort may not increase the rest. All can impale.

Missile Weapons

These weapons are quite different from one another. They are similar only in that it is itself thrown, or else it is a device projecting a deadly object through the air. A hand axe or short spear are examples of the former, and the sling or bow are examples of the latter.

Big Targets

Big things are easier to hit. For monsters of SIZ 30 or more, every 10 SIZ above SIZ 30 adds 5 percentiles to an attacker's base chance to hit with arrow, thrown rock, sling stone, and so on. Point-blank and extended range modifiers apply, not that they're going to do your investigator much good.

Extended Range

A character may fire at up to double a missile weapon's range, with a half-normal chance to hit. He or she may fire at up to triple the weapon's base range at one quarter normal chance. These extensions of range would depend upon neutral or favorable winds.

Point-blank Fire

Point-blank is that distance equal to or less than the firer's DEX in feet. The shooter's chance to hit is doubled at point-blank range. The damage done is unchanged.

Precision Aim

The firer braces the weapon or takes special care in stance or aim, firing once in a round at half normal DEX rank. The effect is to double the point-blank and base ranges for the missile weapon.

Sanity & Insanity

Though spiritual counseling might seem a good substitute, systematic psychoanalysis is unavailable in the Dark Ages, and there are no insane asylums. Every village has its village fool who has been known to the community since childhood. Such a person can be entrusted with simple duties in exchange for food. The insane are often believed to be possessed and therefore qualifiy for an exorcism. In gen-

eral, insane people are not held responsible for any harm they might do.

An insane Dark Age investigator can be assumed to be a wandering derelict. Lacking modern treatment, the indefinitely insane person's only hope is private care at home or in a monastery, protected from upset, kept warm, and fed until he (or she) recovers. A benevolent keeper may consider a caring priest to be the equivalent of a modern-day psychoanalyst (see the *Call of Cthulhu* rules for detailed benefits and risks). After several or many game months of kindliness, the keeper may allow the investigator to re-enter the world.

Most of those who suffer from serious mental illness have done so from an early age, and will be dealing with the illness for their entire lives. In *Cthulhu Dark Ages*, player-characters typically start sane and mentally competent. In the course of play they must confront knowledge and entities of alien horror and terrifying implication. Such experiences shake and then shatter their belief in the normal world, progressively damaging their sanity. They also may shake belief in the holy church, a further complication.

Sanity in the game is modeled after the behavior of characters in Lovecraft's fiction, who faint or go mad more than a few times. Characteristic SAN (Sanity) is the game's register of investigator flexibility and resilience to emotional trauma. Investigators with high SAN find it easier to rationalize traumatic events or to repress horrific memories. Those with less SAN are mentally fragile, susceptible to emotional upset. Though other gruesome, comparatively ordinary sights and events also cause emotional disturbance, center stage in the game belongs to the Cthulhu Mythos.

In an unnerving or horrifying play situation, the keeper will test the resiliency and emotional strength of the player-characters. He does this by calling for Sanity rolls. A success is a D100 roll equal to or less than the current Sanity points. An unsuccessful Sanity roll always costs the character Sanity points. A successful roll costs no points, or relatively few points — see page 49 for "Examples of Sanity Point Costs".

Insanity in a game character is triggered when too many Sanity points are lost in too short a time, causing *temporary insanity* or *indefinite insanity*, defined later in this chapter.

Results of Temporary Insanity

When an investigator succumbs to insanity, it is best to make the result appropriate to the causal event. Keepers may roll 1D10 on the tables below for guidance.

Short Temporary Insanity

Roll 1D10.   **(1D10+4 COMBAT ROUNDS)**

no.	result
1	fainting or screaming fit
2	flees in panic
3	physical hysterics or emotional outburst (laughing, crying, etc.)
4	babbling, incoherent, rapid speech, or logorrhea (a torrent of coherent speech)
5	intense phobia, perhaps rooting investigator to the spot
6	homicidal or suicidal mania
7	hallucinations or delusions
8	echopraxia or echolalia (investigator does/says what others around him do/say)
9	strange or deviant eating desire (dirt, slime, cannibalism, etc.)
10	stupor (assumes foetal position, oblivious to events) or catatonia (can stand but has no will or interest; may be led or forced to simple actions but takes no independent action)

Longer Temporary Insanity

Roll 1D10.   **(1D10 x10 GAME HOURS)**

no.	result
1	amnesia (memories of intimates usually lost first; languages and physical skills engaged, but intellectual skills absent) or stupor/catatonia (see short duration table)
2	severe phobia (can flee, but sees object of obsession everywhere)
3	hallucinations
4	strange sexual desires (exhibitionism, nymphomania or satyriasis, teratophilia, etc.)
5	fetish (investigator latches onto some object, type of object, or person as a safety blanket)
6	uncontrollable tics, tremors, or inability to communicate via speech or writing
7	psychosomatic blindness, deafness, or loss of the use of a limb or limbs
8	brief reactive psychosis (incoherence, delusions, aberrant behavior, and/or hallucinations)
9	temporary paranoia
10	compulsive rituals (washing hands constantly, praying, walking in a particular rhythm, never stepping on cracks, checking one's sword constantly, etc.)

To remain active in the game, the investigator's insanity must be of a sort that can be effectively role-played. If time is of the essence, the keeper can roll on one of the temporary insanity tables (to left). As a matter of course the keeper should choose the insanity to match the situation which prompted it. In this regard, the keeper should consult with any players concerned.

A temporarily insane character may return to sanity after a few game rounds, or may need months to recover. Indefinite insanity may take months or years. If Sanity points reach zero, the character needs lengthy care and protection — who can say if he or she will ever return to play?

A character may regain Sanity points, and even increase his or her maximum Sanity points if POW increases. An increase in the Cthulhu Mythos skill always lowers the character's maximum Sanity points by the same amount.

How the Mythos Causes Insanity

Lovecraft suggests that what we believe to be the immutable laws of time and space are only valid locally, and are only partly true. Beyond our ken are infinities where alien powers and hostile races hold sway. Some encroach upon our world. The real universe, Mythos authors suggest, is one of irrational event, unholy fury, and endless anarchy. Human insanity opens a way into this terrible realm. Through such openings we can glimpse the dark and bloody truth at the heart of everything in a single sweeping cosmic vision. Sanity is lost in a few specific ways.

- The Cthulhu Mythos skill represents knowledge of the true universe. No amount of verbal therapy or bed rest can halt the self-transformation that true knowledge initiates. As Cthulhu Mythos increases, maximum Sanity drops, and points of Cthulhu Mythos limit current Sanity. A cycle begins: failed Sanity rolls become more frequent and current Sanity drops again.

- As the physics of the real universe, Mythos magic is more powerful and more elegant than any earthly science. As investigators work to visualize the unimaginable, their minds absorb alien ways of thought and undermine life as they have known it. Many crises of faith occur.

- Mythos tomes augment the Cthulhu Mythos skill by teaching Mythos spells. This knowledge costs Sanity, as

readers and spell casters deliberately replace what they once believed with the precepts of the Cthulhu Mythos.

- Nearly all creatures and entities of the Mythos cost Sanity points to encounter. Aliens are intrinsically discomforting and repelling. Every human instinctively reacts this way. Even losing Sanity does not erase this antipathy, though it can be repressed.

- Severe emotional shocks come from witnessing untimely death, violence, and other emotional loss. This world's common supernatural events and agents such as hauntings, vampires, zombies, and curses also affect characters.

Using SAN

The investigator sheet records three SAN relationships.

- Characteristic SAN: it equals the investigator's POW x5. Characteristic SAN changes if POW changes.

- Maximum Sanity points: it equals 99 minus present Cthulhu Mythos points. Maximum Sanity points may be more than, equal to, or less than characteristic SAN. Maximum Sanity is a cap amount, indicating the highest possible number of current Sanity points.

- Current Sanity points: this number is circled on the investigator sheet. Players find that this number changes often.

A successful Sanity roll can mean that the investigator either loses no Sanity points, or minimal Sanity points. With a failed roll, the investigator loses from several to many Sanity points. Losing a quantity of Sanity points may cause an investigator to go insane. If an investigator's current Sanity points drop to zero, he or she is permanently insane. That could mean that the investigator drops out of play for a long time, or it might allow the keeper to devise some special fate.

Insanity and the Cthulhu Mythos

Insanity stemming from non-Mythos causes yields no Cthulhu Mythos knowledge. But each time an investigator reels from Mythos-induced terrors, his or her belief in the Mythos is strengthened. The first instance of Mythos-related insanity always adds 5 points to Cthulhu Mythos. Further episodes of Mythos induced insanity each add 1 point to the skill.

Insanity

Insanity is induced by soul-searing experiences and ghastly surmises connected

with the Cthulhu Mythos. The duration of insanity depends upon the number of Sanity points lost, or the proportion of Sanity points lost. Three states of insanity — *temporary insanity, indefinite insanity,* or *permanent insanity* — can result.

Temporary Insanity

If an investigator loses 5 or more Sanity points as the consequence of one Sanity roll, then he or she has suffered enough turmoil that the keeper must test the player-character's Sanity. The keeper asks for an Idea roll. If the Idea roll *fails*, then the investigator has successfully repressed the memory. This is a trick the mind uses to protect itself. Perversely, if the Idea roll *succeeds*, then the investigator recognizes the significance of what was seen or experienced, and consequently goes temporarily insane.

The effects of temporary insanity begin quickly. Your keeper will choose whether they last for 1D10+4 combat rounds, or for 1D10 x10 game hours. Your keeper will also choose the symptoms connected with the insanity — panic, fainting or screaming, hallucinations, an appropriate phobia such as claustrophobia, tremors, sudden blindness, and so on.

Examples of Sanity Point Costs

Sanity lost*	unnerving or horrifying situation
0/1D2	surprised to find mangled animal carcass
0/1D3	surprised to find corpse
0/1D3	surprised to find body part
0/1D4	see a stream flow with blood
1/1D4+1	find mangled human corpse
0/1D6	awake trapped in a coffin
0/1D6	witness a friend's violent death
0/1D6	see a ghoul
1/1D6+1	meet someone you know to be dead
0/1D10	undergo severe torture
1/1D10	see a corpse rise from its grave
2/2D10+1	see gigantic severed head fall from sky
1D10/1D100	see Great Cthulhu

* – the value before the slash is the loss with a successful Sanity roll; the value following the slash is the loss if the Sanity roll fails.

Indefinite Insanity

If an investigator loses a fifth (round up fraction) or more of current Sanity points within one game hour, he or she goes indefinitely insane. Indefinite insanity removes a player character from play for an average of 1D6 game months.

Indefinite insanity represents a massive shock to the afflicted investigator. If no obvious symptoms for indefinite insanity are apparent, the keeper may mull over the choices for a session or two before choosing one. Play can continue. Meanwhile the investigator is haunted by a powerful sense of foreboding.

Some symptoms of indefinite insanity are continuous, such as amnesia, depression, or obsession. They may also be transient or episodic, such as multiple personality, nightmares, appalling emotional numbness, or social detachment.

Permanent Insanity

Investigators who reach zero Sanity points go permanently insane. "Permanently" may mean a year or a lifetime. In real life, a person may make some sort of relative adjustment after three or four months or years, but in the game the duration for permanent insanity is entirely at the keeper's discretion. In the real world, all insanity is indefinite, since no one can actively predict the future.

Nonetheless, many powerful symptoms offer little hope of recovery. Lovecraft concludes more than one story intimating that a lifetime of madness follows for the narrator. Every keeper must decide what end-point for madness best promotes the game.

Playing Insanity

When a player-character has a brush with insanity, the keeper's participation is demanded. The keeper must be able to describe the investigator's emotional state to the player, and suggest the extent of the malady without offering the player any certainty of its duration or depth. He must rouse the player's concern for his investigator while objectively orienting the player within the insanity. Since in this era there is no good terminology for describing fools, the keeper must translate across a thousand years.

If an investigator has even one point of Sanity remaining, the player has firm control of the player character. The aesthetics of how the player chooses to present a mad or nearly mad investigator represents a genuine challenge of roleplaying. Insanity or near-insanity calls for stronger roleplaying, not for less player control.

Once oriented within the role, the investigator will be able to describe his emotions so that other characters understand his situation, and can act with due regard, perhaps with sympathy. A player who can vividly describe his investigator's anxiety or terror deserves applause.

The threat of insanity in *Cthulhu Dark Ages* characterizes the Mythos in a way which allows no compromise. Exposed to it, what sane human would freely choose it? The Mythos is intrinsically loathsome and foul. The connection of Sanity points and Cthulhu Mythos points emphasizes the power of the Mythos, which corrupts and ruins by proximity and association. The sanity rules aim to show human fragility. All that people believe to be strong proves delusory and hollow. Madness becomes a necessary pre-condition for truth.

The Quality of Insanity

Investigator insanity characterizes the power of the Mythos by causing the investigator to adopt behavior which is limited in what it can achieve, yet is expressive and interesting to roleplay. Even an indefinitely or permanently insane investigator does not always need to be shut away, if an intriguing alternative can be negotiated with the keeper.

There is always the chance that a player may act out too many elements of his investigator's insanity, and unintentionally get in the way of the game. If so, the keeper must quash this sort of interruption. Not to do so would be unfair to the other players.

Sample Vessels of the Era

ROWBOAT
10 feet long, 4 feet wide
- crew 1 rower
- cargo 1/2 ton
- draft 1 foot

RAFT / BARGE
15 feet long, 10 feet wide
- crew 1 poleman (only goes down-river)
- cargo 2 tons
- draft 1 foot

Norman War Vessel

VIKING LONGBOAT (DRAKKAR)
72 feet long, 15 feet wide
- crew 40 rowers
- cargo 16 tons
- draft 3 feet

MERCHANT BOAT (KOGGE)
50 feet long, 15 feet wide
- crew 6 sailors
- cargo 50 tons
- draft 10 feet

NORSE KNORR
36 feet long, 10 feet wide
- crew 4 sailors
- cargo 8 tons
- draft 3 feet

BYZANTINE MERCHANTER
72 feet long, 20 feet wide
- crew 12 sailors
- cargo 100 tons
- draft 12 feet

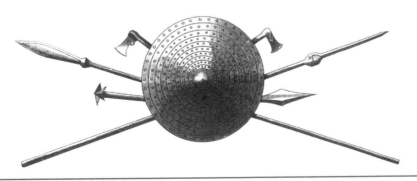

Costs, Equipment & Services

Listed prices are for new goods. Two factors that influence the price of an item are availability and quality.

FOOD

2 pounds of bread	1 denier
2 pounds of cheese	1 denier
3 dozen eggs	1 denier
Food and lodging, 1 day	1–5 deniers
Horse fodder, 1 day	3–6 deniers

CLOTHING

Woolen pelisse—cheap	12 deniers
Hooded cloak or robe	60 deniers
Short cloak—superior	120 deniers
Double cloak, hooded—winter	140 deniers
Marten cloak, bonnet—noble	360 deniers

TOOLS

Bucket	12 deniers
Awl, plane, auger, file, pliers, shears, hammer, saw	4–24 deniers
Sickle, hand ax, pickax, spade	24 deniers
Swing plow	72 deniers
Plow (iron plowshare and colter)	140 deniers

WEAPONS, SHIELDS AND ARMOR

24 arrows or 12 bolts	12 deniers
Fine Scabbard	48 deniers
Helm	100 deniers

Refer also to the weapon tables on pp. 44–46.

MISCELLANEOUS

Resinous torch, lamp oil, candle for 2 hours' worth of light	1 denier
Creeper rope, 30 ft	2 deniers
Fiber rope, 30 ft	12 deniers
6 person tent, incl. 2 10 ft poles	360 deniers
Traveler's pack: outer wear, water-skin, knife, fishing line & hook, felt blanket, sack, flintstone & iron, whetstone	240 deniers
Warrior gear: war-horse, saddle, horn, helm, sword, spear, chainmail, shield	2400 deniers

WEEKLY WAGES

Farmer, priest, servant	1–3 deniers
Craftsman, sailor	3–6 deniers
Guard, cleric, mercenary	4–8 deniers
Warrior, merchant	20–40 deniers

These values represent either equivalent earnings or hiring wages.

ANIMALS

Farm dog	12 deniers
Sheep	12–15 deniers
Cow	24 deniers
Mule	36 deniers
Sow	12–54 deniers
Ox	24–108 deniers
Horse	240+ deniers
War-horse	600 deniers

Young slave, boy or girl	< 3000 deniers

VEHICLES

Wheelbarrow	12 deniers
Two-wheeled cart	120 deniers
Four-wheeled wagon	240 deniers
Four wheeled cart (leathered)	360 deniers

Four-wheeled carts in the Dark Ages lacked a pivoting beam. Oxcarts covered with leather are watertight.

CONSTRUCTIONS

Commoner's hut	72 deniers
Commoner's house	360 deniers
Short wooden bridge	420 deniers
Fishery	480 deniers
Timber hall	720 deniers
Water mill	810 deniers
Small farm with land	4800 deniers
Earth and timber castle: tower, moat, stockade, ditch, bailey and gatehouse	36000 deniers

BOATS

Rowboat	120 deniers
Raft	12 deniers
Viking Drakkar	9000 deniers
Norse Knorr	3000 deniers

Utilities

After day comes night. The time of men will pass and they will return to where they came from.

— The *Necronomicon*.

Players and keepers are not usually acquainted with the Dark Ages era that serves as a setting for *Cthulhu Dark Ages* adventures. This chapter provides some general historical context. Many suggestions for realistic Dark Age settings can be found in the glossary. Particular historical points are dealt with in the scenario. When in doubt, apply friendly stereotypes.

The year 955 was a turning point in the history of the Occident. That year, Otto the Great crushed the Magyar cavalry on the banks of the river Lech, thereby putting an end to the age of invasions.

In the Dark Ages that followed, the Occident struggled hard to recreate its unity, a foundation on which, one century later, a new civilization would grow that would become our modern world.

The Dark Ages describe the twilight zone before the last age of history—ours. And while feudal warlords shared the land, defining a new temporal order, a monastic reform was silently sweeping through the Christian world, bearing a new spiritual order.

The World

Scholars of the Dark Ages pictured the universe as being made of several spheres revolving around a spherical earth, and carrying respectively the stars, the planets, the sun and the moon.

Thanks to the mild climate that prevailed in the Dark Ages, the Occident was covered by one vast primeval forest, except for flatland moors, mountain tops and Mediterranean scrublands. Birches were then covering Greenland and Iceland.

People of that time were basically forest dwellers. Wherever they looked they saw a tree line, and wherever they walked or rode they crossed the forest, and often got lost on the way (maps and compasses were yet to be invented)!

Time

Dark Ages people relied on the cockcrow to give the signal for dawn, or listened to the bells sounding the canonical praying hours in a nearby monastery. Observation of the position of heavenly bodies was often accurate enough to know the time.

The only "clocks" are the sundial, the sandglass, and the *clepsydra*, or water-clock. Nighttime is mainly measured in terms of "candles."

The year is naturally divided into seasons and into weeks with the Sunday rest, punctuated by religious fetes, celebrations and fasting periods.

In the Dark Ages clerics keep track of the year, the month (*kalendes*) and the day of the month, and compute the date of Easter, etc. New Year's Day does not start on January first, but varies from place to place. At the chancery of the king of France it is the first of March. In Germany and England, it is customarily Christmas.

According to the most widely accepted chronology, the world will be 4952 years old in 1000 A.D., and scholars believe they are living history's last age: the sixth age.

Languages

Occidental languages are split into two groups: *Romanic* languages (Italian, French, Spanish) and *Germanic* languages (the languages of the Germanic Empire). Each language group is in turn subdivided into a patchwork of dialects.

Except in Italy and to some extent England, the majority of laymen are illiterate.

Since Latin is the language of the church, of clerics and of monks, it is *de facto* the most widespread of languages. Indeed monastic and Episcopal schools dispense lower and higher education in Latin. Clerics, ministers, ambassadors, interpreters, jurists, and secretaries converse in Latin and write all letters and legal documents in Latin. Monks chant in Latin and priests preach in Latin. Of course, laymen don't grasp a single word of it.

Religion

Catholicism is the official religion of the occidental world. There are churches everywhere. Parishes are landed estates, and the priest is supported by the tithe levied on the believers. The priest is a servant of the parish owner.

Priests implement the mission of the church to baptize, celebrate mass, give the sacraments, communicate the faith and uphold morals in their rural parishes. Besides that, church imposes a few duties like Sunday mass, the observance of *fêtes* and fasting, and rules for births, weddings and deaths. Non-observance of these rules is sometimes followed by physical punishments, like pulling out teeth.

In short, priests are in charge of the *cura animarum* — the care of souls. Most of them live with a concubine. Itinerant officers of the local ecclesiastical authority supervise parish priests in their mission. A priest is not allowed to cross parish lines to administer penance without the bishop's permission.

From the humble parish priests to depraved popes, the whole clergy is integrated with the feudal system. Archbishops have the same worries and ambitions as

---

Tasks & Ranks

The *abbot* is the father for life of the community. All monks obey him without question or delay. He is sometimes seconded in his duties by a prior.

The *hospitaller* insures the service in the hostel, and carefully plans welcoming ceremonies. Other monks and servants assist him in his task.

The *almoner* is in charge of the chaplaincy and cares for the sick of the neighborhood once per week, helped by a few servants. In prosperous monasteries, the almoner also organizes food distribution to the poor. Clothes worn by monks for more than a year are given away.

The *bursar* is the most important officer in a monastery. He is in charge of the clothing, the bedding, and the lighting. He is authorized to collect the rent money coming from the abbey's lands and dues in kind.

The *cellarer* is in charge of the storeroom and has a flock of subordinates. The *refectory monk* directs the service in the refectory; the *loft monk* supervises the corn lofts, the water mill and the bakery; the *constable* runs the stables, and the *gardener* takes care of the vegetables garden and the orchard.

The *sacristan* is the officer responsible for the church and the liturgical furniture. The *preacher* is master of ceremonies and librarian. The *precentor* is the choir master.

The *infirmarian* cares for the sick and performs the ritual bleeding of healthy monks for the Annunciation Day. The most accepted treatment against illnesses consisted of feeding the sick with meat.

Nuns

Nuns, just like monks, are served by lay sisters, but male priests act as chaplains.

their lay counterparts. There are even warrior-bishops who fight with maces!

The most widely accepted Christian belief is in the immortality of the soul, and the concept of eternal punishment in the pits of hell. However, only a few live a pious life in accordance with the Holy Scriptures, while the vast majority of people believe they can buy their way into heaven with testamentary gifts. Another common practice among the most privileged is to obtain salvation of the soul by becoming monks on their dying beds.

Heresies

Around 1000 A.D. appears the Manichean heretic movement, embracing peasants, nobles and clerics alike. Manicheans reject the ecclesiastical hierarchy, and do not believe in the necessity of baptism and other Christian rituals. They do believe however in a self-created universe and in the harmlessness of adultery.

Christianity has not yet eradicated the pagan spirit (*paganum animum*): everywhere people try to invoke rain by way of magic, and worship ancestors, nature's spirits and heavenly bodies. They celebrate New Year's Day on the first of January by offering a feast dressed as stags or cows, and going on a roof or to a road crossing to read the future. They are afraid of the dark and of the demons of the night.

Some women believe that they can fly to the clouds, travel great distances, and combat other flying women. The first records of demon worshippers appear in the tenth century.

Germanic and Slavic people only reluctantly adopt novelties like the wheeled plough and water mills. They fear the nature spirits' anger, and appease them with little effigies, offerings, and invocations.

Conversions

Many pagan kingdoms are Christianized during the Dark Ages. This process is usually initiated at the highest level, and then forced upon the rest of the population through large scale baptism and the eradication of the old cults and their priests or priestesses.

Why do heathen leaders convert to Christianity in the first place? One common problem of paganism is its lack of structure, hierarchy and decorum. Conversely, Christianity has plenty of those, hence it is able to provide newly formed nations with a unified spiritual identity that strengthens the powers in place.

Exorcists

In 250 A.D., the church instituted a new order of low-ranking priests: the *exorcitate*. Upon a successful exorcism the exorcist is promoted to full-fledged priest. Exorcism consists of a solemn address to the demon to leave the body, backed up by three sacramentals: water, salt and oil.

Pilgrims

Pilgrimage, together with the cults of saints and relics, is a characteristic of the Dark Ages. The supreme pilgrimage is the journey to Jerusalem (six months of travel from South France).

Hermits

Hermits live in solitude, working to attain exaltation through cold and hunger, meditation, or through the struggle of accomplishing some exhausting physical labor.

Monks

In the tenth century monasteries experience a rebirth. The reforming movement, the aim of which is to "free the church from the hands of laymen," starts in the abbey of Cluny. Cluny depends directly on the Holy See in Rome, and is not owned by a lord as is still the custom.

Clunisian monks live under the strict Rule of Benedict of Nursia, sixth century founder of Western monasticism. In 1000 A.D., there are hundreds of abbeys and priories, and thousands of monks submit to Cluny. This praying community sets an example of sanctity in the spiritual chaos of the Dark Ages. Great abbots become very famous and very influential men. They are often travelling, accompanied by escorts of armed monks.

The wealth of some abbeys is such that they are not too vulnerable to the vicissitudes of the time, like famine. On the other hand that same wealth sometimes corrupts the good monks, some of whom take wives and indulge in gluttony and sloth. This decline in monastic values eventually prompts the Cistercian Benedictine reform — a return to basics — in 1098 A.D.

Monasteries also function as hostels for the most privileged and the most indigent. Exemplary monasteries like Cluny have a hostel outside their walls, with two dormitories (one for men, one for women), latrines and a refectory. Monasteries also lodge pilgrims, traveling

priests and monks, and the poor in the chaplaincy — the house of the poor — outside the cloister. Indigent travelers and pilgrims are sometimes given a provision of a denier before leaving the monastery.

According to the Benedictine rule monks must spend time in prayer (six to seven hours a day), work pulling up the weeds in the garden, kneading bread at the bakery, and charity. Apart from two short periods of time monks are not allowed to talk to each other (they actually develop a sign language of a few hundred words). Daily chores are entrusted to lay brothers called *conversi*, or *barbati* because they are not required to shave, or *illiterati* because they can not read.

The monastery employs many professional artists to account for the numerous paintings, jewel-stained book covers, ivory carvings, the embroidered fabrics, the crown-shaped lights made of bronze, gold or silver, and so forth. Some abbeys even house workshops that minted deniers — a kingly right inherited from Carolingian times. Many monks are skilled craftsmen.

Monks sleep in a dormitory where candles or oil lamps are left burning at night. A monk's bed consists of a simple wooden frame with a felt carpet, a straw mattress, a linen sheet, and a cushion filled with straw. In winter each monk gets a blanket of hairy fabric or goat or lamb skin.

Monks are required to wash their faces and hands every day. They take two warm baths per year in large vats: once before Christmas and once before Easter. Monks also shave their beards once per month.

Novitiate lasts for about a year. The novice is a man willing to "embrace the rule." The monastic order welcomes "oblate" children — often second-born sons of noble families — brought to the monastery by the parents with an appropriate dowry. Monasteries also educate gifted peasant boys especially chosen by the abbot, such as Gerbert of Aurillac who eventually becomes pope. Boys and novices are not allowed to mingle with monks until they have taken their vows.

One kind of monastic school located outside the cloister is open to peasant children, and another is reserved to oblate children who are taught to read Latin and to calculate. Saint Gall, Reichenau, and Fulda have famous schools. Teaching is strictly oral and consists of simple arithmetic and catechism.

Costume

Monks wear a plain black habit with an outdoor hood or cowl and a *scapular* (a long narrow sleeveless outer cloth draped over the basic tunic). They have simple shoes or sandals, wear a leather belt and carry a knife. The belt also serves as a

The Social Pyramid

Farmers represent about nine-tenths of the population of the Occident (in contrast to three-quarters in Byzantium). Some 45,000 souls therefore support a cathedral city of 5000 souls, working the soil or the sea all about. Such cities are at least 50 miles apart, two to three days' march.

Some 4500 peasants in surrounding villages support a town of some 500 souls, the residence of a local warlord, and his garrison of 10 to 20 warriors. Towns are at least 5–7 miles apart, about two hours walking.

Rural Calendar

March: prune vineyard; **April:** pasture animals, weed fields, plant and prune fruit trees; **May:** gather fodder for horses and fasten vines; **June:** plough fields, shear sheep; **July:** make hay; **August:** harvest; **September-October:** gather and press grapes, sow; **November:** put wine in barrels, thresh wheat, take pigs to graze in the forest; **December:** slaughter pigs.

Huts and Timber Halls

A representative southern European village consists of one street flanked by stone houses, and one tower at each end (Catalonia).

In northern Europe wood prevails and a village is a cluster of huts, silos, ditches and timber halls (Brittany). About one village out of two has a stone church with a cemetery.

Buildings are basic rectangles with a roof of thatch or shingles that sometimes extends to the ground. The only opening is the door. Sizes vary greatly: the smallest huts have no walls as such and larger timber halls have one or two rows of vertical posts supporting roof beams and defining aisles and bays. A central fireplace is at ground level and marked by stones.

Close to the houses and within the village stockades, farmers keep fenced vegetable gardens, fruit trees, and hemp beds.

disciplinary aid in self-flagellation. Each monk also receives from the abbot a pen, a needle, a towel, and a writing tablet.

The nun's costume is similar to the monk's, with the hood being replaced by a wimple and a head veil. Habits are white, black, or mixed.

Diet

Lunch consists of two meals: one of beans or peas, and one of "herbs." Now and then monks are also served eggs and cheese. On Sundays and Thursdays fish is added to the regular menu. Bread — one pound per monk — is a constant as is wine — one cup. Supper (*cena*) consists of bread with fruits or *oublies*, a sort of thin pastry. On fast days (most of the year except for fêtes and the period from Easter to Pentecost) supper is the only meal.

Farmers

Most farmers of the Occident are feudal tenants: their lord grants them plots of land (*tenures*) for cultivation in exchange for certain services, among them the obligation to cultivate the lord's *mansus*.

Every tenant has a few strips of land to cultivate. Ploughing is done with the swing plough or the wheeled plough, and harvesting is done with the sickle. Once the ears of the corn are cut, hay becomes common property until the new harvest. In the Dark Ages rotation of crops is unavoidable, for lack of a proper fertilizer. The biennial rotation widespread in Mediterranean regions consists of sowing a field every other year only. In northern Europe a 3-year rotation prevails.

Farmers actually live across a wide spectrum of social conditions from quasi-slaves — serfs — who can be sold as property, to freemen or colonists who benefit from reduced rents and obligations. A few possess a plough or harrow and a team to pull it, but the majority must rely on their own strength to pull the plough.

The most gifted farmers go into service with their lord as squires or as sergeants (from *serviens*,

A Motte-and-Bailey Stronghold

The stronghold is built on raised ground or a man-made earth hill or *motte*, right over ground water. It consists of a square wooden tower with a first floor hall raised on a basement, and possibly one or two extra stories, all connected by an interior ladder-like stairway. The top of the tower is used by the watch. Windows are simple openings that can be covered with boards. The basic furniture of Dark Ages strongholds includes large beds, long tables consisting of planks laid across trestles, and benches.

The basement is dug into the motte, where food stocks are kept along with the lord's "treasure." The well is usually located in the basement.

The ditch surrounding a motte is reinforced by a wooden palisade (in some rare instances, a stone wall) and a gatehouse. The outer defenses enclose an open area or *bailey*, sometimes including outbuildings such as a communal oven and kitchen, latrines, stables, kennels, and barn.

It takes a hundred workers about a month to build a simple wooden motte-and-bailey stronghold with a 100-foot-diameter and a 50-foot-high motte.

servant) who collect taxes and fines, and deal with merchants. Large abbeys delegate the administration of their domains to a mayor (*villicus*). In the empire there are also "ministers," favored servants who fulfill courtly or knightly functions for their lord.

Farmers sell surplus at village fairs where they can earn a few deniers for paying off taxes: dues, tithe, and "tallage."

Blacksmiths (about one in every other village) are simple tenants like most farmers, and pay their dues in kind to their lord with the weapons and the horseshoes they craft.

Villagers hunt in the surrounding forest, gather fruits, beechnut for oil, moss and dead leaves for litters, wood for their houses, fences, and tools, and for their lord's castle, roadwork and bridges. They leave their animals to graze in the forest.

There are also woodsmen who lead a nomadic life on the fringe of the village community, in the lord's forest: some are coalmen and produce charcoal for ovens, or the ash for making glass and soap. Others make creeper ropes and ground tree bark to produce the tan for tanning leather. A few are specialized in collecting honey and wax from wild bees.

Costume

Men wear breeches and a long shirt that falls down to the thighs, in the fashion of their ancestors. Women wear very simple dresses and children wear one-piece smocks. Wooden-soled shoes and small boots are quite common, but the most common footwear consists of strips of cloth intertwined around feet and lower legs — socks.

Diet

The basic diet consists of rye, oats, barley, and to a lesser extent wheat. Farmers who can afford the lord's oven bake their own bread; the others eat porridge day in and day out, seasoned with herbs or peas. Corn is also used to brew ale, which is safer than water. The fruits of the forest and the products from their vegetable gardens complement the farmers' diet. If they can afford to keep livestock, they might have eggs and milk, and occasionally boiled or salted pork.

Warlords

The feudal anarchy arising after the downfall of the Carolingian Empire seriously eroded the prerogatives of kings, and tore apart the very fabric of their kingdoms. Kingdoms broke up into principalities, and principalities broke up into fiefs: much of the old power of counts and princes shifted to the benefit of small warlords and religious communities. New strongholds and castles sprout everywhere: on the site of an antique institution, an outpost, a *vicus*, etc.

These warlords all have different origins: many descend directly from an ancient lineage of clan chiefs or landowners. Lords either live with their great lord, or were "housed" (*casati*) on a fief of their own. There are also bold adventurers who simply take over land with ten or twenty companions, and settle in before anybody can throw them out. A Dark Ages dictum pronounces: "no land without a lord"!

Housed warlords have two things in common: above all they are knights, heavily armed horsemen and military leaders. Secondly, a warlord possesses a stronghold in which he and his clan can hide from enemies and happily oppress inferiors. This is usually a timber hall with one storeroom and a corn loft or an upper floor for the lord's chamber.

During the Dark Ages however, a new type of fortification appears in France: the motte-and-bailey stronghold.

In his spare time the lord plays war games: he hunts, plays chess, or participates in tournaments. These battlefield simulations, not necessarily reserved to the aristocracy, are far more informal and improvised than later in the Middle Ages. Therefore tournaments are rather dangerous, if not as deadly as the ancient Roman games from which they originated.

Portrait of a Warlord

A shaven man with short hair, tunic falling to his knees, baldric girded around the loins. He is equipped with a horn, a small whip, a sword, a flintstone and the iron to strike it, the branch to set afire, and spurs. For his war-horse: a fur saddle with stirrups, a cloth cover on the croup, and a bridle. His battle gear consists of a sword, a lance, a helmet, chain mail and a shield.

Diet

Unlike his tenants, the lord's table abounds with meat (served by an attendant on a large slice of superior bread) and wine. Apart from one knife, everybody eats with his or her hands.

Princes

Great lords rival kings in terms of power and riches. Their main obligation to the king consists of the military aid they owe him, but in practice they do pretty

much what they want. In fact principalities — not king-doms — are the real political hearts of the Occident.

Portrait of a Great Lord and his Lady

A bearded man, wearing a large lustrous cloak attached to the right shoulder by a precious broach and under the cloak, a blue shirt falling to the calves. He wears red *chausses* (tight leggings) and black pointed shoes with a golden rim. His lady wears a long linen or silk veil (*pallium*) covering the head and closed at the neck by a jewel. The veil opens on a long embroidered shirt hiding the feet, with wide sleeves and golden braids. Underneath she wears a skintight chemise.

During the Dark Ages, war mainly takes place between lords, between princes and vassals, or between king and lords. Apart from a few notable exceptions there are strictly speaking no "international" wars.

The reasons to wage war are material ones: land, strongholds, cities, etc. Therefore war basically consists of sieges, burning down entire villages, and slaughtering and raping at will.

Note that great lords wear heavy armor, ride fast battle horses, and are worth their weight in silver coins. They only die on the battlefield accidentally, and when caught the enemy usually prefers to hold them for ransom.

The Palace

The prince's main residence is his palace. The staff consists of servants, guards, clerics and craftsmen. Princes

are on the move most the year, meeting their peers or making pilgrimages, and stopping off at their many country castles.

Typically a palace consists of a defensive wall enclosing domestic dependencies, a long timber warehouse, a chapel, and a stone or brick building with the ceremonial room (*aula*) on the first floor where the prince discusses matters of politics and religion with visiting vassals, bishops and abbots.

A Castle

The first floor of the stone tower is without openings and is used as storeroom. The second floor is the living room of the lord and his suite and is provided with a fireplace and groined bays. Inside the defensive walls one finds barracks for the garrison (provided in part by vassals and allies), shelters for the servants and the craftsmen, and barns.

Cities & Trade

In the occidental society of the Dark Ages there is little room for trade. Everything is produced or gathered on the spot. Money plays only a small part in the economy.

There are many reasons for this economic stagnation, primarily the downfall of the Carolingian Empire that fragmented centralized power and disrupted established trading routes and posts. Muslims control Spain and Sicily. Vikings devastate ports of the North Sea. The Danube is unsafe for navigation because of the Hungarians, despite their recent conversion to Christianity. Last but not least, the church condemns trading under the principle that "deniers do not produce deniers."

The network of Roman roads is antiquated and only suitable for beasts of burden. Wheeled vehicles are only used for short distances. Moreover, local lords impose tolls on travelers and traders.

Rivers constitute the most practical and dependable communication route. Towns along large navigable rivers are usually situated at regular intervals, corresponding

roughly to a day of travel. The most important towns have a bridge.

In Germany and in the North of France, cities of the Dark Ages only survive as cathedral cities, that is, residences of lay or clergy lords, and all activities are tied to the daily life of these lords.

Just like any feudal lord, the bishop is the master of the people and he owns all the property in his diocese. The city inhabitants are more or less under the same juridical conditions as country tenants. They are lodged, fed, clothed and armed by the bishop.

In Italy the lords prefer to reside in cities rather than in their countryside castles, in the fashion of their Roman ancestors. Cities like Milan and Venice are relatively large and well developed compared to their relatives in the rest of the Occident.

In the Dark Ages, most Jewish merchants are still based in far away countries like Syria, Egypt and Byzantium. Jews who live in occidental cities act as moneychangers or usurers, practices forbidden to Christians but nonetheless essential for society. They buy vital goods, ovens and mills, precious metals, and some even administer the finances of bishoprics.

A Goroda

Russian cities like Novgorod or Kiev (there are about a hundred of them) consist of a wooden palisade enclosing three districts: the merchants, the craftsmen and the soldiers' districts. Craftsmen work metals, leather and bone and make oil and cloth. Around this core grow lively suburbs where hunted, farmed, and gathered products (furs, honey, wax) are exchanged for iron and salt.

Exports

The Occident exports salt, wine, corn, fish (salted or smoked); linen, black woolen cloth from the Rhine, reddish woolen cloth of the Swabs, precious Flemish cloth, wood from the Trentino and Appenino forests, sickles, knives, Frankish weapons, Bohemian tin, copper and silver from Harz and Bohemia and Slovakia, Slavic gold, brass, lead, iron from Brescia and Carynthia and Styria.

Byzantium exports products from the Black Sea and the Orient: silk, spun gold, wines, spices, perfumes, incense, slaves, black fox fur, and so forth.

The Jews form a strong community bound together by language, religion and common interests derived from their mercantile activities.

The Christian attitude towards Jews generally oscillates between indifference and esteem, although a latent anti-Semitism is always there, ready to raise its ugly snout when some natural or unexplained disaster hits the Christian community.

In the Dark Ages Vikings rule the northern seas. They colonize Greenland and discover North America, and they build huge settlements and warehouses in north Germany.

At the beginning of the tenth century, the Swedish Vikings — the Russ — are well established in Russia. As soon as the snow melts, Scandinavian boats navigate the Dniepr from Kiev to the Black Sea and Constantinople. There the Russ trade honey, furs and slaves for spices, wines and silks.

A Cathedral City

The heart of a city is the cathedral district, which features a cathedral (the bishop's palace) and the tower of the lay lord (burgrave). The burgrave is responsible for the city's protection. Monasteries and episcopal schools are supervised by the chancellor, who issues licenses to teach. The schools provide higher education to teach clerics.

Close by one finds the houses of the garrison's *milites*, the shelters for clerics, servants and other laymen in service of the bishop, the covered market and the shops of the craftsmen.

A description of the Arras market of 1000 A.D. lists the following goods: woolen cloth, fish, corn, fruits, dye, ash, wooden platters, salt, wine, cattle, wax, lard, knives, iron, scythes, spears, lamb skins, cat skins, rabbits, leather, honey, butter, cheese, gold and slaves.

The city often still has ancient Roman walls and buildings. Streets are narrow and tortuous, winding in the shadow of two-storied houses.

The Dark Ages sees the advent of outside burgs (*forisburgus*) as merchants' warehouses progressively outgrow the city walls. Merchants obtain new privileges from bishops. In fact, townsmen — burgesses — are about to transform the cities of the Middle Ages into real economic centers.

Technology

The sack of Rome in 410 A.D. marked the end of the Roman Empire, and the beginning of the Middle Ages. Most technological and scientific advances of that thousand-year-old civilization were lost to the barbarian kingdoms, or survived in some crude form — and so it

was in 950–1050 A.D. The Christian Occident only starts to rediscover the lost knowledge via the Arabs of Spain and Sicily, whose science is based on that of ancient Greece, Persia, and India.

The is particularly true of medicine. Although the medical science of the Romans appears rudimentary by today's standards, they do perform simple surgery and dentistry, know how to cauterize and suture wounds, and how to disinfect them with wine (which was incidentally also their anesthetic). In contrast, health and hygiene in the Dark-Ages Christian world devolves to a messy affair of total ignorance, dogmatic misinterpretation of the Roman legacy, and many folkloric half-truths. Occupational diseases and poisonings are commonplace, and child delivery is a death-defying business for both mother and baby. Infectious diseases are completely misunderstood and thus unstoppable, untreated battlefield injuries often result in massive infections and ultimately death.

In the Dark Ages only the Arabs are scholarly enough to preserve the Roman legacy and even to advance it: the first medical faculty ever is established in 978 A.D. in Baghdad, many medical treatises are written, and there are records of surgery to remove tumors and gallstones.

A major technical breakthrough of the Dark Ages is the use of draught horses for ploughing, made possible by the introduction of horseshoes and rigid horse collars. Horses are put to good use in the fields: hitched up in a line, they pull the plough and harrow much faster than oxen, and they are more resilient too. But both horses and oxen are expensive, so most farmers must rely on manpower or donkeys.

Milling corn and hay is done in water mills, there are special beer-mills to mill hops, iron-mills for the iron industry, and fullers' earth-mills for the textile industry. Again, renting the lord's mill is expensive, hence many farmers still rely on the ancient custom of hand-milling. Some mills are floated in the middle of rivers to increase their power.

One corn mill is sufficient to support the needs of about 50 peasant families.

Iron ore, copper, salt, gold and silver are traditionally dug up in opencast mine pits (in some places galleries were dug, and gold was also sought in riverbed sands). Miners are simple tenants like most farmers.

Ore is melted in primitive ovens. Iron is so rare in the Dark Ages that the need for its use in weapons left little for agricultural tools: wooden tools — *ustensilia lignea* — predominate.

Mineral salt is extracted from pits by first dissolving it with water. The mixture is hauled out of the mines with cranes and then boiled in big cauldrons until the water completely evaporates. Salt is of course produced in coastal salterns too.

Textile production is tied to the exploitation of the land, since it depends on wool, linen and hemp. The women dye fabrics with natural dyes like madder and vermilion, and make clothing. Their tools are the distaff, the spindle and a simple upright loom operated by one person.

Leather is typically made from ox, goat, lamb and wolf skins. Fur coats are made from lamb, marten, mole, otter or beaver skins. Both leather and fur are processed by specialized craftsmen.

Glass working is uncommon during the Dark Ages, and most glass artifacts are luxury goods. The technology is not yet advanced enough to produce either clear glass or sizeable glass panels.

A Quick Tour of the World

Arab World

A vast urbanized empire spanning North Africa, two-thirds of Spain, Sicily and the Near East, with its capital in fabled Baghdad. Arabs are unequalled scholars in mathematics, medicine, alchemy, and astronomy. Despite the unifying forces of Islamic culture, the Dark Ages sees political fragmentation in the Arab world. In the Dark Ages, Occidentals consider Muslims as ordinary neighbors, and there isn't any particular animosity directed towards them.

Cordoba

Cordoba in Spain is the second largest city of the Occident, with over one hundred thousand inhabitants, an order of magnitude larger than western capitals like Paris, London, Rome or Aachen. The city counts more than a hundred thousand houses, seven hundred mosques, seventy libraries, and one university (still to be invented in the Occident). The streets are paved and lit at night! Near the Great Mosque and its thousand columns, streets are even covered with carpets. Brick houses are built in the style of North Africa and the Middle East: the largest are two stories high, enclosing gardens and fountains, and equipped with a well or water cisterns.

Baghdad

Baghdad is one of the largest and wealthiest cities of the world. A triple circle of ramparts, 360 towers, and four gates defend the "Round City" as it is also called. On a moat at its very center stands the great palace and the great mosque. Suburbs surround the city, with the huge al-Karkh market to the south and the city wharves to the east on the river Tigris. Two pontoon bridges cross the river to the east bank and its growing suburb. Baghdad has state hospitals and close to a thousand official doctors of medicine.

Byzantium

This is the civilized Eastern Roman Empire, center of religious orthodoxy. The centralized political administration controls the economy via large corporations. Territory is divided into military provinces called "themes," ruled by governors, and provided with a net-

work of castles. The road system is poor, though: goods are carried on the backs of pack animals or women.

By 1020 A.D., the Byzantine Empire rules the Balkans from Hungary to Armenia. Commercial relations between Byzantium and the Occident (especially Italy) are quite frequent, but nonetheless tainted by mistrust.

Constantinople

The capital Constantinople surpasses ancient Rome in size and in beauty. Constantinople is Europe's largest city, counting close to a million inhabitants, and is defended by a fifteen-mile-long triple defensive wall with fifty gates. It has long avenues bordered with countless marble columns, public baths covered with mosaics, many basilicas and forums, aqueducts, cisterns and sewers. Constantinople is the focal point of trade routes to and from the Occident, Scandinavia, Russia, Persia, Ethiopia and even China.

German Empire

Two-thirds of the Holy Roman Empire is still virgin forest in the Dark Ages — *terra incognita*! The empire lays east of the Meuse and reaches as far as Bohemia. The North Sea coast of the empire extends from the fens of the Netherlands to the great northern plain.

The emperor (*imperator Romanorum augustus*) is elected by the nobility of the four duchies: Saxons, Franks, Bavarians and Swabs. Bishops and abbots control much land and provide part of the emperor's army, and hold the highest functions of the state. German bishops even rule the bishoprics of Bohemia, Hungary and Poland.

The eastern marches are Christianized in the tenth century and colonized in the eleventh.

Attempts to restore the grandeur of the Carolingian Empire yields mixed results. Nevertheless, the centralized

power (the emperor, imperial bishops and *pagus* counts [judges]) are quite well respected, thereby delaying the fragmentation of authority by the great nobility, as is already happening in France.

Kingdom of Burgundy

A wealthy kingdom around the Rhone-Saone valley, west of the Jura and the Alps, includes warm Provence and its Roman way of life.

Kingdom of England

A kingdom torn between the Danes, the Anglo-Saxons, and the Normans of the duchy of Normandy in France. The land is divided into shires and "hundreds" (*vap-natak* in Danish areas). The formation of principalities isn't felt in England at the same time, or with the same force, as on the mainland.

Hundreds has the responsibility to enforce local justice (malls are held once per month). The earl is the royal officer of a shire responsible for raising military forces and implementing royal justice. Shire courts are presided over by bishop and sheriff — a minor royal official. The sheriff is also sent on "turns" to the local courts of the hundreds, and collects the royal revenues and taxes.

In some regions Danish farmers have settled, keeping their own laws and customs.

Kingdom of France

A wine and wheat land of the Franks, with numerous cathedral cities like Paris. Formerly Roman Gaul, it extends from the heaths of Aquitaine in the south, to the Ardennes forest in the north. The French kings dispute with the empire about the Dukedom of Lorraine. The power of the king — the duke of France — reposes on the sole domains of the crown. France is the birthplace of feudalism and feudal institutions.

France is a patchwork of strongholds in the Dark Ages, much more so than Germany or Italy. Strongholds are often not more than ten kilometers apart. In the course of the Dark Ages, France moves from anarchy to a state with large territorial principalities and well developed administrations.

Kingdom of Italy

The mountainous land of the Lombards, still attached to an urban way of life inherited from ancient Rome.

Venice

Venice is a city entirely living from trade. Venice exports heathen Slavs kidnapped or bought on the Dalmatian coast to the harems of Egypt and Syria. Except for slaves, the lowest people around were sailors, craftsmen and merchants.

Papal States

The Papal States to the south of the kingdom of Italy are ruled by the pope of the Western Church, bishop of Rome, vicar of Christ, from his Holy See in Rome. The clergy and the people of Rome theoretically elect the pope. In practice however, he is chosen by Roman nobles, which make him the instrument of political factions. Nonetheless, the clerical bureaucracy succeed in maintaining Rome's spiritual power over Christendom.

Rome, the Eternal City

In the Dark Ages, Rome is a vast field of antique ruins, the remnants of Roman civilization. Within the city walls that once sheltered a million inhabitants, a few thousands live in small groups scattered along the banks of the Tiber.

The Eternal City attracts a constant flow of pilgrims, the bread and butter of Rome's clerics, innkeepers,

Mappa Mundi

The few world maps of the Dark Ages picture the earth's surface as a disk. The northwest quadrant represents "Europe" and the southwest quadrant Africa, the two being separated by the Mediterranean Sea. This occidental half-disk is separated from the oriental half-disk — Asia — by the river Don to the North, and by the river Nile to the South. At the center of everything lies Jerusalem.

pawnbrokers, and nobles who live in strongholds built on ruins.

Russia

The Russian Empire — centered at Kiev — is a creation of the Swedish Vikings, and consists of principalities. A prince is a sort of supreme judge with limited powers; otherwise, he is responsible for the defense of the city and the land. An assembly of nobles and bourgeois support the prince in his duty.

The kingdom of Kiev unites Slavs and Vikings into one nation, under the umbrella of Byzantine culture and the Christian faith.

Kiev

A great city, capital of a powerful state, Kiev has eight markets and forty churches. Hagia Sophia was one of the most beautiful monuments of Christendom. Kiev offers large warehouses for storing goods. Craftsmen and merchants are organized into rich guilds called "hundreds," and benefit from special privileges. It is, for instance, possible to obtain credit from local princes or other merchants.

Scandinavian Kingdoms

Denmark, Sweden and Norway. Viking society originally consists of clans of free farmers organized in small isolated communities, each with its own customs and clan leader. The Viking woman holds a social status not found elsewhere in the Occident, except maybe in Britain. She can possess land, strongholds and drakkars.

Denmark is a unified Christian kingdom, where feudal lords hold land. The "Danevirke" is a long earth wall crossing the base of the Jutland peninsula separating Denmark and Germany.

Sweden is the only Scandinavian region that fails to become a united kingdom during the Dark Ages. Also, conversion to Christianity progresses very slowly in Sweden, and urban development stagnates.

Slavonic States

The Dark Ages sees the transformation of the pagan lands of central Europe into unified Christian states: Poland, Hungary and Bohemia. The Hungarians are originally fierce Asian nomads who invaded the region between the Tisza and the Danube around 900 A.D., splitting the Slavic world in two.

Prague

The largest northern city of the Occident, according to Ibrahim Ibn Yakub. A city of whitewashed stone, with an important craft industry (saddles, bridles, shields), and a big slave market. There, great lords can sell their serfs to Jewish and Hungarian traders.

Spanish Kingdoms

There are four Christian states in Spain to the south of the Pyrénées, squeezed between the powerful Arab state and the Christian world.

And Beyond

Obviously the world is not limited to the above. The Vikings colonize Greenland and discover North America, and struggle with the Beothuk Indians and the Inuit. The Arabs establish trading routes to dark Africa and its famed gold. Other trading routes link Byzantium and the Arab world to Russia, East Africa, India, and China.

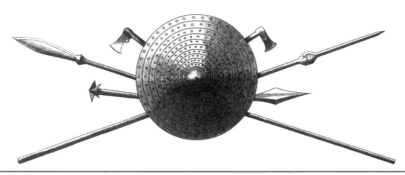

The World
ca. 1000 A.D.

Island

Finnish Tribes

Norway
(Denmark)

Orkney
(Denmark)

Scotland

North
Sea

Sweden

Baltic
Sea

Baltic Tribes

Kievan Russia

Irish
Kingdom

Wales

England

Denmark

Slavic States

LONDON

AACHEN

Holy
Roman
Empire

PRAGUE

Poland

KIEV

PARIS

France

Moldavia

Burgundy

Hungary

Bay of
Biscay

VENICE

Italy

Croatia

Wallachia

Black Sea

Georgia

Leon

Navarre

Serbia

Bulgaria

Armenia

Castille

Adriatic Sea

Emirate
of Cordoba

PAPAL
STATE

Small
Italian
States

CONSTANTINOPLE

CORDOBA

TO BAGHDAD ▶

Byzantine Empire

Arab
States

Idrisid Kingdom

Saracens

Mediterranian
Sea

JERUSALEM

Berber Tribes

Libyan
Tribes

Fatimid Caliphate

CAIRO

Dark Ages Glossary

abbey: important monastery run by an abbot.

alchemy: in the Dark Ages, *Arabian* alchemy or *al-kimia*. Mystical teachings of Arabic scholars and philosophers about the order of nature, the four elements of Aristotle (earth, water, air, and fire), and how to control their transmutation.

ale: alcoholic beverage fermented from yeast, water, and malt. Safer than water!

allod: land held in full ownership. Inheritance regime based on the division of the allod amongst all heirs of equal rank; all sons, for example.

armarius: librarian. Books are put in closets *(armaria)*.

arts: cycle of seven literary and scientific disciplines that form the base of teaching and culture during late antiquity and the Middle Ages (see *Quadrivium* and *Trivium*). Saint Augustine's doctrine states that the sole objective of an art should be a better understanding of the Holy Scriptures.

astrology: scholarly theory by which the celestial movement of the stars and planets constrain "human forces" as well as the forces of nature.

auctores: authoritative classical writers. Cicero is the Dark Ages epitome of the art of writing, and Virgil the epitome of poetry.

automaton: self-acting machine. Mechanical wonder that imitates the movements of life. One example is the animated throne of Emperor Konstantinos VII Porfyrogennetos (941), adorned with a golden tree, singing birds, and roaring golden lions.

ban: power to command, to constrain and to punish. Originally a royal power, the ban was usurped by lesser lords with the weakening of public authority: the right to rent out some-body's bull or boar, to force tenants to use one's mill or oven or wine press for a fee. Above all, the right to exert (arbitrary) justice and levies.

benedictine rule: a monastic rule elaborated by Saint Benedict of Nurcia in the sixth century.

Bible, the: the Septuagint is the first major Greek translation of the Old Testament, written in Alexandria between 250 and 150 B.C. The Vulgate is the major Latin translation of the Bible, written by Jerome late 3rd, early 4th century at the request of Pope Damasus. There

are also scattered and partial English translations attributed to Bede.

boni homines: freemen recipients of local custom (Roman or German), presiding over malls (see page 67). In feudal countries, they merely assist seigniorial courts exercising the ban.

books: primarily bound, copied and stored in abbeys. The catalogue of a monastic library typically contains the books of the Bible, commentaries on the Bible, the works of Flavius Josephus, Horacius, Lucan, Perseus and Juvenal, poets of late antiquity, historiae and the life of saints. In the profane closet, one could find classical theatre pieces, Boece's summary of Plato and Aristotle, books treat-ing the seven arts of the Quadrivium and the Trivium, *quaestiones medicinales* (see page 68), and books on the virtues of plants.

bronze: many monumental bronze doors and statues are produced in the Dark Ages. The most famous bronze workshop is that of Bernard of Hildesheim.

canonical praying hours: prima hora at dawn, tertia in the morning, sexta at noon, nona in the afternoon, vesper at sunset, etc.

castrum: important fortress with many eligible parties, as opposed to lesser — and often more recent — strongholds belonging to one lineage.

chanson de geste: a long epic poem such as "Roland."

charter: manuscript that contains the ownership titles of a physical person or moral person.

clepsydra: very rare clock powered by water from a slowly emptying receptacle.

constable: household officer, headman of the stables, and by extension, garrison officer and keeper of the law.

corn: wheat, rye, oats, and barley grain.

craftsmen: armorers, bakers, blacksmiths, brewers, butchers, carpenters, cooks, furriers, goldsmiths, locksmiths, masons, millers, painters, parchment makers, saddlers, shoemakers, tailors, tanners, etc.

crypt: column-supported, vaulted chapel with curved walls, often situated under a church's choir; usually houses the bodily remains of saints (relics).

custom: the established custom *(consuetudo)* is often the only recourse against arbitrary

Dark Ages Glossary

seigniorial justice (the ban) and unfair taxes (*malas exactiones*).

denier/penny/denarius: silver coin in use in the Occident. Fictitious monetary units are the *sou/shilling/solidus* (12 deniers) and the *livre/pound/librum* (20 solidus). The Byzantines use the *nomisma*, and the Arabs use the *dinar*, both gold currencies.

dues (in kind): sheaves, poultry, honey cakes, livestock, skins, clothing, etc.

exemption: privilege granted by the pope to a monastery that more or less freed it from the control of the bishop.

familia: group of servile workers housed and fed by a master, and who owe him all their work.

fêtes, Christian: the three oldest and most important ones are: Christmas (Christ's birth on December 25th), Epiphany (January 6th), and Easter (Christ's resurrection on the Sunday following the first full moon after the vernal equinox). Lent (40 days of fasting) and the Holy Week before Easter are very important too.

feudalism: relationship that takes place between the dominated class (peasants) and the dominant class (nobility).

feudal system: system of man-to-man ties that structure the dominant class (*potentes*). The practical aspects of this system consist of swearing fidelity (*fidelitas*) and paying homage (*hominium*) to one's lord, in exchange for the fief (*feudum, beneficium*).

fief: administrative domain of a lord.

fish: commonly consumed fishes are salmon, lamprey, cuttlefish, carp, trout, eel, barbel, roach, chub, and also mullet and herring. Fish is traditionally salted or smoked.

forest fruits: apples, pears, plums, chestnuts and hop cones.

frock: outer robe-like garment worn by a monk.

fruits: fruits are very varied including quinces, peaches, medlars, walnuts, hazelnuts, cherries and strawberries.

Greek fire: incendiary substance made of naphtha, quicklime and sulfur, and almost impossible to put out. To be flung at enemy ships and buildings with catapults.

haus/domus: house. In the high aristocracy, the "house" consists of the direct family, a chaplain, household officers (seneschal, constable, etc.) who are sometimes granted a fief for support, a few clerics, servants and even prostitutes.

hawking: hunting sport imported from the plains of Asia, and growing in popularity.

herbs: vegetables; lentils, leeks (eaten raw), cabbage, lettuce, chervil, parsley, watercress.

historiae: history annals (manuscripts). Men of the church who conceive history in a biblical perspective only, write historiae.

immunity: institution that closes a territory (usually a religious domain) to royal officers; the beneficiaries of the immunity fulfill the tasks usually reserved for the public authority, such as justice.

indulgence, partial: the payment of money in lieu of penance. Standard practice from the 11th century onwards.

itineraria: lists of region and city names. Itineraria are inherited from the Romans and regularly updated. Used for military expeditions, travels and territorial divisions.

joculatores: wandering minstrels, professional entertainers. Joculatores might also juggle, ropewalk or sell sexual favors.

languages, written: the most widespread language in the Occident is Latin (Roman Catholic Church). "Vernacular" languages are second best but rising: (Old High) German in the empire, (Old) English in England, (Old) French — a simplification of Vulgar Latin — in France and Burgundy, "Glagolica" script throughout the Slavic world, and Syriac in Western Asia as a replacement of Greek. Arabic is used in the Arab world, including Southern Spain.

magyars: heathen Hungarians.

maleficia: potion, supposedly magical.

mall: public assembly of justice enforcing the "custom," as opposed to seigniorial justice

(the ban). Defendants are rarely acquitted or executed (nobles are beheaded, others hanged), as most are simply banned.

mansus: type of landholding. One distinguishes between the master's mansus (representing up to a half of the arable land) and the farmers' tenures.

mappa mundi: symbolic world map.

mead: alcoholic beverage fermented from honey and water.

miles, milites: "soldier," or mounted warrior. A feudal warlord typically has 10 to 20 milites in service or hired.

music: typical musical instruments are drums, the tambourine, flutes and strings. The Dark Ages are also famous for the monks' Gregorian chants.

ordeal: severe physical test that a crime suspect must endure to prove his innocence in the face of God, such as having no marks from putting one's hand into fire or boiling water, or holding a white-hot iron. Another favorite of the Dark Ages is the "judicial duel," whereby the duelist who dies is decreed guilty *post mortem*.

pagus: "country," district of a county.

parish church: one village out of two possesses one, and none in the frontier marches. Most churches are built of stone, and the dead are buried next to them. Note that stone itself is not used as a decorative element. Rather, mosaics and mural paintings embellish surfaces. Parish churches provide sanctuary to wanderers, fugitives and strangers. Some churches have special huts for that purpose. In theory, no armed or mounted man is allowed to enter the church.

Peace of God: movement started by the church in the 980s. This movement has two objectives: to limit the brutalities of the warrior aristocracy and to protect the victims of these brutalities. The decisions of the assemblies of peace, expressed in council canons, aim above all to protect the persons and properties of non-warring parties (clerics, farmers, and merchants). The "Truce of God" forbids battle from Friday to Sunday, or during Lent or other liturgical events.

Dark Ages Glossary

priory: small monastery — sometimes with only a handful of monks — led by a prior.

privileges, urban: clauses like the inviolability of homes against public officials, the suppression of judicial duels, and the ban on legal proceedings against burgesses outside the city.

quadrivium: scientific disciplines of the liberal arts: music, astronomy, arithmetic and geometry.

quaestiones medicinales: widespread teaching technique for medicine consisting of questions and answers.

reform: aimed at the purification of the morals of the clergy, and the independence of ecclesiastic power with respect to the secular power.

relics: relics come in three classes. First are corporeal parts of saints and artifacts from Christ's passion and death, such as Christ's crown of thorns at the Cathedral of Notre Dame in Paris, chunks of the true cross in Paris (as well as three of the four nails), Rome, Brussels, Oviedo, and the lance that pierced Christ's side (of which the head seems to have been lost). Second, articles of clothing or household artifacts touched by saints. Third, items that have touched first or second class relics.

runes: religious and magical ideograms. The runic alphabet is used in Germany and Scandinavia.

saltus: non-cultivated part of the land (forest or fallow land) used for gathering, hunting and rearing.

Saracens: heathen Arabs from south Spain and Sicily. Unequalled scholars.

scholasticus: literally "that belongs to the school"; person responsible for a monastic or cathedral school. The scholastic philosophy defines all of science and theology in the Middle Ages.

scriptorium: copying workshop in monasteries.

seneschal: household officer, chief officer for the lord (steward), and manager of the household.

sergeant (mayor): servant of the lord (abbot), estate manager, and tax collector.

Slavs: heathen people east of Germany.

tariff penance: ancient judicial custom of the Germans, adopted by the church, in which sins and crimes are inventoried with appropriate punishments such as days of fasting (bread and water), prayers or pilgrimages. Hardly applied in practice. Secular justice is arbitrary or simply lacking, or rooted in personal vengeance and vendettas. God is the ultimate judge of course, and life is cheap indeed!

technographs: authors of *artes* — manuals for the basic and practical teaching of a discipline.

tenure: strips of land attributed to one farmer. A tenant owes dues in kind and labor service to his lord, and the tithe to the parish priest.

treasures: denier chests, jewelry, silver and onyx vases, crucifixes, chalices and other liturgical objects in solid gold, holy relics in precious reliquaries, wooden statues of saints sheeted in gold, ivory sculptures, miniatures, magnificent sacerdotal clothes, all in purple and gold, precious silken cloth, etc.

trivium: literary disciplines of the liberal arts: grammar, rhetoric and dialectic.

tropes: sacred theatre, in Latin, as opposed to the mimed theatre dating back to antiquity, which is partly obscene and strongly reproved.

venison: small game, deer, wild boar, and bear. Meat is spiced with thyme, rosemary and bay leaves. For conservation meat is either salted or smoked.

vicus: new pole of commercial activity that forms the kernel of a budding town; a stopping-off place to cross a river or a mountain pass.

Vikings: heathen Scandinavians, or *Nordmanni.* Unrivalled sailors, terrors of the Occidental world before 950 A.D.

war engines (from *ingenium,* "ingenious contrivance"): battering rams, catapults, wheeled towers, ballistas and trebuchets. Heavy catapults can shoot 50-pound missiles up to several hundred yards, or shoot a 60-pound missile up to two hundred yards. A large hybrid trebuchet can easily hurl a 400-pound stone (or animal carcasses, or bundled humans) 100 yards. For more, see p. 46

wine: reserved to the most privileged and to the celebration of the mass. The largest vineyards are situated in ecclesiastical domains or on the banks of large rivers, since these are major transport routes.

A Hundred Years and More

950–986 .....Harald Blaatand unifies Danemark and imposes his rule on Norway.

951 ....Otto I the Great, king of Germany, is declared king of Italy. He actually manages to impose his authority ten years later.

954 ....Hungarian raids in Germany and Italy.

954–994 .....Following Aymar, Maieul becomes fourth abbot of Cluny (Abbey founded in 909 by William the Pious, Duke of Aquitaine).

954 ....France: death of Louis IV; his son Lothaire succeeds him under the tutelage of Hugh the Great, Duke of the Franks.

955 ....Battle of Lechfeld (August 10th): Otto I vanquishes the Hungarians.

959–975 .....Edgar rules over England. The archbishop Dunstan crowns him in 973.

960–992 .....After the conversion of duke Mieszko I in 966, Poland becomes Christian and has its own bishopric (Posen). Mieszko seeks the support of the empire by becoming the "friend of the emperor." He places his land under the protection of the pope (985).

961 ....The Byzantines, under the leadership of the general Phocas, conquer Crete, then Alep (Syria) in 962. Nicephorus II Phocas is emperor from 963 to 969, and campaigns against the Arabs in Cyprus.

961–972 .....Kingdom of Kiev: Sviatoslav dominates international trade routes and clashes with Byzantium.

961–976 .....In Cordoba, Kalif al-Hakam II, son of Abd al-Rahman III, continues the work of his father who pacified Muslim Spain (al-Andalus).

962 ....Otto I crowned emperor in Rome by the Pope John XII: The Ottonians restore the Holy Roman Empire.

963 Otto I deposes the "unworthy" pope.

969–976 Apogee of the Byzantine Empire under the rule of John I Tzimiskes. Russians thrown out of the Balkans; eastern Bulgaria becomes a Byzantine province. John also conquers Syria and Palestine.

973–983 .....Empire: Otto II succeeds to Otto I, and marries Theophano, the niece of the Byzantine emperor.

975 ....A Pisano-Byzantine fleet attacks Messina.

976–1025 ...Basil II, "the Killer of Bulgarians," defeats the Bulgarian King Samuel after a 20 year war. He promotes the propagation of the orthodox faith in Russia by giving his sister to the Russian prince Vladimir in 989.

977–1002 ...Abusing the youth of the new Kalif Hisham II, son of al-Hakam II, who is only 10, the vizier Almanzor establishes the Arab domination over Spain (Omeyyad dynasty).

978 ....First teaching hospital: medical faculty of 24 physicians established at the al-Bimirastan al-'Adubi by 'Adud-ad-Dawla, in Baghdad.

978–1015 ...Vladimir I, "the Bright Sun," becomes sole ruler over the Russian princes of the Kingdom of Kiev. He marries the sister of Basil II, Princess Ann, and after his baptism in 988, Kiev becomes a religious center of orthodoxy.

978–1016 ...King Ethelred vainly tries to stop the Danish invasion of England, started in 980, by paying them large tributes (the Danegeld). The Danes conquer England in 1013.

982 ....Vikings discover Greenland. In 984, Erik the Red of Iceland reaches Greenland and establishes colonies.

983 ....Spring: Mistav, prince of the Obodrites (Slavs), takes Hamburg, and the Weletabs attack the bishoprics of Havelberg and Brandeburg.

983 ....First custodial prison sentences (Britain): introduced under law of King Alfred for breaking a pledge. Prisoners to be fed by relatives unless they had none.

983–1002 ...Empire: Otto III is ruler. Until 995 though, he is put in minority by his mother Theophano and grandmother Adelaide. In 996 he makes his cousin Bruno pope (Gregory V) and is crowned emperor in Rome.

985 ....The vizier Almanzor takes Barcelona.

985–1014 ...Sven Forked-Beard Christianizes Denmark and leads the Danish army against the Anglo-Saxons in 994. Anglo-Saxon priests establish the Danish Church.

A Hundred Years and More

986............France: death of Lothaire: his son Louis V, "the Lazy," associated to the throne since 979, succeeds him.

987 ....Death of Louis V the Lazy. At the request of the archbishop of Reims Adalberon, the overlords reject Charles, Duke of Lower Lorraine and Lothaire's brother, and elect Hugh Capet, who is crowned by the prelate.

987 ....Crowning in Orleans of Robert the Pious, son of Hugh Capet, "associate" king.

987 ....Institution of the Peace of God.

987 ....Almanzor takes Coïmbra.

988 ....Almanzor takes León.

988 ....Charles, son of Louis IV, Duke of Lower-Lorraine and Carolingian pretender, takes the cities of Laon and Reims with the support of his bishop Arnoul. Laon is taken back in 991 and Charles dies in captivity in Orleans in 992.

988–1004 ...Abbon, abbot of Fleury-sur-Loire.

991 ....June 11th: deposition of Arnoul bishop of Reims and election of the monk Gerbert of Aurillac; formation of the "party of monks" that wishes to relieve their institution from the authority of bishops and only depend on Rome.

992 ....First commercial treaty between Venice and Byzantium.

992–1025 ...Duke Boleslas I Chobry the Brave, son of Mieszko, rules in Poland. Friendly relationship with Germany at first, but from 1003 to 1018 conflicts arise because Germany is opposed to Boleslav's conception of a unified western Slavic state under Poland's rule.

993 ....January 31st, first saint canonization: bishop Ulrich, died 973, canonized by Pope John XV.

994–1049 ...Odilon, abbot of Cluny.

995 ....Eudes II becomes count of Blois at his father's death. He seizes the county of Champagne in 1023 and tries to occupy the kingdom of Burgundy-Provence in 1032.

995–1022 ...Olof Sköttkonung of the Upsal dynasty rules over Sweden and is baptized in 1008.

996 ....Death of Richard the First; his son, Richard II, Duke of Normandy.

996 ....October 24th, France: death of Hugh Capet; Robert the Pious succeeds him.

996–997 .....Uprising in the Champagne country.

997 ....Almanzor takes Compostelle.

997–1038 ...Etienne I founds the Christian kingdom of Hungary, with the help of German knights and Benedictine monks.

999–1003 ...Pontificate of Sylvester II (Gerbert of Aurillac).

1000 ....Leif Erikson, son of Erik the Red, discovers Vinland ("Land of Pastures") in North America on the basis of a rumor, but fails to establish a lasting colony.

1000–35 .....Sancho the Great, king of Navarre, joins Castile and Aragon to his kingdom to better resist Muslim Spain. He extends his influence to Catalonia and León.

1002–24 .....Empire: Henry II the Saint rules (crowned emperor in 1014). He conquers Bohemia and becomes king of Italy in 1004.

1002–31 .....At the death of Almanzor, rival factions fight for power and provoke the fall of the Omeyyad caliphate of Cordoba in 1031. Christians attack — this is the beginning of the *Reconquista*.

1002...........Death of Henry I, duke of Burgundy, without an heir. His nephew, Robert II the Pious, conquers the duchy after a conflict that lasts 14 years. Robert eventually entrusts it to his second son, Henry, in 1018.

1005–29 .....Gauzlin, abbot of Fleury-sur-Loire.

1006–28 .....Fulbert, bishop of Chartres.

1007 ....Foundation of the Bishopric of Bamberg; christening missions to the Slavs in the East.

1016 ....Pisa and Genoa ally to attack the Arabs in Sardinia and Corsica.

1016–35 .....Knut the Great, son of Sven, King of Denmark, of England and of Norway (1028). He marries Ethelred's widow. After his death, his sons rule over England until 1042.

A Hundred Years and More

1016 ....Beginning of the Norman expeditions in South Italy and Sicily.

1017 ....France: Hugh, son of Constance of Arles and Robert the Pious, is crowned and associated to the throne.

1019 ....Kingdom of Kiev: Iaroslav the Wise consolidates the Russian unity. First compilation of the Russian Code (*Russkaja Pravda*), a mix of Byzantine law and Slavic custom.

1023 ....Robert the Pious and the emperor Henry II meet in Ivois (Ardennes).

1024–39 .....Empire: Conrad II rules (crowned king of Italy in 1026 and emperor in 1027).

1024 ....Knut the Great occupies the March of Slesvig.

1025 ....Poland: Boleslas I crowned King.

1025+ ....Decline of Byzantium because of rampant feudalism: the state grants lands to maintain its army, church and bureaucracy.

1025–34 .....Poland: Mieszko II must renounce the crown because of Conrad II's opposition, and recognize Conrad's sovereignty in Poland (1033).

1026 ....France: death of Hugh, designated heir to Robert the Pious. His second son Henry is crowned associate king in Reims (1027).

1031 ....France: Henry I succeeds to Robert the Pious.

1031 ....Spain: after the dislocation of the caliphate of Cordoba begins the reign of the clan kings (*reyes de taifas*). Their short-lived kingdoms have uncertain frontiers.

1033 ....The Kingdom of Burgundy is incorporated to the empire.

1033–36 .....The monk Guido of Arezzo introduces the modern musical notation Ut, Re, Mi, Fa, Sol, La, Si.

1035 ....Spain: death of Sancho the Great. His domains are split among his three sons; Castile and Aragon become independent.

1035–47 .....Magnus the Good becomes King of Norway after deposing Sven, son of Knut the Great.

1038 ....Poland: heathen insurrections and Czech attacks drive Casimir I out of the land. He returns with the help of the Germans, restores the state and the church in Krakow.

1039–56 .....Henry III marries Agnes of Poitou and is crowned emperor in 1047. Bohemia and Hungary become German fiefs.

1040 ....The clergy proclaims the Peace of God.

1040 ....Pagan insurrection in Hungary.

1042 ....Edward the Confessor, son of Ethelred, organizes a centralized administration of England with the help of the Normans.

1044 ....Earliest known formula for gunpowder, published in the Chinese "Complete Compendium of Military Classics."

1046 ....Synod of Sutri: Pope Clement II intends to purify the clergy and forbid the marriage of priests.

1054 ....Schism between the Western and the Oriental Church.

Natural Disasters & Occult Events

Even a god cannot change the past.
—Agathon, c. 445 B.C.

950 ....The Byzantine Theodorus Philetas translates the *Al-Azif* from Arabic to Greek, and renames it *Necronomicon*.

953 ....An Italian monk named Vilgard reads sacrilegious books that make him lose his mind. Encouraged by demons, he starts to teach blasphemous theories and is condemned by the pope. Cultists of this dogma are found all over Italy.

954 ....Abbot Adson writes a "small treaty of the Antichrist" for Gerberge, Queen of France; it prophesies that Judgment Day won't take place "before all the kingdoms of the world are separated from the Roman Empire."

956 ....Great epidemic in France and Germany.

968 ....Famine in the Balkans (land of the Greek).

Natural Disasters & Occult Events

974 ....Earthquakes. A cyclone devastates Rome.

978–984 .....The Chinese compile an encyclopedia of 1000 volumes.

983 ....Rebellion of the pagan Obrodites living along the lower Elbe; they succeed in establishing a pagan state that will last until the twelfth century.

984 ....June 20th: a white comet is seen at noon in Thuringe, moving slowly across the sky.

991–1052 ...First wave of neo-Manicheism (heresies).

992 ....Two "northern lights" (*aurora borealis*) observed above Germany during Walpurgis night and New Year's eve.

994–997 .....Holy Fire epidemic consumes Burgundy and France.

997 ....The anti-pope, John XVI, is made prisoner by the Emperor Otto; his ears, his tongue and his nose are cut off and his eyes are pierced.

998 ....February: In Germany a celestial body moving through the night sky suddenly explodes and falls to earth, while the moon turns to a bloody red.

998 ....Seismic activity felt across the northern part of the Germanic Empire. Feast of All Souls celebrated for the first time in Cluny.

1000 ....Millennium of the incarnation of Jesus: terrible earthquake in Europe. Radiant comet. The remarkably preserved body of the emperor Carolus Magnus is miraculously exhumed, and the relics are elevated in Aix. A man possessed by "bees" spreads Manichean heresies and eventually drowns himself in a well.

1002 ....December: one evening people in the duchy of Burgundy observe "the apparition or the body of an enormous dragon throwing bundles of lightning."

1003 ....Strange floods. Birth of a monster drowned by his parents. A leviathan as large as an island is spotted offshore in Berneval.

1005–06 .....Droughts and floods cause major famine in occidental Europe.

1006 ....In a church in Auxerre, monks fall asleep in their cells and wake up in completely different locations.

1008 ....A criminal claiming his innocence sees a stream of an unknown fluid pour out of his abdomen.

1010 ....Destruction of the church of the Holy Sepulchre in Jerusalem by the "prince of Babylon" (caliph of Baghdad). Cosmic signs, disastrous droughts, excessive rains, epidemics, and horrible plagues.

1014 ....Bright comet visible from September to December.

1016 ....A huge wolf enters a church in Orléans and sounds the bells.

1017 ....Manichean heretics corrupt the people of Aquitaine. Ten Manicheans are sent to the pyre; no bones are found amongst the ashes.

1023 ....January 24th: solar eclipse; two "stars" are seen battling around the constellation of the Lion.

1023-24 ......Heresy in the Capetian capital Orleans: a sect of 14 Manichean "clerics"—who worship a devil appearing either as a black man or as an angel of light — refuse to be converted and choose to die on the pyre.

1028 ....Impious Christians burn down Jerusalem. A witch, accused of cursing Count Guillaume of Toulouse, is tortured and crucified.

1030–33 .....Millennium of the redemption of Christ: Apocalyptic climate and locust swarms waste crops from the Orient to the Occident and cause the Great Famine. Widespread cannibalism; "ghouls" desecrate cemeteries.

1033 ....June 29: Solar eclipse; nobles try to kill the pope.

1040 ....Widespread pagan revolt in Hungary.

1044 ....The star "Bosphorus" (Lucifer) is observed "moving up and down".

1045 ....Holy Fire epidemic in the North of France.

1046 ....November: a heavenly body falls onto the fortified town of Saint Florentine; crops are two months late.

1050 ....Patriarch Michael of Constantinople condemns the blasphemous *Necronomicon*.

Who's Who

God

The One and Only Almighty Creator, known to Christians as God the Father, YHVH (pronounced "Yahveh") in Hebrew, and Allah to Muslims (Koran 29:46).

Monks

Abbon of Fleury (945–1004): monk, scholar and abbot of the monastery of Fleury-sur-Loire (988). Very learned in the liberal arts, especially the Quadrivium, and author of numerous educational pamphlets. Abbon and Odilon of Cluny are the leading figures of the reforming monks around 1000 A.D. Mortally wounded in a fight with rebellious monks.

Adalberon (c. 920/30–989): bishop of Reims (969). He played an important role in the political intrigues that marked the beginning of the reign of Hugh Capet.

Aimoin of Fleury (970–?): successor and biographic author of Abbon. Author of a history of the Fleury abbey and the "Miracula Sancti Benedicti."

Anselm of Canterbury (1033/34–1109): Famous scholasticus who tried to explain faith by using the ontological proof of God's existence.

Fulbert of Chartres (960–1028): founder of the school of Chartres, and bishop of Chartres in 1006. High quality teacher.

Gerbert of Aurillac (940–1003): first scholasticus of Reims and friend of the archbishop Adalberon of Reims, Gerbert soon went into service with the Ottonians. Under the name of Sylvester II he was pope between 999 and 1003. As a scholar, he specialized in the Quadrivium. Using the works of Boece, Gerbert taught his students notions of logic and Aristotle's ten categories: substance, quality and quantity, relations, position, place, time, state, action and emotion. Gerbert brought back from northern Spain a treasury of Muslim science in mathematics, astronomy and music, and diffused this knowledge into Christendom. Gerbert also taught the Occident how to calculate, by reintroducing the abacus.

Ibn Sina or "Avicenna" (980–1037): last famous Arab philosopher and doctor, perhaps the most remarkable man of the Orient. Author of numerous books, including the *Book of Healing* (a scientific encyclopedia) and the *Canon of Medicine.*

Liutprand of Cremone (912–972): bishop of Cremone, cleric and writer at the service of Otto I and Otto II, author of the "History of Otto."

Maieul (906–994): fourth abbot of Cluny (954). Famous for being captured by the Saracens in 972.

Oddon of Meung: author of a long epic poem on the virtues of plants.

Oliba (971–1046): count of Berga and Ripoll (988–1002), abbot of Ripoll, Cuxa and Bishop of Vic, in Catalonia. Prestigious clergyman, founder of Monserrat (1023), and reformer of numerous monasteries.

He took part in the creation of the Truce of God.

Peter Damian (11th century): cardinal notorious for writing a manual praising flagellation, in spite of Saint Augustine's advice to congregates not to flagellate themselves too enthusiastically nor frequently.

Kings & Emperors

Charlemagne's Descendants

Louis IV, King of France, 936–954

Lothaire, King of France, 954–986

Louis V the Lazy, King of France, 986–987

Capetian Kings (France)

Hugh Capet, 987–996

Robert the Pious, 996–1031

Henry I, 1031–1060

Kings of Germany

Otto I the Great, 936–973

Otto II, 973–983

Otto III, 983–1002

Henry II, 1002–24

Conrad II the Salian, 1024–39

Henry III, 1039–56

Spanish Kings

Sancho, King of Castile, Navarre and Aragon, 970–1035

Ferdinand, King of Castile, 1033–65

Garcia, King of Navarre, 1035–54

Ramiro I, King of Aragon, 1035–63

The Cthulhu Mythos

Lovecraft once wrote, "All my tales are based upon the fundamental premise that common human laws and interests and emotions have no validity or significance in the vast cosmos-at-large." He further imagined that the fundamental truths of the universe were so alien and horrifying that mere exposure to them might result in madness or suicide. While humanity might crave both comfort and the truth, only one or the other was possible to it.

The human mind was an inflexible container. It could not maintain both more truth and complete sanity — more of one poured in must spill out more of the other. Humans desperate for the power cloaked within truth might choose to forgo all remnants of sanity in exchange for becoming adept at manipulating the secrets of time and space. Their devil's bargains made, these merciless sorcerers would whistle down devastation and doom to this world in new exchange for yet more knowledge and power.

Lovecraft's working-out of these ideas in his fiction became known as the Cthulhu Mythos. The term encompasses a complex and broad group of sometimes contradictory narratives, stories, essays, letters, and deductions, so extensive as to be impossible to summarize in detail — not the least because new Mythos material continues to be written around the world. Adding to the confusion, one of his perceptions was that the truly alien is genuinely unknowable. The Mythos becomes not just mysterious, but protean and contradictory: not only do we not know it, we never can know it.

As it transpires, we have only our own names for most of these things. We do not even know their names for themselves, or if they have names.

Whatever of this that is known in the Dark Ages occident generally is completely misunderstood and reinterpreted under the rubric of a Christian universe. Player characters should reflect this. Keepers must remind their players that the very nature of the world and even the night sky is understood differently in this time.

A General Summary

Though their interrelations are dim, we know that some entities of the Cthulhu Mythos are clearly superior or inferior in their powers. Gods are the mightiest, followed (at some distance) by the Great Old Ones. Both may be attended by lesser servitor races, often of a characteristic species.

Outer Gods, Elder Gods, Other Gods

Depending on which author one reads, the universe is ruled by beings variously known as the Elder Gods, Outer Gods, or Other Gods. Only a few of these deities are known by name. The majority are both blind and idiotic. They are all extremely powerful alien beings, and some may be of extra-cosmic origin.

The Outer Gods rule the universe and have little to do with humanity, except for Nyarlathotep. Humans meddling with these entities suffer for it, usually ending mad or dead. Names for a few Outer Gods are known. They appear almost to be true gods, as opposed to the alien horror of the Great Old Ones, and some may personify some cosmic principle. Only a few of these deities seem to take interest in human affairs or to acknowledge the existence of the human race. When they do, they often are shown trying to break through cosmic walls or dimensions in order to wreak new destruction. All the races and lesser deities of the Mythos acknowledge the Outer Gods, and many worship them.

The Outer Gods are controlled to some extent by their messenger and soul, Nyarlathotep. When the Outer Gods are discomforted, Nyarlathotep investigates. Azathoth, the daemon sultan and ruler of the cosmos, writhes mindlessly to the piping of a demon flute at the center of the universe. Yog-Sothoth, either a second-in-command or co-ruler, is coterminous with all time and space, but locked somehow outside the mundane universe. Yog-Sothoth can be summoned to this side only through the use of mighty spells, whereas Azathoth theoretically might be met by traveling far enough through space. A group of Outer Gods and servitors dance slowly around Azathoth, but none are named.

The term Elder Gods sometimes refers to another race of gods, neutral to and possibly rivals of the Outer Gods. The Elder Gods, if they exist, do not seem to be as dangerous to humanity as Azathoth and its ilk, but they have even less contact with humanity. Nodens is the best known Elder God.

Outer and Elder Gods sometimes have been lumped together and confusingly called the Other Gods, though primarily gods of the outer planets and not of our Earth. They would seem seldom called here, but when they do appear they are second to nothing in horror. (And, just to thoroughly confuse you, a set of minor Outer Gods are known collectively as the Lesser Other Gods!)

Species associated with these deities (shantaks, hunting horrors, servitors of the Outer Gods, dark young of Shub-Niggurath) are correspondingly rare on Earth.

The Great Old Ones

They are not as supernatural as the Outer Gods, but are nonetheless god-like and terrible to human eyes. Humans are much more likely to worship Great Old Ones, who are comparatively near at hand and who occasionally participate in human affairs or contact individual humans, than they are to worship Outer Gods. Entire clans or cults may secretly worship a Great Old One. Lone madmen, on the other hand, seem to prefer the Outer Gods. Beings serving the Great Old Ones frequently inhabit the remote fastness of the Earth. Investigators most often encounter their worshipers and alien servants.

The Great Old Ones themselves appear to be immensely powerful alien beings with supernatural-seeming abilities, but not to be true gods in the sense that the Outer Gods are reported. Each Great Old One is independent of the rest, and many seem to be temporarily imprisoned in some way.

It is said that "when the stars are right" the Great Old Ones can plunge from world to world. When the stars are not right, they cannot live. "Cannot live" need not mean death, as the famous couplet from the Necronomicon suggests.

That is not dead which can eternal lie,
And with strange aeons even death may die.

Cthulhu, the most famous creation of Lovecraft, is a Great Old One. With the rest of his race, he sleeps in a vast tomb at the bottom of the Pacific Ocean. Cthulhu seems to be the most important Great Old One on Earth. Others of differing forms exist, and they are recorded as being both less powerful and more free. Ithaqua the Windwalker roams at will across Earth's arctic latitudes. Hastur the Unspeakable dwells near Aldebaran, and Cthugha near Fomalhaut. Other Great Old Ones doubtless infest other worlds, and it may be common for a world to be ruled by dominant Great Old Ones. All those known on Earth are invoked or worshiped by humans but, by the evidence of the stories, Cthulhu is worshiped more than the rest

put together. Minor Great Old Ones such as Quachil Uttaus usually have no worshipers, but wizards may know spells to summon them. Such entities fill the role of demons within the hierarchy of the Mythos.

But even Cthulhu is known of by few, and interventions by Great Old Ones in human affairs are isolated. Some commentators suspect that these greater beings rarely think about human beings or take them into account. Humanity is negligible and unimportant.

Servitor Races

Particular species are often associated with particular Great Old Ones or Outer Gods — byakhee with Hastur, for instance, or nightgaunts with Nodens. These are servitor species, and frequently a god or Great Old One manifests accompanied by several such servitors. Representatives may act as assassins, messengers, spies, and couriers, frightening off investigators and bulking out confrontations. In comparison, Outer Gods and Great Old Ones should be met with exceedingly infrequently.

Independent Races

Other alien species are also important, and sometimes have been able to hold their own against Great Old Ones. The independent races vary in power, and some are extinct. They are intimately connected with our planet, as described in "At the Mountains of Madness" and "The Shadow Out of Time". In these stories Lovecraft gives the true history of the Earth. Some species, such as dholes or flying polyps, make no association with particular gods or else, as with elder things and the Great Race, take no special interest in magic. Whether one is greater or lesser seems to depend on the relative danger posed by the average individual.

At the dawn of the Cambrian age, beings known only as the elder things flew to the Earth. They inhabited much of the land, warred with other species, and finally were pushed back to Antarctica. The elder things, perhaps by mistake, bred organisms eventually to evolve into the dinosaurs, mammals, and humanity. They also bred the horrible shoggoths, whose ultimate revolt led to the near-extinction of the elder things.

Eons ago, indigenous cone-shaped beings had their minds taken over by the Great Race of Yith, mental beings from the stars. The Great Race survived in their adopted bodies until about 50 million years ago, when they were defeated by terrible flying polyps not native to this Earth, which the Great Race had imprisoned in vast caverns beneath the surface. However, the Great Race had already transmitted their minds forward in time to escape their doom.

The star-spawn of Cthulhu came down upon the Earth and conquered a vast reach of land in the primordial Pacific Ocean, but were trapped when it sank beneath the surface.

The beings referred to as the fungi from Yuggoth (or mi-go) established their first bases on the Earth in the Jurassic period, about a hundred million years ago. They gradually reduced their bases to the tops of certain mountains, where they maintain mining colonies and such.

Dozens of other races also participated in this antediluvian parade, such as the serpent people who built cities and a civilization in the Permian, before the dinosaurs had evolved, and a winged race which succeeded the Great Race of Yith. Even species from Earth's future are mentioned, such as the beetle-like organisms which succeed man, and the intelligent arachnids who are prophesied to be the last intelligent life on Earth, billions of years hence.

At present, humans share the planet with deep ones and ghouls (which seem related to humanity in some fashion), and with a handful of mi-go. Other species occasionally visit Earth, or are sleeping, or are dormant.

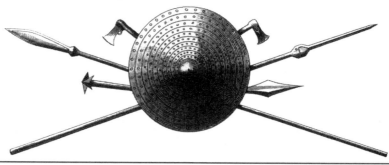

The Old Grimoire

Happy is the tomb where no wizard hath lain, and happy the town at night whose wizards are all ashes.

—*Reflections* of Ibn Shacabao.

A miracle does not happen in contradiction to nature, but in contradiction to what is known to us of nature.

—Saint Augustine.

Not all magic originates from the Cthulhu Mythos. Other earthly magic or religion-based effect exists and is represented in *Cthulhu Dark Ages* by the Old Grimoire of spells. The Old Grimoire is the product of centuries of shamanic tradition, religious cults, and witchcraft. Mechanics and procedures for non-Mythos magic are the same as those for Mythos magic, and both representations of the world overlap to some extent. For instance, many spells of the Old Grimoire relate to Limbo, a primitive human rationalization of Yog-Sothoth's abode "between the spheres." Some Mythos creatures and deities possess supernatural powers resembling Old Grimoire spells (see the Bestiary, pages 97–123).

Magus, Magi

In the Dark Ages there remain very few practitioners of old magic. The church fought pagan rituals and beliefs for centuries, and is slowly winning the battle. Magi, witches and healers of the Dark Ages lead a precarious life on the fringes of society: although they are not yet openly hunted down, they are often feared and ostracized.

Magi, for instance, constitute an outcast elite, cast off precisely because of their knowledge of the occult history of the world, their magic, and their familiarity with the true nature of spirits and Limbo.

The Keeper's Dilemma

Isolating the investigators with magic and then introducing a greater power to overcome leads to a sad and pointless conclusion: acquiring magical or holy powers should never be bland or routine. A new spell should come as the reward for some outstanding deed or after great perseverance only. Learning a spell from a supernatural entity may even require the sacrifice of an eye, an arm, or some other disfigurement. Introduce spells into your campaign carefully!

The keeper must realize that pursuing arcane powers eventually leads investigators to madness, exclusion and premature doom.

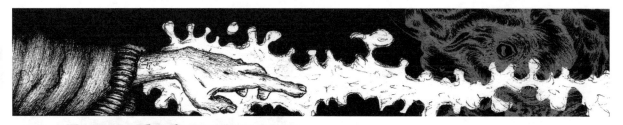

The Priest, the Witch, & the Healer

The first two entries below are occupations accessible to new investigators (see "Occupations," pages 18–22). The last two entries are the province of the keeper, not the players:

Healers have a fixed role in rural society. They perpetuate the belief in spirits and ancestors, and often revere some form of fertility goddess (Shub-Niggurath?).

Hermits and "exorcist" priests sometimes perform Old Grimoire magic, albeit under a religious guise. They may be actively anti-religious, as far as heretics are concerned.

Magi are secret practitioners of the "eight disciplines" after the Quadrivium and the Trivium, under the elusive patronage of some "magician king" (Yog-Sothoth's avatar Tawil at'Umr, see "Bestiary," page 122).

Witches and sorcerers are cultists worshipping the Black Man (probably a form of Nyarlathotep).

At the end of the day, it is up to the keeper to decide whether investigators have access to supernatural powers, and at what cost. An interesting way to temper power-craving players not deterred by the Sanity-reducing hazards of spell casting is to improvise malicious side effects. Side effects may be passing, or they may develop into full-blown subplots. Here are a few examples:

- the caster is plagued by a disturbing disease, a malformation, aging, nightmares or hallucinations;

- the magic liberates an unseen creature that stalks the caster and/or perpetrates terrible crimes in his neighborhood (innocent people are mysteriously slaughtered or vanish forever);

- the caster's perceived reality undergoes an alienating change — people don't know him anymore or a recently visited place seems to have vanished from the surface of the earth.

The Occult Skill

The Occult skill is to non-Mythos magic and spirits what the Cthulhu Mythos skill is to Mythos magic and monsters. Any evidence of Old Grimoire spell-casting and ingredients calls for an Occult roll. Succeeding, the investigator is able to recognize the signs of occult intervention for what they are (odd spell components, pale nimbuses, the rushing of winds, howling and hissing animals, murmuring voices, etc.). The Occult skill also helps in identifying spirits (see the Bestiary) and major occult texts, and provides knowledge of astrology and (Arabian) alchemy concepts.

Learning Spells

Learning a Mythos spell does not of itself cost Sanity points. Casting a spell generally does, as stated in the spell description.

Any individual can learn a spell. Studying the Mythos is an activity best done cautiously — increasing Mythos knowledge always brings a character closer to the time when sanity fails or the Mythos stakes its claim.

Knowledge of a spell can be gained in three ways: from another person, from a spirit or a Mythos entity, or from a book. The few precious books in the Dark Ages are jealously guarded, and this is the least-likely route to greater magical proficiency.

There is no limit to the number of spells that a single individual can know. The keeper determines the number of spells to which investigators are exposed; judicious keepers guard spell learning as jealously as monasteries guard their books.

Learning a Spell from a Person

Spells of the Old Grimoire depend upon oral tradition. To learn a spell, the student must be taught by another person or an entity knowing the spell.

To learn a spell from another person, roll D100 equal to or less than the student's INT x3 for each game week studying the spell. A single spell requires at least a week of study. Succeeding, the student knows the spell and may teach it to others.

Learning a Spell from a Spirit

A spirit possessing the student or captured by him (and many of the entities of the Mythos) can telepathically implant a spell's knowledge in the student's mind by means of a vision or a dream. This method is alienating and disturbing, and may happen more or less quickly as the story requires. Having the Mythos gnaw away at the will and psyche of the student invokes the need for a Sanity roll for seeing or perceiving the entity inside of him (use the particular entity's Sanity loss statistics). The student must then receive a successful Idea roll to retain knowledge of the spell. Failing, the process must be begun anew.

Learning a Spell from a Book

This is the least-likely source of spell knowledge, since there are so few books in the world of the Dark Ages.

To learn a spell from a book requires first that the book has been read and comprehended. The keeper will indicate the presence of spells, and describe them in only the most general terms. The investigator chooses which spell to learn based on this incomplete knowledge.

Following 2D6 game weeks of study, the player then rolls D100 equal to or less than the investigator's INT x3 (or as the keeper sees fit). With success the spell has been learned. Failing, the study time is lost but the player character may begin anew.

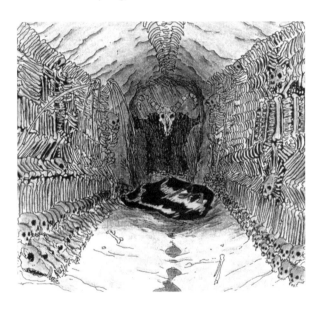

Casting Spells

Manipulating the forces of the Mythos and changing the nature of the world demands knowledge, time, and energy of the caster, and taxes the sanity of those who would cast spells. If the result of the spell is the arrival of some horrible monster or deity, the caster's sanity is further taxed, as well as the sanity of each and every witness. Having no Sanity points does not prohibit the casting of spells — otherwise there would be no cultists. Players lose control of investigators lacking Sanity points, becoming instead creatures of the keeper. Clever keepers discover unnerving ways of re-introducing lost (living but insane) investigators to the story.

All spells need time to cast, from a few moments to many days or weeks. The caster must reiterate some-times complex and lengthy formulae and chants in authoritative tones and manner. He or she must also have complete freedom of movement, since gesture can be as important as chant.

How Sorcerers Get That Way

Though investigators rarely get the chance, sorcerers and cultists sometimes swagger around with unseemly amounts of Power. Where did it come from?

Increasing POW increases the SAN characteristic but does not increase current Sanity points.

- When a character successfully casts a spell requiring magic points or POW to be matched on the Resistance Table (indicated by the "**Resistance Table:** Yes" entry in the spell description), a chance exists for the caster's POW to increase from this exercise. Subtract the caster's POW from 21 and multiply the difference by five: the product represents the percentage chance that the caster's POW increases by 1D3. Roll 1D100 equal to or less than that percentage chance to effect the increase.

- As a reward for any Luck roll result of 01, POW can be said to be exercised. Subtract current POW from 21 and multiply the difference by five: the product represents the percentage chance that the caster's POW increases by 1D3.

- Engaging in and surviving spirit combat with a spirit of POW greater than the player character also exercises that character's POW. Again, subtract current POW from 21 and multiply the difference by five: the product represents the percentage chance that the caster's POW increases by 1D3.

- A character may be able to arrange a gift or a trade for POW from some Great Old One or Outer God. This rationale is best left to the keeper. Such a bargain inevitably increases Cthulhu Mythos and surely costs additional Sanity points besides those lost in communicating with such a being.

Spell Description Format

All Old Grimoire spell descriptions include the following features:

SPELL NAME: Each spell is given a generic name that distinguishes it from other spells. Avoid using it during play. Instead call the spell something appropriately imprecise, poetic, or circumstantial. Some spells include a discretionary specification in brackets. Tailor the spell to affect a particular species, substance or characteristic.

- **Creature:** specific animal species, fabulous creatures, spirits, deep ones, etc.

- **Skill Class:** Communication, Manipulation, Perception, Physical Movement, and Thought.
- **Characteristic:** Strength, Constitution, Intelligence, Power, Dexterity, and Appearance. Power, Size, and Education can not be manipulated.
- **Spirit:** ghosts, nature spirits, Limbo creatures, etc.
- **Substance:** natural substances (water, silver), magic, invisible creatures, or evil effluvium (poison, enemy).

The specialty of the spell must be specified when the spell is learned, with the assent of the keeper. For instance, Find Gate is a different spell from Find Gold, but both spells work in the same manner. Knowing one variant of these spells is of no use in attempting to cast a similar spell.

SPELL RANGE: Range defines the distance from the caster within which the effects of the spell occur. Spells are described as having one of three ranges: *touch*, *sight* or *indefinite*.

- **Touch spells** only affect a target which is physically being touched by the caster. The caster must touch the location to be affected; this needn't be skin-to-skin contact for the effects of the spell will pass through intervening clothing and armor.
- **Sight spells** can be cast within about 300 feet and the caster must be able to see (physically or magically) the target of the spell.
- Spells of **indefinite range** do not fit into either of the above catagories. They generally feature an effect that may take some time to manifest, such as summoning a creature to the caster.

DURATION: The magic point or POW cost of a spell generates an effect that endures for the listed duration. Sample standard durations are *Instant*, *One Round*, *One Day* and *Permanent*.

Instant spells take effect immediately upon completion of spell casting, and then their effects are completed. This may effect a change upon the world, such as Healing a wound. Such change is permanent and immutable, and will not dissipate or fade with time.

Spells lasting for One Round or more take effect the moment that casting is complete, but expire at the end of the round specified. The spell ceases to be effective and the target is freed from its effects.

Spells lasting for One Day or more remain in effect for at least twenty-four hours. The effects of the spell cease with the following dawn, or as the keeper requires

for the story. The spell ceases to be effective and the target is freed from its effects.

If applicable, doubling the basic cost doubles the duration, tripling the cost triples duration, etc. Magic points are committed before the spell is cast and are expended weather or not the spell successfully takes effect.

MAGIC POINT or POW COST: All spells take time to cast — a single round by default — and they all require the expenditure of magic points or POW. Spells take effect at the end of the casting period after all required magic points or POW have been sacrificed. The cost of some spells can be scaled up for greater effect. If the caster is distracted while casting (by an upsetting event, a loud noise, a blow, etc.), a successful Idea roll is necessary to maintain his casting. If the roll fails, both the spell effects and the magic points or POW invested are lost.

SANITY COST: Successfully liberating magical forces usually costs Sanity points, in amounts varying from spell to spell. Note that the horrific outcome of many spells may cost yet more Sanity points to the caster, to the spell's target, or to witnesses.

RESISTANCE TABLE: Being affected by a spell is anathema to the human condition. A magician casting spells at characters or entities having magic points must overcome them with his or her own current magic points on the Resistance Table in order for the spell to take effect. No one can adequately prepare themselves to be affected by magic so as to lessen all resistance; a caster with a willing subject will have no worse than a 50% chance of a spell succeeding.

Failing, the spell does not take effect and the magic points invested in the spell are wasted.

Note that if the target is the spell caster himself, no roll is needed.

SPELL DESCRIPTION: Spells should not be described as having common or usual effects; each spell should be appropriately described by the keeper for the circumstance. The keeper and the player may come up with intriguing modifications or add specific details. The physical components of a spell, how they are acquired or prepared, is left almost entirely to the keeper. Here follows a list of usual components:

- **Organic:** ashes, blood, bones, a corpse, flowers, flesh, herbs, intestines, liquids, a small animal, etc.
- **Mineral:** gold dust, mercury granules, powder, rocks, saltpeter, salt water, sulfur, etc.
- **Crafted:** brazier, bronze disk, copper bowl, leaden seal, monolith, painted or drawn lines, pipes, small figurine, stone arrangements, wooden boxes, etc.

The evidence of the casting of a spell is up to the keeper. As the keeper wishes, spell castings might include pale nimbuses, the rushing of winds, howling and hissing animals, murmuring voices, alarming moans, and so on.

Ritual Magic

Routinely, spells are cast by a single caster in a single round. If a caster wants to cast a spell whose magic point cost exceeds his resources, then he must spend additional hours in casting. He may also join forces with other casters who know the spell. This is *ritual magic*.

Solitary Ritual

Humans naturally regenerate all their magic points in twenty-four hours, or one-fourth of a spell-caster's POW every six hours. Through ritual magic, a magician can prolong the casting of a powerful spell until he or she generates the magic points needed to complete casting — and the generated magic points must go to casting the spell and to no other purpose. The caster must be undisturbed during this process and must maintain concentration. There is no allowance for eating, drinking, or dodging blows. Should anything threaten the caster's concentration, an Idea roll is sufficient to ignore the distraction.

> **EXAMPLE:** *Mirabel, a witch with a Power of 12, naturally recovers 3 magic points every 6 hours. She can cast a 15-point spell in six hours by using the 12 she began with and the 3 she generates during the ritual (12 + 3 = 15 magic points). The ritual demands exclusive use of these generated magic points. At its conclusion the spell is cast but poor Mirabel collapses, unconscious, until at least one more magic point is recovered (or two more hours, in her case).*

Note that magic points are of no use for spells that demand POW expenditure; the only way to cast a spell with a higher POW cost than the caster can sacrifice is to share Power with others.

Group Ritual

A group or crowd of people can help power spells. The caster acts as the focus for the group. Each member of the group also knowing the spell may also expend magic points or POW points as desired. The remaining members of the group aid the ritual by forming an outer circle about the casters — chanting, holding candles or lanterns, burning incense, and so forth. Such an outer circle may forestall interruptions or distractions to the casters.

Each group caster is subject to a separate Sanity roll, and each may incur the full Sanity point loss attached to casting the spell.

Because lengthy rituals carry a greater risk of interruption it is wise to perform them in a place of relative calm, like a remote clearing in the woods.

Magical Artifacts

Magical artifacts are items permanently altered by one or more spells from the Old Grimoire. Creating such items always requires the expenditure of one or more points of permanent POW, plus a number of magic points amd Sanity points. Creatures described as being immune to all but magical weapons are vulnerable to any item qualifying as a magical artifact, whether or not the magical effect imbued in the item is specifically combat in nature.

If the artifact bestows use of a spell by the wielder, the casting of that spell conforms to standard spell casting procedures and conditions. In particular, the wielder of the item must spend magic points or POW and Sanity in order to activate the spell.

The Bind Soul spell can be used to create a freakish magical artifact that contains an imprisoned spirit. Such artifacts are in essence "possessed," having INT, POW and a will of their own. The wielder can use its magic points in casting spells; and those magic points will regenerate of their own accord. Having gotten to know the imprisoned spirit (as sometimes happens after long

ownership), the wielder may make use of its knowledge and experience, as allowed by the keeper.

To access the magical powers of an artifact, the wielder must first master the item: using the resistance table he or she must overcome the Power of the creator of the item or the POW of the captive spirit (unless known, randomly generate this value using 3D6+3).

Success yields mastery, which persists so long as the master wields the item once per day. Failure drains the wielder of 3D6 magic points and triggers a Sanity roll, loss 1/1D8, as the imprisoned spirit psychically expresses it's rage. Mastery may be attempted again.

The Old Grimoire

The Old Grimoire spells included in *Cthulhu Dark Ages* are not meant to be exhaustive. Many are variants of spells in the *Call of Cthulhu* grimoire, and occasionally *Call of Cthulhu* spells are referred to that are not presented here. The keeper is free to add more non-Mythos spells to the list or to create new spells as seems fitting, but keep in mind that when dealing with Mythos magic, there are frequently costs to casting greater than mere magic point or POW expenditures or Sanity point losses.

The Spells

Augur

Range: Indefinite   **Duration:** Instant

Cost: 4 MP

Sanity: 1D2   **Resistance Table:** No

The caster receives portents of the future. Such portents are generally cryptic, and it is up to the caster to be clever enough to understand them (use POW x5). The components and methods of augury vary, from the examination of animal entrails to the casting of stalks or coins. A portent may come as a misty vision, an otherworldly murmur, an overpowering emotion, or a sudden insight.

The keeper should prepare the portent with care. Revealing too much can easily rob players of their sense of free will and can limit the keeper's freedom of action. Revealing too little is pointless and frustrating. A well-balanced portent can add meaningful thrills and chills to the game when the keeper stages events that the players think they can correlate with the portent.

Become Spectral

Range: Touch   **Duration:** One Round

Cost: 1 MP per round of duration, chosen at casting

Sanity: 1D4   **Resistance Table:** Yes

This spell hides one target from mundane observers by shifting his or her body into Limbo. The target and personal possessions become invisible to all but spirit senses. The target's own sight and hearing remain attuned to our material plane but with a distant, less distinct character, as if a cold mist surrounds the target. The spectral target can move normally.

Becoming spectral carries an inherent danger: Limbo creatures can sense the presence of a spectral body and spiritually or magically attack. Generally, succeeding with a Luck roll the target escapes spirit attack from a random spirit of 2D6+4 POW. Keepers may use this opportunity to present more powerful opponents.

Bind Soul

Range: Touch   **Duration:** Permanent

Cost: 10 MP plus 1 POW

Sanity: 3   **Resistance Table:** Yes

Allows the caster to imprison a soul in a specially prepared vessel. The caster must find a soul to bind: engaging in spirit combat, driving the opponent spirit to zero magic points, then casting this spell is the common route.

The special vessel for the soul must be prepared ahead of time, a ritual requiring three days, the stomach of a sentient being, and the expenditure of one POW point. Anything that can be permanently etched or inscribed is suitable; the spirit is released by opening or breaking the vessel (it can then do as it will).

If the victim spirit is tethered to a physical body (is currently disembodied), its body begins to die at 2 CON per day, once bound. CON reaching zero, the body dies and the soul is trapped forever.

Bless Blade

Range: Touch   **Duration:** Permanent

Cost: 1 POW

Sanity: 1D4   **Resistance Table:** No

Creates a weapon capable of damaging or killing entities which cannot be harmed by ordinary weapons. This spell requires the blood sacrifice of an animal of at least SIZ 10. The blade of the weapon must be forged of an elemental metal such as iron or silver. The blade may be of any size, but larger weapons do greater damage. If the blade is broken, melted, or otherwise damaged it permanently loses this ability, but it will not be harmed in attacks against supernatural creatures.

Bless (Characteristic)

Range: Sight   **Duration:** One Day

Cost: 2 MP per 1D3 Characteristic points added

Sanity: 1D6   **Resistance Table:** Yes

Should the caster overcome the target's magic points with his own, the target gains 1D3 points in the specified characteristic. These points may alter some derived values: adding CON may increase hit points, for example. This spell may not be used to alter the POW or EDU characteristics.

Bless (Skill Class)

Range: Sight   **Duration:** 1D6 Rounds

Cost: 2 MP per 5 percentile improvement to skill class per 1D6 rounds.

Sanity: 1   **Resistance Table:** Yes

Bless temporarily increases one target's chance to successfully use skills of the specified skill class. The number of magic points committed to the spell can be used to increase the percentile improvement or the number of D6 rolled to determine duration in any combination.

The skill classes are Communication, Manipulation, Perception, Physical Movement, and Thought.

Blindness

Range: Sight   **Duration:** 1D6 Rounds

Cost: 3 MP per 1D6 rounds of duration

Sanity: 1   **Resistance Table:** Yes

Blindness makes a single target temporarily sightless. The duration of the spell must be decided at the time of casting. The experience costs the target 0/1D4 Sanity points.

Body Warping

Range: Touch   **Duration:** One Week

Cost: 1 POW per week duration, plus a number of magic points equal to the magic points of the target.

Sanity: 2D6   **Resistance Table:** Yes

Body Warping transforms the target's physical form to that of another species. The species target of the transformation must be fully known to the caster.

Upon completion of the spell, that target gains the natural abilities of the new species at base percentage chances; he or she will not gain any magical or supernatural abilities of the new shape. INT, POW and SIZ of the target remains constant and does not change; this may result in a creature that is significantly smaller or larger than the average specimen of that species. The memories and experiences of the target are not transformed.

If emulating a person, the target's APP becomes that of the individual emulated. A stern keeper may rule that Body Warping is never quite accurate, and when the target returns to his or her natural appearance there remains some difference, health problem, or minor deformity.

Cast Out the Devil

Range: Touch   **Duration:** One Day

Cost: 10 MP

Sanity: 0   **Resistance Table:** Yes

Frees the target of possession by an alien spirit or entity. Taking a full day to cast, this elaborate ritual requires no Sanity points. After a contribution of 10 magic points to energize the spell, match the POW of the exorcist against the POW of the foe possessing the victim. Willing assistants who also know the spell may add half their POW (round fractions down) to the effort, and this spell is seldom attempted without such help.

Cloud Memory

Range: Touch   **Duration:** Permanent

Cost: 1D6 MP

Sanity: 1D2   **Resistance Table:** Yes

Cloud Memory blocks the target's ability to consciously remember a particular event. The caster must overcome the target's magic points and must have an understanding

of the events to be blocked; he or she can not dictate something so broad as "Forget what you did yesterday". This understanding may be imparted either by being a witness to the event or through information offered by a (sane) third-party witness. The keeper may determine that the target's recollection of the event is sufficient, but the target must be able to relate this to the caster.

If the incident was terrifying, the victim may thereafter still have nightmares vaguely and symbolically relating to it. If the spell fails, the event in question becomes even more vivid in the target's mind and no longer is susceptible to this spell.

This spell cannot reverse a Sanity loss, or temporary or indefinite insanity.

Compel (Creature)

Range: Sight   **Duration:** Until Completed
Cost: 1 MP
Sanity: 0   **Resistance Table:** Yes

The caster achieves command over one specimen of the specified species. The target is compelled to obey one order by the caster, even to attacking its own kind. Upon completion of the command the target is freed and can not be again compelled for one day.

The caster's verbal and mental order must be specific, visualized, and limited in duration. It must be stated while the caster is within line-of-sight of the target. The target will begin to act in the round following the completion of the command-giving. It must be something which the creature could naturally accomplish and comprehend. "Protect me from harm forever" would not be a valid command, but "slay that sorcerer" would be. Orders might include carrying someone somewhere, presiding at some ceremony, or going to a specific location to appear as a warning.

As a rule of thumb, the command to a compelled monster should not have more words to it than the target has points of INT. To keep life simple, postulate that the thing compelled is able to understand the gist of what the player intends.

Contact (Creature)

Range: Indefinite   **Duration:** One Day (or more)
Cost: At least as many MPs as possed by the target
Sanity: 1D3   **Resistance Table:** No

Expending at least as many magic points as possessed by the target, the caster compels one individual of the specified species to approach the spot where the spell is cast.

Some creatures face limitations as to the location at which to appear (a fish will not appear on land). The entity may or may not appreciate this compulsion. This spell is not instantaneous; it will take a day or more for the contactee to appear. Those entities living nearby walk, swim, or fly to the place where the spell was cast. Things from other dimensions form in or enter our world in a characteristic manner. A specific individual can be contacted if the caster knows its True Name (see the Bestiary).

Once the contactee reaches the place of summoning it is then freed of the spell's compulsion. There is no guarantee that a contacted entity would rather bargain than devour the caster; it may also have some other goal in mind and it is free to act as it will.

Create Limbo Gate

Range: Touch   **Duration:** Permanent
Cost: 3 POW
Sanity: 0   **Resistance Table:** No

A Limbo Gate does not lead to another land, but instead to Limbo. Entering this dimension costs 0/1D4 Sanity

points. Visible as far as the traveler cares to go are glowing geometric diagrams suspended at various angles. These things can be entered — they are the Gates leading out of Limbo, and each costs another 3 magic points to use. The keeper may choose where and when each leads to.

Limbo is coterminous with many times and spaces, and is inhabited by ghastly things and many spirits of the dead who lost their way traveling to the "eternal reward" promised by whatever religion they practiced while living. Explorers who do not understand the pathways through the various dimensions can also become lost.

Limbo Gates have an inherent danger: they work both ways. Ghastly Limbo creatures may discover the Gate's existence, and step through to our world.

Create Mystic Portal

Range: Touch   **Duration:** Permanent

Cost: POW as indicated on the table below

Sanity: 0   **Resistance Table:** No

A Gate is a magic passageway connecting to a single other location. A Gate may take many forms, common ones being indicated by a pattern of scribed lines on a floor, a peculiar arrangement of stones in a field, or a grove of trees planted and grown in a specific pattern. Using the Gate costs that number of magic points equal to the POW originally used to make the Gate.

Lacking enough magic points for the trip, the keeper might rule that the traveler is lost in Limbo, unconscious and drained of magic points. Gates allow return at the same magic point cost.

The far end of the Gate resembles the initial end. Ordinarily, anyone or anything can move through a Gate, though some have been built so that a certain word or gesture is needed to activate the portal.

Some magi believe Gates are porous and that spirits can squeeze through the ends of a Gate and intrude into our world.

POW/magic points	Distance in miles
1	not to exceed 1
2	10
3	100
4	1,000
5	10,000

and so on: add another POW point, add another zero to distance.

Note that Dark Ages scholars believed that the world's size did not exceed several thousand miles. Anything beyond that was thought to belong to transcendental spheres.

Curse (Characteristic)

Range: Sight   **Duration:** One Day

Cost: 1D3 POW if failing to overcome target

Sanity: 1D6   **Resistance Table:** Yes

Should the caster overcome the target's magic points, the target loses 1D3 characteristic points and the caster gains as many magic points. The effect lasts for one day, and the target may not be brought below one point in the affected characteristic. If the caster fails to overcome the target, the caster loses 1D3 magic points instead.

Curse (Skill Class)

Range: Sight   **Duration:** One Day

Cost: 2 MP per 5 percentiles subtracted from skill class per 1D6 rounds

Sanity: 1   **Resistance Table:** Yes

Curse temporarily decreases one target's chance to successfully use the skills of the specified skill class. The number of magic points committed to the spell can be used to increase the percentile reduction of the number of D6 rolled to determine duration in any combination.

The skill classes are Communication, Manipulation, Perception, Physical Movement, and Thought.

Deafness

Range: Sight   **Duration:** 1D6 Rounds

Cost: 3 MP per 1D6 rounds of duration

Sanity: 1   **Resistance Table:** Yes

Deafness makes a single target temporarily deaf. The duration of the spell must be decided at the time of casting. The experience costs the target 0/1D4 Sanity points.

Death's Breath

Range: Touch   **Duration:** 1D6+4 Rounds

Cost: 2 MP for every 3x3x3 cubic yards

Sanity: 0   **Resistance Table:** No

A dense shadowy mist exudes from the person of the caster to fill an area of about 1000 cubic feet per 2 magic points invested; each measure of volume requiring one game round to exude. The spell's duration measures

from the completion of the mist formation. This mist can douse small lights such as candles and only the strongest light penetrates at all. Within the mist sight is impossibly clouded, the senses of touch and hearing are benumbed, freezing air blunts the sense of smell, and it unnaturally withstands even the force of wind. At expiration the mist dissipates without trace.

It is believed that the mist flows directly out of Limbo, and sometimes hides ghastly things (see the Nameless Mist description in the Bestiary).

Demon Hearing

Range: Sight   **Duration:** 1D6 Rounds
Cost: 2 MP per 1D6 duration and 5% increase to Listen.
Sanity: 1   **Resistance Table:** Yes

Demon Hearing doubles the target's hearing sensitivity, bringing sounds twice as close and also granting the target a five percentile increase in Listen for the duration of the spell.

At the time of casting the caster can increase the magic point expenditure and, for 2 additional MP, increase by 1D6 the duration — or increase by 5 additional percentiles the Listen bonus.

Trebling the cost of this spell allows the target to hear another whisper across line of sight.

Demon Sight

Range: Sight   **Duration:** 1D6 rounds
Cost: 3 MP
Sanity: 1   **Resistance Table:** Yes

Demon Sight doubles the target's visual acuity, bringing sights twice as close and also granting the target a five percentile increase in Spot Hidden for the duration of the spell.

At the time of casting the caster can increase the magic point expenditure and, for 2 additional MP, increase by 1D6 the duration — or increase by 5 additional percentiles the Spot Hidden bonus.

Disembodiment

Range: Touch   **Duration:** 1D6+3 Hours
Cost: 15 MP
Sanity: 1D4   **Resistance Table:** Yes

Disembodiment tears the target's soul out of its material envelope, instigating a Sanity test for the target of 1/1D6. While disem-

bodied, the target's body remains unconscious, and the spirit and body maintain a magical connection (commonly imagined as a silvery filament) over any distance. The spirit will know if its body suffers damage, and the body reacts if the spirit loses magic points or POW. If the spirit is destroyed, the body dies.

A disembodied spirit can sense the mundane world as if viewed through a light mist or gauze, can sense other spirits — embodied or not (and can sense that a particular spirit is embodied) — and can initiate spirit combat with either an embodied or disembodied spirit. Sensing that two or more spirits inhabit the same body, the spell's target spirit may choose to initiate spirit combat with either. If winning, it can drive a possessing spirit from the body.

The disembodied spirit can also cast spells, but can not otherwise physically interact with the mundane world.

Dismiss (Spirit)

Range: Sight   **Duration:** Instant
Cost: MP equal to the POW of the spirit
Sanity: 0   **Resistance Table:** Yes

Causes a spirit to return whence it came, presumably back to Limbo or back to its body in the case of a disembodied spirit. Match the magic points spent by the caster against those of the target on the Resistance Table. This yields the chance that dismissal succeeds.

This spell fails to dismiss spirits bound to a magical artifact.

Enthrall

Range: Sight   **Duration:** Until Disturbed
Cost: 2 MP
Sanity: 1D6   **Resistance Table:** Yes

Speaking soothingly to the target, the caster entrances his or her victim once the target's magic points are overcome on the Resistance Table. Enthrall causes the target to stop anything it was doing and stand struck, numb, and dumb. An enthralled target may not attack for the duration of the spell. An enthralled target is incapacitated

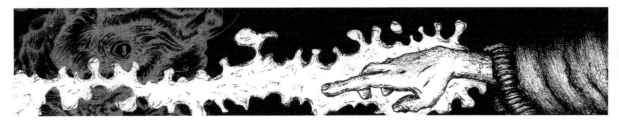

until retrieved from the trance by direct physical force or a similarly shocking event.

Exaltation

Range: Sight **Duration:** One Day

Cost: 12 MP per 1D6 Sanity increase and/or Temporary Sanity relief; +1 POW for Indefinite Insanity relief.

Sanity: 1D6 **Resistance Table:** Yes

With an impassioned appeal lasting five game rounds, Exaltation floods the target with a soul-lifting feeling of well being that grants the target extra Sanity points. The spell may be cast on a sleeping target, causing him or her to experience a wonderful dream and restful sleep.

Exaltation lasts 24 hours or until the imparted Sanity points are lost.

A casting of Exaltation can permanently calm one incidence of temporary insanity, and with the additional expenditure of 1 POW can permanently relieve indefinite insanity.

Fear

Range: Sight **Duration:** Instant

Cost: 12 MP for every 0/1D6 Sanity loss

Sanity: 1D6 **Resistance Table:** Yes

An intense, incapacitating fear grips the target if the caster overcomes the target's current magic points with his or her own. The sudden unexpected feeling of dread costs the target Sanity points with a failed Sanity roll and tests concentration.

The spell may be cast on a sleeping target, causing him or her to experience a horrible nightmare and a poor night's sleep.

Find (Substance)

Range: Sight **Duration:** 1D3 Rounds

Cost: 1 MP

Sanity: 1 **Resistance Table:** No

In learning the spell, the caster crafts a fetish used as a location indicator, and must define the substance to be found. The substance may be anything familiar to the caster and of a clear and definable nature: water, silver, deep one spoor, and so forth. The fetish may be a peculiarly-bent twig, a bauble on a string, a sliver of wood floating on water, or other device as appropriate to the nature of the substance sought. The effects of the spell penetrate up to 3 feet of intervening material. Find has the ability to make unseen things visible to the caster, as in Find Magical Things, Find Invisible Things, but seeing what Find exposes may cost extra Sanity points.

Flesh Ward

Range: Touch **Duration:** One Day

Cost: 1 MP per 1D6 points of protection

Sanity: 1D4 **Resistance Table:** Yes

Each magic point invested in this spell grants the caster or his or her target 1D6 points of armor against non-magical attacks. This protection is degraded as it absorbs damage. If a character has 12 points of Flesh Ward and is hit for 8 points of damage, the strength of the Flesh Ward is reduced to 4 points but no damage passes through.

Only one instance of this spell can benefit any one target at any one time, until the previous casting expires or is completely degraded.

Fury

Range: Touch **Duration:** Until CON Roll Failed

Cost: 2 MP

Sanity: 1D4 **Resistance Table:** Yes

Fury induces a berserk rage and causes the caster or his target to fight unceasingly and without care for personal safety. When the first opponent is dispatched, the target rolls 1D20, adding the number of opponents already fought under the spell. If this roll exceeds the target's CON, then the spell expires and the target slumps, exhausted. If less than CON, the target searches out the next-nearest opponent to engage. The target always chooses whom to attack, but will attack a friend if all foes have been slain.

The spell increases by one the number of attacks that the maddened target can make in each round, the second coming at the end of the round.

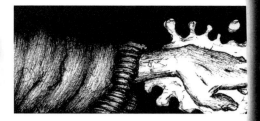

The berserk ignores unconsciousness stemming from a major wound or from hit points that fall to 2 or less. A fatal wound is still fatal, but he or she fights on until the end of the round of death, striking blows while spewing the body's vital fluids.

A furious target may not actively defend (dodge or parry) for the duration of the spell.

Sorcerers sometimes know this spell as "the Curse of the Wolf."

Corpse Reanimated with the Gray Binding Spell

Gray Binding

Range: Touch   **Duration:** Until target decays
Cost: 8 MP
Sanity: 1D6   **Resistance Table:** No

This spell forms an uncontrolled vampire. A ritual liquid must be poured over a corpse and left to marinate for five minutes. During this time the caster intones the binding chant, after which the corpse rouses. The keeper determines the ingredients of the liquid: at least one part should be difficult to obtain and reprehensible to the morals of the local culture.

The corpse is nearly mindless and unhappy, and not under the control of its creator. The thing continues to rot after its creation, and so eventually decays into incapacity. In statistics, the risen corpse is otherwise identical to a vampire, except lacking the vampire's spells (see page 100).

Heal

Range: Touch   **Duration:** One Week
Cost: 3 MP
Sanity: 0   **Resistance Table:** Yes

Heal maximizes the patient's healing rate. Requiring lengthy preparation (25 game rounds to cast), Heal maximizes the patient's natural healing rate at three hit points per week. With successful application of the Medicine skill the maximum total rises to six hit points per week. If the patient also receives a successful use of First Aid, then the first week healing totals 9 points. Thereafter the spell must be re-applied and Medicine used for 6 points healing each week.

In addition each casting of Heal can cure one disease or one poisoning.

Levitate

Range: Sight   **Duration:** 1D6 minutes
Cost: 1 MP for every 1 SIZ levitated
Sanity: 1D6   **Resistance Table:** Yes

Levitate causes the caster or a chosen target to float slowly through the air, 3–5 feet off the ground or floor; if the target is inanimate and lacking magic points then no Resistance Table roll is needed. If falling from a height, the target falls in slow motion and halts several feet off the ground. Maintaining concentration after casting, each additional magic point expended allows the caster to move the target one yard horizontally or vertically.

The target floats as the caster wills, helpless to stop moving except by grabbing a tree limb or similar brace: in that case match target STR against the caster's magic points (both those invested in the spell and those still unspent). If the target wins, the spell is broken — and the target falls, of course.

Moonlight

Range: Sight   **Duration:** 50 Rounds
Cost: 1 MP per 3x3x3 cubic yards
Sanity: 0   **Resistance Table:** No

Causes a small silvery ball emitting light of full-moon intensity to illuminate the target area. Moonlight dissipates darkness, shadows and mist for 10 minutes (even the spectral mist invoked by the Death's Breath spell). Moonlight can also reveal the outline of invisible Limbo

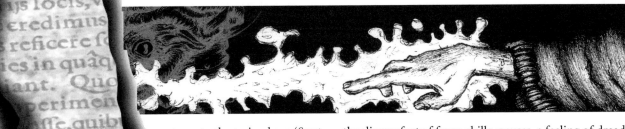

creatures to the trained eye (Spot Hidden required).

Nyhargo Dirge

Range: Sight **Duration:** Instant
Cost: 12 MP
Sanity: 1D6 **Resistance Table:** Yes

A modified version of the Resurrection spell (see *Call of Cthulhu*) used to destroy corporeal undead such as skeletons, zombies, vampires, and servants of Glaaki (among others). The caster sings an eerie, droning chant. If the undead fails a POW versus POW roll on the Resistance Table, it immediately turns to dust.

Pact of Quachil Uttaus

Range: N/A **Duration:** Instant
Cost: 1D50 MP, 3 CON, and 3 POW
Sanity: 0 **Resistance Table:** No

This rare spell is found only in the *Testament of Carnamagos*. The "Forbidden Words" from that text are deadly to read and the only way to summon Quachil Uttaus into our world. The pact is dangerous but powerful as it protects the caster from all forms of death. As his sign, Quachil Uttaus will deform the contractee's spine. Once the pact is complete, the contractee neither ages naturally nor can he or she be killed by any physical force nor by most magical means. However, if this spell is cast in the presence of someone already pacted with Quachil Uttaus, the Treader of the Dust appears and takes that person already pacted and known to him, leaving behind only a pile of ash. If contacted via the Forbidden Words and with no contractee ready to pact, the Great Old One takes whoever read the words unless the reader is willing to enter into the pact.

Poison Blood

Range: Touch **Duration:** variable
Cost: 2 MP for every day of "poisoning"
Sanity: 0 **Resistance Table:** Yes

Poison Blood exposes the target to an infectious agent. Following two weeks of preparation, the caster must then touch his or her victim — a light brush is all that is needed. The disease rules apply if the Resistance Table roll is failed. Symptoms start after a 12-hour incubation period, and cost the target 1D3 hit points per day plus the discomfort of fever, chills, nausea, a feeling of dread, rashes in uncomfortable places, and so forth.

Power Drain

Range: Touch **Duration:** Instant
Cost: 1D6 MP if failing to overcome target
Sanity: 1D8 **Resistance Table:** Yes

Drains magic points from the target. If the caster wins the resistance test then the target loses 1D6 magic points and the caster gains them. If the caster fails to overcome the target, the caster loses 1D6 magic points to the target.

Power Source

Range: Touch **Duration:** One Day
Cost: 1D6 MP, as granted to the target
Sanity: 1D8 **Resistance Table:** Yes

Grants magic points to the target. If the caster overcomes the target's resistance, then the target gains 1D6 magic points and the caster loses as many. Granted magic points dissipate after one day unless used.

Return Follower of Mad Cthulhu

Range: Sight **Duration:** Instant
Cost: Variable MP
Sanity: 1D6 **Resistance Table:** Yes

Redirects a compelled star-spawn of Cthulhu at the person who summoned it. Using the Resistance Table, match the number of magic points spent by the caster against the number of magic points spent by the summoner of the star spawn. If the caster of the Return spell wins, then the creature will return to and attack its original master with all due haste. This spell has no effect against an unbound star spawn.

Scrying Window

Range: Touch **Duration:** Permanent
Cost: 10 POW plus 98 MP
Sanity: 1D3 **Resistance Table:** No

This enchantment results in the creation of a magic window which looks into the past. Using it costs the viewer 1D3 Sanity points per ses-

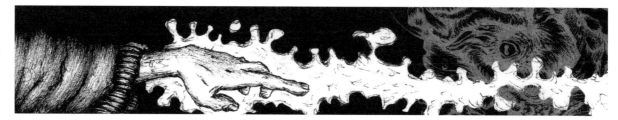

sion, as well as incidental Sanity losses for viewing particular monsters.

To make a Scrying Window, enchant a central viewing pane of tanned and scraped leather stretched in a wooden frame with 10 points of POW. When the pane is enchanted, it must be keyed to a specific time in the past, relative to the date of casting. As a key, one could say, "1000 years past", but not "48 B.C." After the central pane is enchanted and keyed, 98 colorful stones are enchanted requiring one magic point each, and are fitted carefully in a geometric mosaic around the viewing panel. When finished the pane achieves transparency, showing the site at which it rests though at the appropriate time in the past.

The window has an obvious limitation: a given scene can be viewed only once, for time passes on both sides of the window, and the pane must be trained to a spot where things actually happen.

The Scrying Window has an inherent danger: any being viewed for which the keeper rolls POW minus 20 or less on D100 realizes that it is being observed and spies the window. It could then cast a spell through the window, including a spell that could manifest a monster on the observer's side.

Seal of Nephren-Ka

Range: Sight   **Duration:** One Day or until crossed
Cost: 1 MP per point of Seal
Sanity: 1   **Resistance Table:** No

Following an hour of preparation, this spell creates a barrier with an area equivalent to a 50-foot cube that resists spirits (embodied or not) and most spells. An entity can cross the Seal by defeating the magic points invested in the Seal with the current magic points of the entity on the Resistance Table; multiple beings cannot combine magic points to attempt passage. Crossing, the Seal is destroyed. It dissipates in one day otherwise.

A Seal resists all spells except for Summonings by the caster of the Seal (entities are frequently summoned within a Seal to protect the caster and any bystanders). A spell caster must overcome the magic points invested in the Seal with his or her own magic points; success and the spell reaches its target and the Seal is destroyed.

A Sealed area may take many forms, commonly indicated by a pattern of scribed lines on a floor, a peculiar arrangement of stones in a field, or a grove of trees planted and grown in a specific pattern. Other aspects of a Seal's appearance are left to the appreciation of the keeper.

Shield

Range: Sight   **Duration:** One Day or until dissipated
Cost: 1 MP per point of armor
Sanity: 1   **Resistance Table:** No

Creates a barrier about the area of a 50-foot cube that blocks physical movement and attack from either direction. A physical being can cross the Shield by overcoming the magic points invested in the Shield with its STR on the Resistance Table; multiple beings cannot combine STR to attempt passage. Passage dissipates the Shield.

The strength of the Shield also resists damage directed at targets on the opposite side. Match damage generated by the attack against the magic points invested in the Shield on the Resistance Table. Damage overcoming the Shield is dissipated but also dissipates the Shield.

The Shielded area may take many forms, common ones being indicated by a pattern of scribed lines on a floor, a peculiar arrangement of stones in a field, or a grove of trees planted or grown in a specific pattern. Other aspects of the Shield's appearance are left to the appreciation of the keeper.

Shrivelling

Range: Touch   **Duration:** Instant
Cost: 1 MP for every hit point subtracted
Sanity: 1/2 MP cost   **Resistance Table:** Yes

A powerful attack, this spell injures the target. It takes two rounds to intone. To succeed, the caster must overcome the target's magic points with his own current

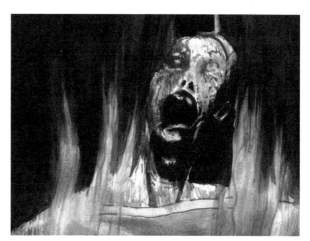

A Victim of Shrivelling

magic points (after investing the MPs in this spell) on the Resistance Table. If successful, the spell blasts and blackens the target — subtract one hit point from the target for each magic point invested in the spell.

Soul Singing

Range: Sight   **Duration:** One Round
Cost: 8 MP
Sanity: 1D4   **Resistance Table:** Yes

Soul Singing causes the target to see and hear only what the caster desires. The caster must (through successful skill use) sing, chant, or play some musical instrument to accompany the spell. Soul Singing is aimed at a single victim who, seeing what the caster wishes him to, is led entranced to the doom or destruction desired. Others present cannot hear the tune unless their players succeed in D100 rolls of POW x3 or less. Then they hear a faint, non-directional, strange melody.

Winds of Desolation

Range: Sight   **Duration:** 20 Minutes
Cost: 8 MP for every point of wind force increase
Sanity: 1D8   **Resistance Table:** No

Causes winds to increase in intensity. Cast at sea this spell causes waves to break at the caster's direction. These winds could also cause fires to spread at the caster's direction. Needless to say, people swallowed up by powerful waves or caught in a large firestorm take the appropriate damage.

To evaluate the spell's cost, consider the difference between the desired wind force and that of the wind at the moment of casting. For instance, 56 magic points need be invested to obtain a gale when a breeze is already blowing.

It is believed that the Winds of Desolation blow from Limbo, often carrying raging spirits with them.

(Wind STR)	Description	Effect on Land	Effect at Sea
(1–2)	Light Air	Leaves rustle	Choppy seas
(3–6)	Breeze	Branches wave	Full sail
(7–12)	Wind	Branches snap	Sails strain
(13–21)	Gale	Structural damage	Masts snap
(22–30+)	Hurricane	Widespread damage	Ship capsizes

The best winds for sailing are breezes. Gales knock down average humans. Hurricanes are a great menace to ships and boats: poor ship handling may cause the vessel to capsize.

Limbo

It was needful to sail over the Ocean that goes round the lands, to leave the sun and stars behind, to journey down into chaos, and at last pass into a land where no light was and where darkness reigned eternally.

—Saxo's History, Book VIII.

And beyond that abyss I saw a place which had no firmament of the heaven above, and no firmly grounded earth beneath it: there was no water upon it, and no birds, but it was a waste and horrible place.

—Book of Enoch, 17:12.

Limbo (literally meaning "border" or "prison") represents the interstices between the spheres that compose the universe. Limbo has many names depending on each system of belief: (the first circle of) Hell, Hades, the primordial Chaos or Void, Sheol, Nilfheim, etc. Limbo is an extension outside of time and of our material world, and borders many times and places of our world. The Nameless Mist permeates Limbo, making it "the land of gloom and chaos, where light is like darkness" (Job 10:22). It is a living yet mindless entity that may have originally spawned Yog-Sothoth.

The Sixth Sense

Ordinary senses are useless in Limbo, and position, duration, and motion have no meaning. Limbo creatures are generally spirits — bodiless and possessing

only INT and POW. Spirits do have a special ability, a sixth sense, that perceives the approach of other spirits or beings while in Limbo.

Spirits that manifest in the mundane world perceive in general terms physical objects and can easily perceive embodied spirits. As Lovecraft wrote in "Through the Gates of the Silver Key", "[Carter] had no stable form or position, but only such shifting hints of form and position as his whirling fancy supplied."

Each being generates an aura with a size or intensity roughly proportional to its POW. Its "force of personality" can be perceived by other spirits and Limbo creatures. A spirit will not know the exact value of the POW it observes, but will know if that POW is within five points of its own or if it is more than five points greater than or inferior to its own. Perceiving a creature in Limbo through this sixth sense invoke a Sanity test for seeing the creature as listed in the Bestiary.

The Ultimate Abyss

From Limbo the Ultimate Gate leads to the Ultimate Abyss, the Last Void outside all worlds. This gate is guarded by the Ancient Ones and Tawil at'Umr, avatar of Yog-Sothoth. The Ultimate Abyss is hell in the strictest sense of the word: Yog-Sothoth's *hole* or *hidden place*.

The *Necronomicon* tells that the Abyss is haunted by the Old Ones, dimensional shamblers, and the tomb-herds, and that there are six-hundred-forty Gates at which they wait "to feast upon the souls of the dead." One of these Gates probably leads to the Dreamlands.

The keeper is advised to read Lovecraft's tale "Through the Gates of the Silver Key" for more context.

Sanity Loss

Entering Limbo or the Nameless Mist costs 0/1D4 Sanity points. Entering the Ultimate Abyss, to learn that *illusion is the one reality, and that substance is the great impostor*, and to have one's *self* annihilated into a *legion of selves*, costs 1D10/1D100 Sanity points.

Spirit Attacks & Possession

Disembodied spirits naturally possess the ability to engage in *spirit combat*. The spirit identifies and engages one other spirit in a contest using the magic points of the attacker and victim on the Resistance Table. A success

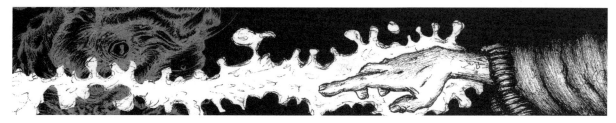

during any one round inflicts losses on the opponent of 1D3 magic points.

Only a disembodied spirit can initiate spirit combat. If attacking a physical creature the spirit manifests on the mundane plane and becomes visible to the naked eye.

Once initiated, spirit combat can not be disengaged unless agreed to by both parties, or until one has no chance of success on the Resistance Table (a difference in magic points of 10 or more). The greater combatant can ignore or engage the lesser as it sees fit; the lesser has no such choice.

- If a spirit loses all its magic points it dissolves within one round and cannot reform for a day. A defeated spirit freed from its body through the Disembodiment spell snaps back to its host body, suffers a Sanity loss of 0/1D6, and is unconscious.
- If a spirit loses all POW it is dispelled forever.
- If a human loses all magic points he or she falls unconscious until at least one magic point regenerates.
- If a human loses all POW he or she either dies or maintains a vegetable-like existence until POW can be raised again, at the keeper's discretion.

In the last two cases the attacking spirit may possess the target: a possessing spirit can dominate the identity of the victim at will, and use the body as its own (replace the INT, POW, EDU, and memories of the victim with the possessing spirit's own). A possessing spirit can only be dislodged by future spirit combat.

A subjugated spirit can be forced to provide information and cast spells.

What's in a Magic Point?

Loss of magic points may leave minor emotional sensations such as sadness, numbness, and anxiety. The inventive keeper may also want to associate loss of POW with nightmarish hallucinations or visions appropriate to the situation, leaving the target disoriented, nervous, terrified, or gray-haired.

Books of the Mythos & More

Below are listed a few tomes of arcane lore that are contemporary to the Dark Ages. Others circulate that are unlisted here. Manuscripts are usually found in the libraries of abbeys, where they are translated and copied by punctilious and often unwary monks.

Specific spells that may be found in the listed tomes are left to the keeper's discretion; listed spells are merely meant as guidelines; not all spells listed are presented in this work and are derived from the spells list given in the *Call of Cthulhu* rulesbook.

al-Azif

In Arabic, by Abd al-Azrad, c. 730 A.D. Original form unknown but numerous manuscript versions circulated among scholars. Immense compendium on nearly every aspect of the Mythos. *Sanity loss 1D10/1D20; Cthulhu Mythos +18 percentiles; 68 weeks to study and comprehend.* **Spells:** Call/Dismiss Azathoth, Call/Dismiss Cthugha, Call/Dismiss Hastur, Call/Dismiss Nyogtha, Call/Dismiss Shub-Niggurath, Call/Dismiss Yog-Sothoth, Contact Ghoul, Contact Sand Dweller, Contact Deity/Nyarlathotep, Dominate, Dread Curse of Azathoth, Dust of Suleiman, Elder Sign, Powder of Ibn-Ghazi, Resurrection, Shrivelling, Summon/Bind Byakhee, Summon/Bind Fire Vampire, Summon/Bind Servitor of the Outer Gods, Voorish Sign.

Black Rites

In Greek, by Egyptian high priest Luveh-Keraph, trans. unknown, Thirteenth Dynasty (c. 1786–1633 B.C.). Rare Greek translation of secret scrolls concerning Bast and other Egyptian gods. Contains a cautionary note on Nyarlathotep

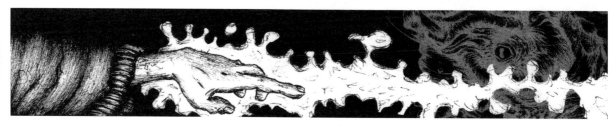

and the Dark Pharaoh. *Sanity loss 1D6/2D6; Cthulhu Mythos +11 percentiles; 41 weeks to study and comprehend.* **Spells:** Bring Forth the Faceless Master of the Sands (Contact Nyarlathotep, Faceless God Form), Call the Black Pharaoh (Contact Nyarlathotep, Black Pharaoh Form), Call Forth the Terrible Lord of the Riverbanks (Contact Sebek), Contact the Goddess of Cats (Contact Deity/Bast), Summon/Bind Cat, Summon and Abjure the Children of the Riverbanks (Summon/Bind Crocodile), Summon the Carrion-Feasters of the Desert (Contact Ghoul).

The Black Tome

In Latin, by Alsophocus of Erongill, trans. unknown, c. 200 A.D. Includes the secret of the Shining Trapezohedron and the call of Cthulhu. *Sanity loss 1D6/2D6; Cthulhu Mythos +10 percentiles; 37 weeks to study and comprehend.* **Spells:** at the keeper's discretion.

Cabala of Saboth

In Hebrew, author or authors unknown, c. 100 B.C. Esoteric book of "angel" lore. *Sanity loss 1D3/1D6; Cthulhu Mythos +3 percentiles; 16 weeks to study and comprehend.* **Spells:** at the keeper's discretion.

Confessions of the Mad Monk Clithanus

In Latin, by Clithanus, c. 400 A.D. Contains formulas for calling a Cthulhu-spawn, sending it back, and protecting against its wrath. Also relates how Slavonic priests imprisoned a large number of star-spawn. *Sanity loss 1D6/2D6; Cthulhu Mythos +9 percentiles; 29 weeks to study and comprehend.* **Spells:** Bring Forth Follower of Mad Cthulhu (Summon/Bind Star Spawn of Cthulhu), Return Follower of Mad Cthulhu, Warding Mark (Elder Sign).

Cthaat Aquadingen

In Latin, author unknown, c. 11th century A.D. Extremely rare study of the deep ones. Bound in human skin. *Sanity loss 1D8/2D8; Cthulhu Mythos +13 percentiles; 46 weeks to study and comprehend.* **Spells:** Bring Forth the Great One (Call Bugg-Shash), Call to the Drowner (Call/Dismiss Yibb-Tstll), Dreams from God (Contact Deity/Cthulhu), Dreams from Zattoqua (Contact Deity/Tsathoggua), Dreams of the Drowner (Contact Deity/Yibb-Tstll), Elder Sign (requires Idea roll to understand), Nyhargo Dirge, Speak with Father Dagon (Contact Dagon), Speak with God-Child (Contact Star-Spawn of Cthulhu), Speak with Mother Hydra (Contact Hydra), Speak with Sea Children (Contact Deep Ones).

Daemonolorum

In Latin, author unknown, c. 200 A.D. Account of an Egyptian sect which believed its gods could take on human form. *Sanity loss 1D4/1D8; Cthulhu Mythos +8 percentiles; 28 weeks to study and comprehend.* **Spells:** at the keeper's discretion.

Hierón Aigypton

In Greek, author unknown (Ieron of Egypt?), c. 200 A.D. Scrolls describing the fearsome rites of the Dark Folk; there is also mention of the Dark Pharaoh Nephren-Ka and of prodigious ruins "where the sun rises." *Sanity loss 1/1D3; Cthulhu Mythos +2 percentiles; 6 weeks to study and comprehend.* **Spells:** at the keeper's discretion.

Liber Ivonis

In Latin, trans. Caius Phillipus Faber, 9th century A.D. Presumed original author: Eibon, wizard of Hyperborea. Bound manuscript version. *Sanity loss 1D4/2D4; Cthulhu Mythos +13 percentiles; 36 weeks to study.* **Spells:** Call/Dismiss Azathoth, Call/Dismiss Rlim Shaikorth, Contact Formless Spawn of Zhothaqquah (Tsathoggua), Contact Kthulhut (Contact Deity/Cthulhu), Contact Yok-Zothoth (Contact Deity/Yog-Sothoth), Contact Zhothaqquah (Contact Deity/Tsathoggua), Create Barrier of Naach-Tith, Create Gate, Create Mist of Releh, Deflect Harm, Eibon's Wheel of Mist, Enchant Brazier, Enchant Knife, Levitate, Voorish Sign, Wither Limb.

Necronomicon

In Greek, trans. of the Al-Azif by Theodorus Philetas, c. 950 A.D. Hand-written copies circulated until 1050, when the Patriarch Michael of Constantinople condemned the blasphemous tome. Many copies were confiscated and burned. *Sanity loss 1D10/1D20; Cthulhu Mythos +17 percentiles; 68 weeks to study and comprehend.* **Spells:** Call/Dismiss Azathoth, Call/Dismiss Cthugha, Call/Dismiss Hastur, Call/Dismiss Nyogtha, Call/Dismiss Shub-Niggurath, Call/Dismiss Yog-

Sothoth, Contact Ghoul, Contact Sand Dweller, Contact Deity/Nyarlathotep, Dominate, Dread Curse of Azathoth, Dust of Suleiman, Elder Sign, Powder of Ibn-Ghazi, Resurrection, Shrivelling, Summon/Bind Byakhee, Summon/ Bind Fire Vampire, Summon/Bind Servitor of the Outer Gods, Voorish Sign.

Pnakotica

In Greek, author, trans. and date unknown. Disparate collection of pre-human stories, myths and legends. Papyrus version, more complete than the one referred to in the Keeper's Companion 1. *Sanity loss 1D10/1D20; Cthulhu Mythos +17 percentiles; 60 weeks to study and comprehend.* **Spells:** Contact Winged One (Contact Elder Thing), Contact Walker in the Waste (Contact Gnoph-keh).

Praesidia Finium

In Latin, by Lollius Urbicus, 183 A.D. Parchment rolls relating the mysterious events that took place during the Roman occupation of Britain, including the killing of a faceless winged being (over fifty soldiers lost their lives too). *Sanity Loss 1/1D2; Cthulhu Mythos +1 percentile; 2 weeks to study and comprehend.* **Spells:** at the keeper's discretion.

Rasul al-Albarin

In Arabic, by Ibn el-Badawi, c. 900 A.D. Book dealing with the Great Old Ones and the being Huitloxopetl. *Sanity loss 1D6/2D6; Cthulhu Mythos +11 percentiles; 36 weeks to study and comprehend.* **Spells:** at the keeper's discretion.

Reflections

In Arabic, by scholar Ibn Shacabao, date unknown. Conversations with the Jinn (Old Ones). Cited twice in the *Al-Azif! Sanity loss 1D4/1D8; Cthulhu Mythos +8 percentiles; 27 weeks to study and comprehend.* **Spells:** at the keeper's discretion.

Sapientia Maglorum

In Latin and Greek, by the Persian fire-mage Ostanes, date unknown but no later than 1st century A.D. Rare volume containing rituals to raise Hastur and Shub-Niggurath, and a possible formula of immortality. *Sanity loss*

1D6/2D6; Cthulhu Mythos +10 percentiles; 40 weeks to study and comprehend. **Spells:** at the keeper's discretion.

Song of Yste

In Greek, trans. by the Dirka magicians, date unknown. Amongst other things, discusses the adumbrali entities. *Sanity loss 1D3/1D6; Cthulhu Mythos +5 percentiles; 11 weeks to study and comprehend.* **Spells:** at the keeper's discretion.

Testament of Carnamagos

In Greek, trans. by anonymous monk, c. 935 A.D. Presumed original author: Carnamagos, Cimmerian oracle. Testament of events past and future, and an invocation to Quachil Uttaus, less complete than the edition referred to in the *Keeper's Companion 2*. The book purportedly distorts the reader's passing of time. *Sanity loss 1D3/1D6; Cthulhu Mythos +6 percentiles; 23 weeks to study and comprehend.* **Spells:** Apportion Ka, Call Slithering Shadows (Summon/Bind Formless Spawn of Tsathoggua), Call Unseen Horror (Summon/Bind Star Vampire), Create Sign of Barzai, Pact of Quachil Uttaus, Touch of Quachil Uttaus (Wither Limb).

The Three Codices

In Latin, authors and trans. unknown, c. 400 A.D. Three books ("Leprous Book", "Codex Maleficium", and "Codex Dagonensis") similar in content to *Cthaat Aquadingen*. Each volume contains at least one set of summonings and wardings of the Sathlattae series. *Sanity loss 1D8/2D8; Cthulhu Mythos +13 percentiles; 46 weeks to study and comprehend.* **Spells:** Bring Forth the Great One (Call Bugg-Shash), Call to the Drowner (Call/Dismiss Yibb-Tstll), Dreams from God (Contact Deity/Cthulhu), Dreams from Zattoqua (Contact Deity/Tsathoggua), Dreams of the Drowner (Contact Deity/Yibb-Tstll), Elder Sign (requires Idea roll to understand), Nyhargo Dirge, Speak with Father Dagon (Contact Dagon), Speak with God-Child (Contact Star-Spawn of Cthulhu), Speak with Mother Hydra (Contact Hydra), Speak with Sea Children (Contact Deep Ones).

Tupsimati

In a dead language, author, trans. and date unknown. Tablets of destiny in Mesopotamian myth, said to belong to the Babylonian Serpent Tiamat, alias Great

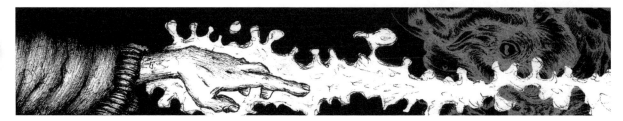

Cthulhu. The tablets are allegedly older than Earth, and of formidable power. Two almost inaccessible copies are said to exist on Earth. It is rumored that the tablets — sometimes known as the Elder Keys — constitute the single most important source for many later Mythos texts. *Sanity loss 1D10/1D20; Cthulhu Mythos +20 percentiles; 75 weeks to study and comprehend.* **Spells:** Call/Dismiss Azathoth, Call/Dismiss Cthugha, Call/Dismiss Hastur, Call/Dismiss Nyogtha, Call/Dismiss Shub-Niggurath, Call/Dismiss Yog-Sothoth, Contact Ghoul, Contact Sand Dweller, Contact Deity/Nyarlathotep, Dominate, Dread Curse of Azathoth, Dust of Suleiman, Elder Sign, Powder of Ibn-Ghazi, Resurrection, Shrivelling, Summon/Bind Byakhee, Summon/ Bind Fire Vampire, Summon/Bind Servitor of the Outer Gods, Voorish Sign, plus any others at the keeper's discretion.

Tuscan Rituals

In Latin, author unknown, date unknown but no later than 1st century A.D. Rites of the Great Old One Summamus. *Sanity loss 1/1D3; Cthulhu Mythos +2 percentiles; 3 weeks to study and comprehend.* **Spells:** at the keeper's discretion.

Non-Mythos Occult Books

Beatus Methodivo

In Latin, attributed to St. Methodius of Olympus, c. 300 A.D. Relatively short prophetic apocalypse. *No Sanity loss; Occult +2 percentiles.* No spells.

Canon Episcopi

In Latin, by Reginon of Prum, archbishop of Treves, c. 900 A.D. Part of a guide of ecclesiastic discipline intended for bishops. The Canon mentions flying women, witch cults, and witchcraft. Will be used in later centuries by the Inquisition to justify its merciless witch-hunts. *No Sanity loss; Occult +1 percentile.* No spells.

Kitab al-Kimya

In Arabic, by Abu Musa Jabir ibn Hayyan (c. 750–803), also known in the Occident as Geber. One of Geber's 22 monumental treatises of alchemy, "the book of alchemy." Remarkable "gibberish" style. *No Sanity loss; Occult +3 percentiles.* No spells.

Sibylline Books

In Latin, by Amalthaea of Cumae, c. 6th century B.C. Compilation of prophecies of the Cumaean sibyl Amalthaea, who offered these books for sale to Tarquinius Superbus, last of the seven kings of Rome. The sibyl burned the first six books after he refused to pay her price. The last three disappeared in a fire in 83 b.c. *No Sanity loss; Occult +1 percentile.* No spells.

Tabula Smaragdina

Aramaic or Greek original, author unknown, c. 200 A.D. The Emerald Tablet is part of the Corpus Hermeticum, the central alchemical text for medieval Europe. Attributed to Hermes the Great III (aka Hermes Trismegistus). *No Sanity loss; Occult +1 percentile.* No spells.

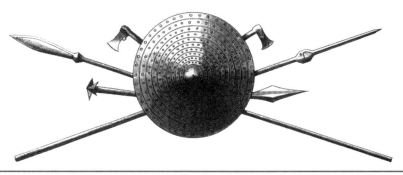

Bestiary

There you will serve gods . . . that neither see, nor hear, nor eat, nor smell.

—Deuteronomy 4:28.

A relatively sparse human population and the increase in blasphemous sects and heresies favors the proliferation of Mythos creatures in the Dark Ages. Humans share the earth with ghouls, deep ones, a handful of mi-go, and pockets of serpent people. Beyond the thin veil of sanity lurk the Outer Gods: Azathoth, Nyarlathotep, Shub-Niggurath and Yog-Sothoth.

Needless to say, all Mythos creatures have their place in the Dark Ages. Notable Mythos creatures in *Cthulhu Dark Ages* are: the Ancient Ones, Bugg-Shash, the dark folk, the doels, Lilith, the Nameless Mist, the Old Ones, Tawil at'Umr, the tomb-herd, and the worms of the earth.

Some version of creatures, such as vampires, miri nigri, and werewolves, are very different from those presented in the *Call of Cthulhu* rules. The keeper should choose between the versions as he or she wishes, perhaps using both versions to add confusion and uncertainty.

Mythos or Not Mythos?

A given Mythos entity may be known under many different names and given different descriptions, in accordance with various systems of beliefs. As it transpires, we only have *our* names for Mythos creatures — we do not even know the names they give themselves, or if they have names at all.

Angels

. . . Wheels within wheels . . . .

—Ezekiel 1:15-19.

Some early descriptions of angels are rather intriguing, like Ezekiel's, who saw the Cherubim as many-colored wheel-like structures, and Saint Basil's, who saw the Seraphim ("Burning Ones") as vaporous fireballs. In ancient times, the concept of angels (from the Greek *angelos,* equivalent to the Hebraic *mal'akh,* meaning "messenger") was intimately related to that of fallen gods, an idea which, in our Mythos context, reminds of even less religiously correct entities.

Dagon (& Hydra)

DEEP ONE GREATER SERVITORS

They put his armor in the temple of their god, and fastened his head in the temple of Dagon.

—1 Chronicles 10:10.

> *Vast, Polyphemous-like, and loathsome, it darted like a stupendous monster of nightmares to the monolith, about which it flung its gigantic scaly arms.*
>
> —H. P. Lovecraft, "Dagon."

Obscure deity linked with the ancient Philistine city of Ashod. Ancient coins depict Dagon as a god with a fish-tail. Dagon is a well-known god among Dark Ages scholars, for his name appears many times in the Bible.

Father Dagon and Mother Hydra are deep ones who have grown enormously in size and age, each over 20 feet tall and perhaps millions of years old. They rule the deep ones and lead them in their worship of Cthulhu. This pair is active and mobile, unlike Cthulhu and his minions, but are rarely met. Dagon's and Hydra's characteristics are identical. It is possible that more than two deep ones have grown to the enormous size and strength comparable to that described in Lovecraft's "Dagon."

DAGON or HYDRA, Rulers of the Deep Ones

STR 52	CON 50	SIZ 60	INT 20	POW 30
DEX 20	Move 10			HP 55

Damage Bonus: +6D6.

Weapon: Claw 80%, damage 1D6 +6D6

Armor: 6-point skin.

Spells: each knows all spells to summon/bind the lesser servitor races of the Mythos.

Sanity Loss: 1/1D10 Sanity points to see Dagon or Hydra.

Father Dagon

Beasts & Demons

Descriptions of creatures below are purposely archetypal. The listed statistics in particular are only averages. The keeper should craft each individual being for the circumstance. For most beings, knowledge of a spell should be considered an inborn magical ability. Usage of such ability entails the expenditure of magic points, as prescribed in the corresponding spell entry. Sanity loss does not apply.

Animals

The following are a few of the animals commonly encountered in the wild:

BEAR: STR 15+, CON 14, SIZ 15+, INT 5, POW 10–11, DEX 13, Move 11, HP 15+, db +1D4, Armor 3-point fur and gristle; Bite 25%, damage 1D10; Claw 40%, damage 1D6+db; Track by Smell 80%.

LARGE DEER: STR 10+, CON 13, SIZ 15+, INT 4, POW 10–11, DEX 15, Move 14, HP 14+, db +1D4.

WOLF: STR 10, CON 12, SIZ 8+, INT 6, POW 10–11, DEX 14, Move 14, HP 10+, db none; Bite 30%, damage 1D8, Armor 1-point fur; Spot Hidden 60%, Track by Smell 80%.

FALCON: STR 2, CON 2, SIZ 1, INT 3, POW 13, DEX 15, Move 32, HP 2, db N/A; Beak/Claw 45%, damage 1; Spot Hidden 90%.

WILD BOAR: STR 10, CON 12, SIZ 10, INT 6, POW 7, DEX 14, Move 11, HP 11, db none; Armor 3-point hide; Gore 30%, damage 1D4; Track by Smell 80%.

Basilisks

What good is it that poor Murrus spitted a basilisk with his spear-tip? In a flash, its venom shoots up the shaft and

Encounter Tables

Encounter tables are included as an optional help for the keeper. The resourceful keeper should prefer crafting meaningful events to using random encounters. Even so, the tables provide realistic frequencies of "animal" species in different habitats, and as such can help the keeper to populate his world.

attack humans. Predators represent at most 5% of all animals in any environment. Large predators include wolves, bears, lynxes, badgers, and of course men. Small carnivores (SIZ 1) include foxes, wild cats, weasels, owls, falcons, etc. Small herbivores include various sorts of mice, moles, hedgehogs, squirrels, hares, etc.

Wilderness

D100	Result
01–05	Human or Carnivore
06–95	Herbivore
96–00	Roll twice or switch to Gate area at the Keeper's discretion

Large Herbivores

Animal	av. STR/SIZ/HP	Forest	Moor
Buffalo	32	01–20	01–05
Auroch	32	21–35	06–15
Wild horse	28	36–50	16–50
Moose	28	51–55	51–55
Large Deer	16	56–80	56–85
Wild Boar	10	81–90	86–95
Small Deer	4	91–00	–
Beaver	5	–	96–00

In Dark Ages Europe, forests covered about 40–60% of the land. The Herbivores table indicates the relative bio-mass of wild herbivores in ancient and early-medieval Europe. Most animals are unlikely to

Gate Area

D100	Result
01–05	Servitor/Independent Race or Spirit
06–10	Magical* Human or Carnivore
11–90	Magical* Herbivore
91–95	Roll twice or switch to Wilderness
96–00	Nameless Mist and/or Gate to Limbo at the keepers discretion.

* Being with innate magical ability, such as a spell.

Limbo

D100	Result
01–05	Old One, Dimensional Shambler or Tomb Herd
06–90	Spirit (incl. disembodied human)
91–95	Roll Twice or Gate to Gate area
96–00	Ancient Ones/Tawil at'Umr—Ultimate gate, at the keeper's discretion

invades his hand — which he, drawing his sword, strikes clean off from the upper-arm at a single blow; stands and stares at the pitiful paradigm of his own demise, safe himself, while his hand is destroyed . . . .

—*Pharsalia* 9.824–833, Lucan.

You will tread on the lion and the basilisk, the young lion and the serpent you will trample under foot.

—*Psalm* 91:12.

The basilisk serpent (meaning "kinglet") is a 2-to-3 yard long snake so venomous that the creature dwells in a self-created desert. Pliny wrote in his *Natural History* that the basilisk is "adorned with a bright white marking

on the head like a sort of diadem . . . and does not move its body forward in manifold coils like the other snakes but advancing with its middle raised high." Basilisks are the personification of venom: if a basilisk bites a victim, that individual dies after one heartbeat of a major paralysis. There is no chance to resist the poison, except maybe by immediate amputation of the bitten limb to prevent the venom from reaching the heart. Legend says that the basilisk's breath is venomous: this is a misinterpretation of the fact the basilisk can spit its venom at up to 6 yards. The attack is aimed at the target's eyes!

Basilisks are native to Cyrenaica to the west of Egypt. It is likely that these creatures were originally created by the serpent people.

BASILISKS, Kinglets

STR 1	CON 1	SIZ 1	INT 3	POW 1
DEX 10	Move 6			HP 1

Other Name: cockatrice.

Damage Bonus: N/A.

Weapon: Bite 30%, damage 1D4; if armor is penetrated, automatic death after one heart beat. Virulent Spit 30% (base range 3 yards), potency 3D6: a victim must successfully resist against that on the Resistance Table with his CON or take damage equal to the 3D6 roll. If the target successfully resists, he or she still takes half damage. An impale means the spit found the target's eyes: blindness!

Armor: 4-point scales.

Sanity Loss: none.

Unicorns

The unicorn is perhaps the most famous of all fabulous beasts, a massive — usually placid — white thing with a single horn and allegedly an admiration of virgins. It appears to have disappeared from the northern parts of the world but is quite common in Africa and Asia. Use the rulebook statistics for the white rhinoceros.

Other fabulous antediluvian beasts that are sporadically sighted are giant stags, boars, hyenas, bears, wolves, aurochs, vultures, owls, and sharks. For these, use the normal-sized version statistics, but multiply STR, SIZ, damage and hit points by two.

Vampires

LESSER INDEPENDENT RACE

For crouched within that centuried coffin . . . was the bony thing my friend and I had robbed; not clean and placid as we had seen it then, but covered with caked blood and shreds of alien flesh and hair, and leering sentiently at me with phosphorescent sockets and sharp ensanguined fangs . . . .

—"The Hound," Lovecraft.

Vampires are the dead who crawl out of their tombs at night to quaff the body fluids of the living or sup on the flesh of the dead. They are related to the Arabic *ghûl* (ghouls) who are partly human, partly dog. The *strigae* or *striges* of the Old World were half woman, half owl. In the Dark Ages monks believed these creatures to be the *lilim* — depraved daughters of Lilith the she-devil (see page 121). In many cultures, vampires are capable of constantly changing form and may appear as humans, wolves, birds or even insects. Vampires are quite common in central Europe, Russia, the Balkans and Arabia.

It is said that these creatures become invisible by standing still, and can move in complete silence. Only blows to the skull or to the heart can harm a vampire.

Vampires are incomplete creatures lacking POW (hence they cannot regenerate lost magic points). Some vampires are animated by grim magic (see "Gray Binding" on page 88).

Optional Rule: vampires gain 1 magic point for every SIZ point of corpse that they devour, or for every hit point of body fluids they drink. They must expend a magic point every daybreak; for each hour in the sun vampires must spend an extra magic point. This process represents the corpse's decay: at 0 magic points, a vampire rots into incapacity and is destroyed.

Vampire Attacks: if the vampire strikes home, then it hangs on and worries its victim with its fangs, continuing to do 1D4 bite damage automatically. A successful STR against STR Resistance Table roll dislodges the vampire, ending the bite damage.

VAMPIRES, The Undead

char.	rolls	averages
STR	3D6	10–11
CON	3D6	10–11
SIZ	2D6+6	13
INT	3D6	10–11
POW	0	(1+ magic points)
DEX	3D6	10–11
Move 4–8		HP 12

Other Names: lilu/lilitu (Mesopotamian vampires), revenants, ghouls, ogres, strigae or striges, succubae, whores of hell, lamia.

Damage Bonus: none.

Weapon: Bite 30%, damage 1D4+automatic worry.

Armor: Impales do normal damage to a vampire; other attack results do half of rolled damage, round up any fractions.

Spells: at the discretion of the keeper, one or more appropriate spells and Body Warping and Become Spectral.

Skills: Burrow 75%, Hide 80%, Listen 70%, Scent Blood/Decay 75%, Sneak 80%.

Sanity Loss: 0 to 0/1D6 Sanity points to see a vampire, depending on its state of decay.

Creatures of the Mythos

Dark Ones

SERVITOR RACE

...But in the hills a still wilder and infinitely more terrible people dwelt — the Strange Dark Folk (Miri Nigri)

who held the monstrous Sabbaths on the Kalends of Maius and November.

—Letter, Lucius Caelius Rufus.

Thor said: "What is this man? Why is your nose so pale? Did you spend last night with the dead? It seems to me that you have the shape of a Thurs; you were not born to have this bride." Alviss said: "Alviss I am called, I live under the earth, under a rock I have my home."

—"Edda."

The dark ones are a race of "dwarfs" (Germanic *zwerc,* Norse *dvergr,* old English *dveorg;* original meaning "twisted" or "bent") that serve Loki (Nyarlathotep) and the Magnum Innominandum (the Nameless Mist). Twice a year the Dark Folk follow barbarous rites, lighting pale bonfires on remote hilltops, beating drums, and fetching humans to feed the Magnum Innominandum and "what lies within."

The dark ones are generally encountered in groups of ten or more.

Legend says the dark ones originally lived off the corpses of dead Great Old Ones. The dark ones' true shape remains a mystery, as they only survive by living as parasites inside dead bodies (some texts — like the *Apocalypse* of Paul — suggest their true form is that of an oversized, two-headed maggot, probably 1 – 3 feet long). Although the host remains dead and continues to rot, a dark one can animate it into a parody of the living. Before the host decays into incapacity, the dark one will find another body (or kill a living being) and occupy it. The dark ones are thus effectively shape-shifters, and despite customary belief, they are not small.

On earth, dark ones often seek the bodies of dead humans that were mummified before burial. They consequently hide in the cool and dark underworld of burial mounds, tombs and caverns that preserve their bodies best (legend wrongly assumes that daylight turns dwarves into stone). Otherwise, the dark folk can be found in peat bogs or near glaciers. The dark ones have an unexplained bond with horses and can apparently ride them.

Lacking POW (and with it any recognizable form of emotion, fear or sanity), the dark ones cannot exercise magic. Instead, the dark folk seem to be able to forge all kinds of ominous artifacts, which allow them to open Gates without spells, to animate lifeless machines, and to modify living beings in forbidding ways. To Dark Ages humans, the dark folk's science would appear as magical and utterly frightening. How the dark ones'

inferior intelligence can account for such rarities is yet another mystery, unless one adds Nyarlathotep in the balance — the dark folk may very well be his Million Favored Ones! Mythos deities or alien races like the mi-go often utilize the vile crafts of the dark ones.

The myth of Germanic and Norse dwarves living under the hills and hoarding treasures can easily be explained by the modus operandi of the dark ones. Still older myths seem to suggest that the dark folk and the Old Ones (or the tomb-herd) may be related or even complementary. "Ancestor," "He-who-enters-the-tomb," "Buried-under-the-cairn," and "Dead-man-of-the-mound" are typical names given to dark ones.

DARK ONES, The Strange Dark Folk

Use the dead host's statistics as defaults, with INT 0 and POW 0, and add the dark one's following characteristic points and hit points:

char.	rolls	averages
STR	n/a	1
CON	3D6	10–11
SIZ	n/a	1
INT	2D6	7
POW	n/a	0
DEX	n/a	1
Move 1		HP 6

Deep One

The keeper may rule that the decay reduces the host's characteristics over time, forcing the dark one to find another host. Incidentally, the increase to the host's SIZ is purely one of weight, not height or width; the increase in other characteristics is biochemical, as the dark one takes over and misuses the host's bodily functions — thus the myths that say dwarves are supernaturally strong.

Weapon: any weapon 75%, damage as per weapon.

Armor: none.

Spells: none, but may possess non-magical artifacts to open Gates, to contact mythos creatures, to invoke mist, winds, etc., at the keeper's discretion.

Skills: Sneak 90%, Ride 75%, and any number of appropriate skills.

Sanity Loss: 0/1D2 Sanity points to see a dark one.

Other Names: miri nigri, children of the fire mist, dwarves, black elves, afanc, korr.

Deep Ones

I think their predominant color was a greyish-green, though they had white bellies. They were mostly shiny and slippery, but the ridges of their backs were scaly. Their forms vaguely suggested the anthropoid, while their heads were the heads of fish, with prodigious bulging eyes that never closed. At the sides of their necks were palpitating gills and their long paws were webbed. They hopped irregularly, sometimes on hind legs and sometimes on four . . . their croaking, baying voices . . . held all the dark shades of expression which their staring faces lacked.

—H. P. Lovecraft, "The Shadow over Innsmouth."

Deep ones are an amphibious race serving primarily Cthulhu and two beings known as Father Dagon and Mother Hydra. Locked in the timeless depths of the sea, their alien, arrogant lives are coldly beautiful, unbelievably cruel, effectively immortal. They come together to mate or to worship Great Cthulhu, but do not crave touching or being touched as humans do. They are a marine race, unknown in freshwater environments, and globally have many cities, all submerged beneath the waves. One is Ahu-y'hola off the coast of Cornwall.

Some deep ones interact with humans. They appear to have a monstrous lust to produce human/deep one hybrids. The reason may lie in the breeding cycle of these beings, of which little is known. Deep ones may be worshiped by humans with whom they regularly interbreed, for deep ones are immortal, unless slain, and so are any hybrid offspring. Typically, hybrids inhabit remote coastal villages.

Such a hybrid begins life as a human-looking child who gradually becomes uglier and uglier. Suddenly, over a period of a few months, the human undergoes a monstrous transformation into a deep one. The changeover usually takes place at the age of 1D20+20 years, but some individuals change earlier or later, or only partially.

Data from the *Encyclopedia Cthulhiana* reveals that encounters with Deep Ones gave rise to sailors' tales of "mermaids" . . . and that the Romans and Merovingians of France claimed that their ruling dynasties came about from mating between humans and sea beings.

DEEP ONES, Gilled Humanoids

char.	rolls	averages
STR	4D6	14
CON	3D6	10-11
SIZ	3D6+6	16-17
INT	2D6+6	13
POW	3D6	10-11
DEX	3D6	10-11
Move 8/10 Swim		HP 13-14

Av. Damage Bonus: +1D4.

Weapons: Claw 25%, damage 1D6 + db
Hunting Spear* 25%, damage 1D6 + db
*impaling weapon.

Armor: 1-point skin and scales.

Spells: at the discretion of the keeper, deep ones with POW 14 or more know at least 1D4 spells.

Sanity Loss: 0/1D6 Sanity points to see a deep one.

Other Names: men/women from the sea, mermen/mermaids, sea devils, etc.

Dragons

Tiamat [Leviathan] that shapes all things made also invincible weapons: she gave birth to monstrous serpents, sharp-toothed, with unforgiving jaws.

—Akkadian verse.

"Dragon" — from the Greek *drakon* ("large serpent") —could be the Dark Ages name for "star-spawn of Cthulhu." In Dark Ages symbolism, dragons are the enemies of man and terror-inspiring manifestations of the Serpent — the archetype of all evil, alias Leviathan. Dragons are said to reside in underground or underwater megalithic chambers, there to guard the secret of immortality. This representation disturbingly resembles living-dead Cthulhu and his minions, entombed in the stone vaults of R'lyeh below the surface of the oceans.

The description of dragons confirms this match: their huge bodies are clawed and winged, some appear to be poison-blowing or exhibit numerous serpent heads (hydras), a possible misinterpretation of the giant squid-like heads of star-spawns.

Manifestations of "worms" (dholes, flying polyps and hunting horrors), shantaks, and lloigors, may also have contributed to the myths of the dragon and the sea serpent.

The names given to many dragons suggest that they are considered to be devourers of corpses.

Dimensional Shamblers

LESSER INDEPENDENT RACE

Shuffling towards him in the darkness was the gigantic, blasphemous form of a thing not wholly ape and not wholly insect. Its hide hung loosely upon its frame, and its rugose, dead-eyed rudiment of a head swayed drunkenly from side to side. Its forepaws were extended, with talons spread wide, and its whole body was taut with murderous malignity despite its utter lack of facial description.

—H. P. Lovecraft and Hazel Heald, "The Horror in the Museum."

Dimensional Shambler

Little is known about these beings save their name and a description of a hide. It is assumed that they are entities capable of walking between the planes and worlds of the universe, spending little time at an one planet, but wandering about. They occasionally serve an Outer God or a Great Old One. They can leave a plane at will, signaling the change by beginning to shimmer and fade. This transition costs them 4 magic points and takes a round to complete. During this time they may be attacked, but they may not attack back.

A shambler can take objects or beings with it when it fades into another dimension. By clutching the desired object in its talons and expending an additional magic point per 10 SIZ points

of the object or creature, that which is held makes the transit also. Objects and victims lost are never found again.

DIMENSIONAL SHAMBLERS, the Murderously Malign

char.	rolls	averages
STR	2D6+12	19
CON	3D6+6	16-17
SIZ	2D6+12	19
INT	2D6	7
POW	3D6	10-11
DEX	3D6	10-11
Move 7		HP 18

Av. Damage Bonus: +1D6.

Weapons: Claw* 30%, 1D8 + db
   *can attack with both foreclaws at once, at the same DEX rank.

Armor: 3-point thick hide.

Spells: a shambler knows one spell per point of INT over 9.

Sanity Loss: 0/1D10 Sanity points to see a dimensional shambler.

Ghouls

LESSER INDEPENDENT RACE

These figures were seldom completely human, but often approached humanity in varying degree. Most of the bodies, while roughly bipedal, had a forward slumping, and a vaguely canine cast. The texture of the majority was a kind of unpleasant rubberiness.

—H. P. Lovecraft, "Pickman's Model."

Ghouls are rubbery, loathsome humanoids with hooflike feet, canine features, and claws. They speak in what are described as gibberings and meepings. They are often encrusted with grave mold collected as they feed.

Lovecraft's ghouls are horrible creatures dwelling in tunnel systems beneath many cities. They have ties to witches and occasionally attack humans. It may be possible for a human to transform into a ghoul over a prolonged period of time.

GHOUL ATTACKS: it may attack with both claws and its bite in a single combat round. If the ghoul's bite strikes home, then it hangs on instead of using claw attacks and worries the victim with its fangs, continuing to do 1D4 Bite damage automatically. A successful STR against STR Resistance Table roll dislodges the ghoul, breaking what amounts to a successful Grapple, and ending the Bite damage.

Ghoul

GHOULS, Mocking Charnel Feeders

char.	roll	averages
STR	3D6+6	16-7
CON	2D6+6	13
SIZ	2D6+6	13
INT	2D6+6	13
POW	2D6+6	13
DEX	2D6+6	13
Move 9		HP 13

Av. Damage Bonus: +1D4.

Weapons: Claws 30%, damage 1D6 + db
   Bite 30%, 1D6 + automatic worry

Armor: missile weapons do half of rolled damage; round up any fraction.

Spells: roll D100 — if the roll is higher than the ghoul's INT, it knows no spells; if equal to or lower than INT, it knows that many spells, as chosen by the keeper.

Skills: Burrow 75%, Climb 85%, Hide 60%, Jump 75%, Listen 70%, Scent Decay 65%, Sneak 80%, Spot Hidden 50%.

Sanity Loss: 0/1D6 Sanity points to see a ghoul.

Other Names: vampires, eaters-of-the-dead.

Giants

And now, the giants, who are produced from the spirits and flesh, shall be called evil spirits upon the earth, and on the earth shall be their dwellings. Evil spirits have proceeded from their bodies. . . .

—Book of Enoch 15:8.

The definition of giants is ambiguous. According to the Greek poet Hesiod, they were sons of Ge ("earth") and Uranus ("heaven"). The Bible, the Book of Enoch and the *Necronomicon* either suggest that they are the product of a blasphemous union between intermediary beings (Old Ones) and daughters of men, or that they "fell out of the sky" (Great Old Ones). Medieval folklore often saw giants as cannibal monsters or "demons," said to reside most of the time underground.

In all cases, the reference to the Great Old Ones of the Cthulhu Mythos is obvious.

Other names given to giants: grigori, nephilim, thurs, iötunn, risi, trolls, leshy.

Halflings

Results of the crossbreeding between humans and non-human creatures, *e.g.* elves (Old Ones). Notable Mythos halflings are human-deep one, human-ghoul and human-Old One.

Leviathan

Who can open the doors of its face? There is terror all around its teeth. Its back is made of shields in rows, shut up closely as with a seal. One is so near to each other that no air can come between them. . . . When it raises itself up the gods are afraid.

—Job 41:14–16, 25.

Leviathan — the Coiled Serpent — came out of the primal chaos. Once vanquished, he took refuge in the sea and lies in wait, feigning sleep. He is a personification of evil, a protagonist in the cosmic battle that has raged since the beginning of time and will finish only when everything has been consumed.

The myth of the Serpent or the Dragon is so universal that it can only hold one inescapable truth: the Serpent is not a myth, and Great Cthulhu *is* the Serpent.

Other names given to Cthulhu: Lotan, Yamm, Tiamat (Chaldean chaos-dragon), Kul (Syrian water spirit).

Loki

Loki is handsome and good-looking, of bad spirit and very unstable in his ways.

—Snorri Sturluson, "Gylfaginning", XXXII.

Loki or Loptr is the archetype of the trickster god, the father of lies and of monsters. Loki will ultimately cause the Twilight of the Gods: in the last battle, "the Wolf will swallow the sun . . . [the Serpent] will walk the land." Then Loki, as the black fire giant Surtr, "casts fire on the earth and burns all the worlds."

Loki is a thief, an adulterer, a shape-shifter and a magician. Loki's symbolism clearly relates him to Hermes, Lug, and Thot, and therefore to Nyarlathotep. We may infer that Loki is one of the thousand forms of Nyarlathotep, namely the Black Man, so often confused with the Judeo-Christian Devil.

There is no evidence of Loki's worship among men.

Goblins

"You may get a bit of a shock tonight when you see us naked, though. We've gone down below to his place, to a region I won't describe to you, and to live longer we've had to . . . change. You've probably heard about it in a different way, though — the young of the Black Goat? Gof'nn hupadgh Shub-niggurath? But the dryads and fauns and satyrs are a lot different from the classical descriptions, so don't think you're prepared."

—"The Moon Lens," Campbell.

. . . The sylphs and the fauns, commonly called "incubus," showed themselves shamelessly to certain women. . . .

—Saint Augustine, "The City of God," XV, 23.

Cthulhu Mythos scholars believe that goblins are the "Goff'nn Hupadgh Shub-Niggurath," *i.e.* favored worshippers of the Black Goat of the Forest that have been ritualistically devoured by the goddess and then disgorged transformed.

Goblins (from the Greek *kobalos*, "rogue") are considered short creatures, but they can grow and take on

the nature of an animal or even of a breeze. They have fluctuating forms, shiny black skin, clawed hands, and are given various names depending on the region in which they are found. Goblins usually live in haunted forests and ruins. They steal children, cook poisoned food that they try to sell to unwary humans, raid hapless travelers, and are prone to unspeakable depravity. They sometimes appear in large groups. Goblins may fight with gnarled clubs and all sorts of improvised weapons.

The goblins know group rituals called "Scarlet Circles" that tear the fabric of space like a temporary Gate does, and allow them to travel between distant places. They have been known to let the hounds of Tindalos use the Circles to break into our world.

GOBLINS, The Thousand Young

char.	rolls	averages
STR	1D20	10–11
CON	1D20	10–11
SIZ	1D8	4–5
INT	4D6	14
POW	1D20	10–11
DEX	2D20	21
Move 8		HP 7–8

Damage Bonus: –1D4.

Weapon: improvised weapons 25%, damage 1D3 to 1D6.

Armor: no natural armor.

Spells: most goblins know at least one spell besides Body Warping, Become Spectral, and Gate ("Scarlet Circles").

Skills: Hide 90%, Sneak 70%.

Sanity Loss: it costs 0/1D6 Sanity points to see most goblins. An especially vile specimen might cost more.

Other Names: dusii (demons), sylvani (forest spirits), schrats (shouters), fauns, satyrs, pilosi (hairy ones), incubi, etc.

Gugs

LESSER INDEPENDENT RACE

It was a paw, fully two feet and a half across, and equipped with formidable talons. After it came another paw, and after that a great black-furred arm to which both of the paws were attached by short forearms. Then

two pink eyes shone and the head of the awakened Gug sentry, large as a barrel, wabbled into view. The eyes jutted two inches from each side, shaded by bony protuberances overgrown by coarse hairs. But the head was chiefly terrible because of the mouth. That mouth had great yellow fangs and ran from the top to the bottom of the head, opening vertically instead of horizontally.
—H. P. Lovecraft, "The Dream-Quest of Unknown Kadath."

In worshiping various Great Old Ones, the gugs of the Dreamlands indulged in ceremonies so abhorrent that somehow they have been banished into the Dreamlands' Underworld. Gugs gleefully eat any surface dwellers they can lay their four paws upon. Gugs are huge — an average gug is at least 20 feet tall.

In combat, a gug may either bite, or hit with one arm. Each arm has two forearms, and thus two claws, so that the arm strikes twice when it hits. Both claws must strike at the same opponent.

an average Gug

GUGS, Unclean Giants

char.	rolls	averages
STR	6D6+24	45
CON	3D6+18	28–29
SIZ	6D6+36	57
INT	2D6+6	13
POW	3D6	10-11
DEX	3D6	10-11
Move 10		HP 43

Av. Damage Bonus: +5D6.

Weapons: Bite 60%, damage 1D10
Claw(s) 40%, damage 4D6 each (no db)
Stomp 25%, damage 1D6 + db

Armor: 8-point skin, hair, and cartilage.

Spells: Few gugs know spells. To simulate this, roll D100 for each random gug. Only if the die roll is equal to or lower than the gug's POW does it know magic, that number of magic spells equal to the die roll.

Sanity Loss: 0/1D8 Sanity points to see a gug.

Hounds of Tindalos

GREATER INDEPENDENT RACE

"They are lean and athirst!" he shrieked . . . . "All the evil in the universe was concentrated in their lean, hungry bodies. Or had they bodies? I saw them only for a moment, I cannot be certain."

—Frank Belknap Long, "The Hounds of Tindalos."

The hounds of Tindalos dwell in the distant past of the earth, when normal life has not yet advanced past one-celled animals. They inhabit the angles of time, while other beings (such as mankind and all common life) descend from curves. This concept is hard to imagine, and only seems to be used with respect to them. The hounds lust after something in mankind and other normal life, and follow victims through time and space to get it. They are immortal.

Just what these creatures look like is unknown, since those who meet them seem not to survive. A hound of Tindalos is hardly likely to look like a hound dog, but the name from the story is so evocative that is how they always are pictured.

Because of their relationship with the angles of time, they can materialize through any corner if it is sharp — 120° or less. The rooms of most human houses have walls that meet at 90°. When a hound manifests, it first appears as smoke pouring from the corner, from which the head and then the thing's body emerges.

Once a human has become known to one of these creatures, it will follow through anything to get to him. To figure the time before the hound of Tindalos reaches its prey, determine the number of years between the prey's present time and the time when spotted by the creature. Then divide the number of years by

Tindalos

100,000,000 to get the number of days travel time for the hound. Driven off by a target, a hound of Tindalos usually gives up. Unfortunately, such a creature is difficult to drive off. Friends who come to a target's aid also will be attacked.

ATTACKS: it may use its paw or its tongue to attack within a round, but not both. It usually attacks with its paw. For random determination, roll 1D6. On a result of 1-4, it uses its paw. A result of 5-6 indicates a tongue attack.

A hound of Tindalos is covered with a sort of bluish pus. When a victim is struck by a paw attack, a gout of this mucoid stuff is smeared over him. This pus-like stuff is alive and active, doing poison damage to the target as if he or she had ingested a poison of POT 2D6, and new damage is done in the same amount for each round that the ichor remains on the victim's body. The ichor can be wiped off with a rag or towel with a DEX x5 or less roll on D100. It could also be rinsed off with water or some other agent. Fire would kill the ichor, though 1D6 hit points would be lost to burns from the flame.

With a successful tongue attack, a deep penetrating (though bloodless and painless) hole is formed. The victim takes no physical damage, despite his peculiar wound, but loses 1D3 POW permanently.

HOUNDS OF TINDALOS, Scavengers of Time

char.	rolls	averages
STR	3D6+6	16-17
CON	3D6+20	30-31
SIZ	3D6+6	16-17
INT	5D6	17-18
POW	7D6	24-25
DEX	3D6	10-11
Move 6 / 40 fly		**HP** 23-24

Av. Damage Bonus: +1D6.

Weapons: Paw 90%, damage 1D6 + ichor + db
Tongue 90%, damage 1D3 POW drained per round

Armor: 2-point hide; regenerates 4 hit points per round, unless dead; mundane weapons have no effect on a hound, though enchanted weapons and spells do full damage.

Spells: each knows at least 1D8 spells, as the keeper finds appropriate.

Sanity Loss: 1D3/1D20 Sanity points to see a hound of Tindalos.

Other Names: Tind'losi hounds.

Mi-Go, the Fungi from Yuggoth

LESSER INDEPENDENT RACE

They were pinkish things about five feet long; with crustaceous bodies bearing vast pairs of dorsal fins or membranous wings and several sets of articulate limbs, and with a sort of convoluted ellipsoid, covered with multitudes of very short antennae, where a head would ordinarily be . . . . Sometimes [they] walked on all their legs and sometimes on the hindmost pair only.

—H. P. Lovecraft, "The Whisperer in Darkness."

The fungi from Yuggoth are an interstellar race, with a main colony or base on Yuggoth (Pluto). There are mining colonies in the mountains of Earth, where the mi-go seek rare ores. The mi-go have definite connections with fungi, and are clearly not animal. They communicate with each other by changing the colors of their brain-like heads, but they can speak human tongues in buzzing, insect-like voices. They worship both Nyarlathotep and Shub-Niggurath, and possibly others. They hire human agents to simplify their operations, and are sometimes connected to cults.

They are unable to eat terrene food, and must import theirs from other worlds. They are able to fly through the interstellar aether on their great wings. but maneuver clumsily in an atmosphere. After death, a mi-go dissolves in a few hours.

They are capable of astounding surgical feats, including the placing of living human brains in life-sustaining metal tubes. They can then attach speaking, listening, and seeing devices to the tubes, so that the brains

can interact with those about them. This way they can carry with them those who cannot withstand the vacuum and cold of space.

Fungi from Yuggoth may attack in hand-to-hand combat with two nippers at once. If the target is hit, the mi-go will try to grapple the victim (roll STR against STR on the Resistance Table to break free), and fly into the sky to drop the victim from a height or take the victim so high that his or her lungs burst.

Encyclopedia Cthulhiana: word of the mi-go actions usually spreads despite the secrecy, and references to these curious creatures are often found in the legends of the countryside surrounding the creatures' lairs.

Bear in mind that a special breed of mi-go is described in "The Tomb" scenario.

Mi-go

MI-GO, the Fungi From Yuggoth

char.	rolls	averages
STR	3D6	10-11
CON	3D6	10-11
SIZ	3D6	10-11
INT	2D6+6	13
POW	2D6+6	13
DEX	4D6	14
Move 7 / 9 fly		HP 10-11

Av. Damage Bonus: +0.

Weapons: Nippers 30%, 1D6 + grapple

Armor: none, but the extraterrene body causes all impaling weapons to do minimum possible damage.

Spells: each has an INT x2 chance to know 1D3 spells.

Sanity Loss: 0/1D6 Sanity points to see a mi-go, from Yuggoth or elsewhere.

Other Names: many, dependent on what mountainous regions they are found in.

Satan

He seized the dragon, that ancient serpent, who is the Devil and Satan, and bound him for a thousand years, and threw him into the pit, and locked and sealed it over him, so that he would deceive the nations no more, until

the thousand years were ended. After that, he must be let out for a little while.
—Revelation 20:2.

In Hebrew "satan" means "enemy" in a generic sense, and doesn't convey the idea of a personified prince of evil. Rabbis usually referred to the Devil only as a symbol of man's moral evil. Satan with a capital "S" is a Christian creation. The first versions of the Old Testament made Jehovah, the Lord of the Universe, the *sole cause of all good and evil*. The figure of Satan as the personification of sin — the serpent of Genesis — is posterior to 700 B.C. In fact, the name Satan can apply to any despotic ruler just as well as to a Mythos deity.

A sixth century mosaic depicts Satan wearing a glorious halo, a red robe, and feathered wings. The slow transformation of Satan into a monster over the centuries was the consequence of Christian propaganda.

Nameless Mist

INDEPENDENT BEING

From the slopes and peaks above us a crackling chorus of daemoniac laughter burst, and winds of ice swept down to engulf us all.
—Letter, Lucius Caelius Rufus.

The Nameless Mist was created by Azathoth to fill the interstices between the spheres that compose the universe, and to spawn Yog-Sothoth.

The Nameless Mist is served by the gugs and worshipped by the Dark Folk, and may intrude into the material world when certain conditions are met. These emanations of the otherworldly mist resemble the mist invoked by the spell of the same name and are preceded by icy

Lost in the Nameless Mist

winds. Living beings engulfed by the Nameless Mist lose all senses except touch (modify skill rolls appropriately). Cognitive skills and in particular the Occult skill function normally. The outlandish experience costs 0/1D4 Sanity points.

The Nameless Mist is likely to hide befitting creatures at the keeper's discretion, *e.g.* one dimensional shambler, 1–2 gugs, 1–3 old ones, 1–10 dark ones, and any number of doels, etc.

NAMELESS MIST, Milk of the Void

SIZ infinite **INT** 0   **POW** 24   **Move** 24

Other Names: Magnum Innominandum.

Weapon: none, but possible attacks by "what lies within" (see corresponding creature entries).

Sanity Loss: 0/1D4 Sanity points to be engulfed by the Nameless Mist.

Serpent People

LESSER INDEPENDENT RACE

They walked lithely and sinuously erect on pre-mammalian members, their pied and hairless bodies bending with great suppleness. There was a loud hissing of formulae as they went to and fro.
—Clark Ashton Smith, "The Seven Geases."

They resemble upright serpents, with ophidian heads and scales, but with two arms and legs. They possess tails and in their great days often dressed in robes. Yig is the greatest god of the serpent people, for he is the father of all snakes. Some blasphemers chose instead to pray to Tsathoggua in ancient times, but they were destroyed by a vengeful god millions of years ago.

The serpent people's first kingdom — Valusia — flourished before even dinosaurs walked the Earth, some two hundred and seventy-five million years ago. They built black basalt cities and fought wars, all in the Permian era or before. They

Serpent Person

were then great sorcerers and scientists, and devoted much energy to calling forth dreadful demons and brewing potent poisons. With the coming of the dinosaurs two hundred and twenty-five million years ago, the first kingdom fell, and serpent people retreated in strongholds far underground, the greatest of which was Yoth. In these times the serpent people became great scientists as well, able to manipulate life itself.

In human prehistory the serpent people raised their second kingdom at the center of the

Thurian continent. It fell even more rapidly than the first Valusia, overthrown this time by humans, who later claimed the land as their own. Again and again the serpent people retreated before the human hordes until their last citadel of Yanyoga was destroyed in 10,000 B.C.

A few lurking sorcerers survive, as do pockets of dwarfed degenerates. These diminutions are likely to include an occasional atavistic, fully capable serpent person who is still favored by Yig. Degenerate serpent people are likely to have characteristics lessened by as much as a third. In addition there are certain hibernating serpent people — the sleepers — who have rested for thousands of years or more. On occasion these serpent people wake, to humanity's regret. This third class of serpent people is typically more intelligent and powerful than their lurking brothers, and often know great sorcery.

Serpent people may use all weapons known to man, clutching them effectively in taloned hands. Use the same base chances as for humans. In hand-to-hand combat the Bite attack can be made simultaneously with most weapon attacks.

A common spell among them is an illusion which transforms the caster's appearance into that of a normal human, allowing him to mingle in human society.

SERPENT PEOPLE, Full Atavism

char.	rolls	averages
STR	3D6	10-11
CON	3D6	10-11
SIZ	3D6	10-11
INT	3D6+6	16-17
POW	2D6+6	13
DEX	2D6+6	13
Move 8		HP 10-11

Av. Damage Bonus: +0.

Weapon: Bite 35%, damage 1D8 + poison*
  * POT equals the serpent person's CON.

Armor: 1-point scales.

Spells: full serpent folk know at least 2D6 appropriate spells; degenerate forms are not likely to know magic.

Sanity Loss: 0/1D6 Sanity points to see a serpent person.

Shoggoths

LESSER SERVITOR RACE

The nightmare, plastic column of fetid, black iridescence oozed tightly onward . . . . A shapeless congerie of protoplasmic bubbles, faintly self-luminous, and with myriads of temporary eyes forming and unforming as pustules of greenish light all over the tunnel-filling front that bore down upon us, crushing the frantic penguins and slithering over the glistening floor that it and its kind had swept so evilly free of all litter. Still came that eldritch mocking cry — "Tekeli-li! Tekeli-li!"

—H. P. Lovecraft, "At the Mountains of Madness."

Shoggoth

Shoggoths are among the most horrible of all the monsters of Lovecraft. Abdul Alhazred himself attempted desperately to claim that there were none on Earth itself, save in crazed dreams. Shoggoths are often found as servants of deep ones and other races, and are amphibious. They are surly servants at best, ever becoming more and more intelligent, more and more rebellious, more and more imitative. They fought their former creators, the elder things, in a rebellion. They communicate in whatever manner their master race wishes, forming special organs for the purpose.

A typical shoggoth is roughly a 15-foot diameter sphere when floating free. In combat, it covers an area 5 yards square. All within the area are attacked separately, and each must receive a successful match of STR against the shoggoth's STR on the Resistance Table, or be sucked apart. If the shoggoth attacks more than one target, it must divide its STR among all targets. Those held within the shoggoth's black bulk can strike back only on rounds in which their players successfully roll STR or less on D100. Each round a victim is held within a shoggoth, he or she loses hit points equal to the shoggoth's damage bonus, the damage describable as rupturing, crushing, and being sucked into pieces.

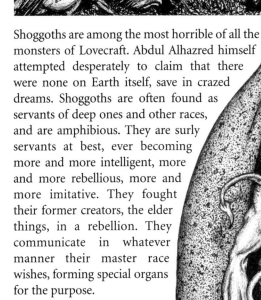

Star-Spawn

SHOGGOTHS, Fetid Iridescences

char.	rolls	averages
STR	18D6	63
CON	12D6	42
SIZ	24D6	84
INT	2D6	7
POW	3D6	10-11
DEX	1D6	3-4
Move 10 roll		HP 63

Av. Damage Bonus: +8D6.

Weapons: Crush 70%, damage is db

Armor: none, but (1) fire and electrical attacks do only half damage; (2) physical weapons such as firearms do only 1 point of damage, impaling or not; (3) a shoggoth regenerates 2 hit points per round.

Spells: none, normally.

Sanity Loss: 1D6/1D20 Sanity points to see a shoggoth.

Star-Spawn of Cthulhu

GREATER SERVITOR RACE

They all lay in stone houses in their great city of R'lyeh, preserved by the spells of mighty Cthulhu for a glorious resurrection when the stars and the earth might once more be ready . . . .

—H. P. Lovecraft, "The Call of Cthulhu."

These gigantic octopoid beings resemble Cthulhu himself, but are smaller. Not all the inhabitants of R'lyeh were trapped when it sank. Some still live on in the deep trenches beneath the ocean, where they are tended by deep ones. Related entities dwell in the stars, such as the beings said to infest the lake of Hali on a planet near the star Aldebaran, in Taurus.

A star-spawn may attack with tentacles or with claw. It may use 1D4 tentacles each round, or a single claw. Tentacle damage equals half the creature's damage bonus, while claw damage equals its full damage bonus.

STAR-SPAWN OF CTHULHU, Satraps of The Sleeper

Char.	Rolls	Averages
STR	2D6x10	70
CON	3D6x5	52-53
SIZ	3D6x10	105
INT	6D6	21
POW	6D6	21
DEX	3D6	10-11
Move 20 / 20 Swim		HP 79

Av. Damage Bonus: +11D6.

Weapons: Tentacles 80%, damage equals 1/2 db
Claw 80%, damage equals db

Armor: 10-point hide & blubber; regenerates 3 hit points per round.

Spells: each knows 3D6 spells.

Sanity Loss: 1D6/1D20 Sanity points to see a star-spawn.

Werewolves

SERVITOR RACE

I am he who howls in the night; I am he who moans in the snow; I am he who hath never seen light; I am he who mounts from below.

—"Psychopompos," Lovecraft.

…His men went without mailcoats, and were frantic as dogs or wolves; they bit their shields and were as strong as bears or boars; they slew men, but neither fire nor iron could hurt them.

—"Ynglinga Saga," 6.

Werewolves are men or women possessed by a kind of spirit ("wolf-shadow") normally found in Limbo. Tawil at'Umr may impart such a spirit to a warrior who caused great carnage in battle, or to a cultist in return for mass sacrifices. Alternately, a *woelcyrge* (Old One) may embed the wolf-shadow into a newborn's mind.

Werewolf

In the heat of a battle, the wolf-shadow tries to take over the mind of his host using the sacred Fury (*Wut*) spell — see page 87 for further details.

Werewolves have been around for a very long time, for Virgil and Saint Augustine already spoke of them. The Vikings consider wolf-men (*berserks*) to be elite warriors of Odin (alias Tawil at'Umr) awaiting the final battle against the forces of Chaos on the Last Evening. Berserks — who dye their bodies black — are known to have formed the household guard of Norway's King Harald I Fairhair (872–930). Berserk warriors wear wolf skins into battle or fight naked, and are in the habit of raping and murdering at will.

Two anonymous texts written around 1000 A.D., "The Dialogue of Solomon and Saturn" and "The Poem of Widsith," attest the existence of a mythical nation of wolf-men —the *hundigas* ("those-of-the-dog"). They appear to be ruled by an enigmatic giant sorcerer named Marculfus (Tawil at'Umr), "the raging wolf known in the whole world," messenger of an ambiguous god whose kingdom is beyond the reach of humans and animals (Yog-Sothoth).

WEREWOLVES, The Army of the Dog

Use the human statistics as defaults, except when the wolf-spirit takes over: switch then to INT 6 and add the spirit's POW 11 to the human's POW, thus forming a common pool of magic points.

Other Names: wolf-men, wolf-coats, versipellis ("turn-skins"), hundigas, berserks.

Weapon: Bite 30%, damage 1D8+db (in wolf-form).

Armor: add an extra 1 point of hide if in wolf-form.

Spells: Fury, Body Warping.

Skills: Hide 60%, Track by smell 90%.

Sanity Loss: 0/1D3 Sanity points to witness the shape-shift; 0/1D3 to see a giant wolf form (SIZ 12+).

Worms of the Earth

LESSER SERVITOR RACE

The worms of the earth are the remains of the serpent people who turned away from worshipping their father Yig, and turned to Tsathoggua instead. Cursed by Yig, they have devolved from humanoid form toward snake form. They withdrew into Britain during their people's decline. When the Picts first arrived on the isles, they fought against the worms and made them retreat deep into the hills. Before long, the worms entered human legend as the "little people" under the hills.

The worms worship an artifact of obscure origins, the Black Stone, marked by symbols of terror. It is said that anybody succeeding in stealing the Black Stone may be granted a service in return, although in the end he or she will still incur the wrath of the worms.

There are three stages to the serpent-men's devolution and one "family" of degenerates may breed true to their stage for many centuries before devolving further.

STAGE ONE

> . . . A brief impression of a broad, strangely flattened head, pendulous writhing lips that bared curved, pointed fangs, and a hideously misshapen, dwarfish body that seemed mottled—all set off by those unwinking reptilian eyes.
>
> —"Worms of the Earth," Robert E. Howard.

The serpent people are dwarves compared to their non-devolved kin, averaging only three feet six inches in height with shortened arms and legs. Their intellect also drops sharply. Stage one degenerates are capable of speech and spell use.

STAGE TWO

> This thing was more like a giant serpent than anything else, but it had aborted legs and snaky arms with hooked talons. It crawled on its belly, writhing back mottled lips to bare needle-like fangs, which I felt must drip with venom. It hissed as it reared up its ghastly head on a horribly long neck, while its yellow slanted eyes glittered with all the horror that is spawned in the black lairs under the earth.
>
> —"People of the Dark," Robert E. Howard.

Worm of the Earth
(stage two degenerate)

These degenerates are essentially large snakes with rudimentary

arms and legs, but with no guarantee of both sets of limbs. They move by slithering like snakes and pulling/pushing themselves with any limbs they may possess. Again intellect takes a sharp drop. Some stage two degenerates may still speak and very rare ones may cast spells.

STAGE THREE

The serpent person has now devolved into a snake looking almost like a natural one. They still possess more intelligence then natural snakes but have lost all spell use.

Worms of the Earth, Children of the Night

STAGE ONE

char.	rolls	averages
STR	3D6	10–11
CON	3D6	10–11
SIZ	2D4	5
INT	3D6	10–11
POW	3D6	10–11
DEX	2D6+6	13
Move 8		HP 8

Other Names: little people.

Damage Bonus: +0 (never negative).

Weapon: Bite 35%, damage 1D6 + poison (POT equal to CON); may use weapons.

Armor: 1 point scales.

Spells: at the discretion of the keeper, those with POW and INT greater than 11 may know 1D4 spells.

Sanity Loss: 0/1D6.

STAGE TWO

char.	rolls	averages
STR	2D6	7
CON	3D6	10–11
SIZ	2D4	5
INT	2D6	7
POW	3D4	7–8
DEX	3D6	10–11
Move 8		HP 8

Other Names: none.

Damage Bonus: +0 (never negative).

Weapon: Bite 35%, damage 1D4 + poison (POT equal to CON); may use weapons if it possesses hands.

Armor: 1 point scales.

Spells: at the discretion of the keeper, those with POW and INT greater than 11 may know 1D2 spells.

Sanity Loss: 0/1D6.

STAGE THREE

char.	rolls	averages
STR	1D6	3–4
CON	2D6	7
SIZ	2D4	5
INT	1D6	3–4
POW	2D6	7
DEX	3D6	10–11
Move 8		HP 6

Other Names: none.

Damage Bonus: +0 (never negative).

Weapon: Bite 35%, damage 1D3 + poison (POT equal to CON).

Armor: 1 point scales.

Spells: none.

Sanity Loss: none.

Spirits & Limbo Creatures

Souls are immortal and there is another life among the dead.
—Diodorus of Sicily, V, 28.

Spirits are immaterial and invisible (they only have INT and POW), and cannot interact with physical objects (though they may initiate *spirit combat*). They can walk or float through the air as easily as the living walk across the ground. They are immune to physical damage, disease, and poison. Spirits are essentially immortal, and their character is often unpredictable and bizarre.

In heathen countries, mortals frequently revere or worship at least one type of spirit (as in ancestor cults or sacrifices to nature spirits). Most powerful spirits (POW 10 or more) have secret True Names by which they may be summoned specifically. Spirits normally reside outside our material world, in Limbo.

The keeper should craft each spirit to fit the circumstances of the adventure.

Spirit Attacks & Possession

Disembodied spirits naturally possess the capacity to engage in spirit combat. An observer would glimpse the spirit clawing at, enveloping, or constricting its physical target.

Spirit Combat: a process whereby a spirit attacks and attempts to drain magic points from its target, which may be either another incorporeal spirit or a spirit incorporated within a living being. The target is able to return the attack, in kind.

Each matches its magic points against its opponent's magic points on the Resistance Table. D100 rolls for each side are made simultaneously. Each side receiving a success on the die roll reduces the magic points of the

opponent by 1D3 points; both sides may be successful. There is no effect with an unsuccessful die roll.

Spirit combat continues until one side or the other is reduced to zero magic points. A living being reduced to zero magic points faints and may be possessed by the attacking spirit during the combat round that follows. An incorporeal spirit reduced to zero magic points may be bound into the service of its opponent during the combat round that follows. If neither possession nor binding occur then the combat is over. A defeated spirit must return to Limbo (or whence it came) for at least one day. A being defeated in spirit combat remains unconscious until at least one magic point has been naturally regained.

- A spirit losing all magic points dissolves within one round and cannot reform for a day.

- A spirit losing all POW is dispelled forever.

- A human losing all magic points falls unconscious until at least one magic point regenerates.

- A human losing all POW either dies or maintains a vegetative state until POW can be raised again, at the keeper's discretion.

Possession: if an attacking spirit drives its target's magic points to zero, it may possess the target's body during the round that follows. A possessing spirit suppresses the natural identity of the victim. The possessed can be forced to perform deeds such as providing information, casting spells, attacking innocent people, etc., until the possessing spirit releases its spiritual hold or is driven out. A possessing spirit can only be dislodged by magic attacks (Disembodiment, Dismiss) or the loss of all magic points in a future spirit combat.

GHOSTS are the spirits of the dead. They can take on very diverse appearances, from the exact form of the dead person or animal, to a mere shadow. Ghosts are usually tied to a specific place and seem to be created by overwhelming emotions at the time of death, like fear, desire or madness. Some ghosts are adept at augury, and other manifest innate abilities that mimic effects of spells. *Spells: Augur, Cloud Memory, Enthrall, Exaltation, Fear, Fury and/or Soul Singing, sometimes one Bless/Curse (characteristic) or (skill class) spell.*

NATURE SPIRITS are personifications of the powers of nature. Their personalities and abilities are focused and shaped by their nature-identity: forest, earth, wind, water, fire, sea, river, disease, and so forth. Each nature spirit should know at least one spell appropriate to its function. Nature spirits are sometimes tied to a specific natural feature such as a tree (dryad), a pond (naiad), or a hill (oread), etc. *Spells: Heal, Moonlight, Death's Breath, Poison Blood, Power Source, and/or Winds of Desolation.*

TOMB-HERD are lesser servitors of Yog-Sothoth, and normally reside in Limbo. They possess the bodies of other creatures in order to enter our world and feed upon the occupants of tombs. See below.

DOELS are mysterious entities that crowd Limbo. In our world they have the unpleasant ability to "dissolve" material life forms. See below.

OLD ONES are powerful spirits cited in the *Necronomicon*, cohabiting in the Ultimate Abyss "between the spheres" with Yog-Sothoth. See below.

ANCIENT ONES are godlike Old Ones doing the command of Yog-Sothoth. See below.

Doels

INDEPENDENT BEINGS

Simultaneously there developed something like a cold draught, which apparently swept past me from the direction of the distant sound . . . . At another time I felt the huge animate things brushing past me and occasionally walking or drifting through my supposedly solid body . . . . Foremost among the living objects were inky, jellyfish monstrosities . . . . They were present in loathsome profusion, and I saw to my horror that they overlapped; that they were semi-fluid and capable of passing through one another and through what we know as solids. These things were never still, but seemed ever floating about with some malignant purpose. Sometimes they appeared to devour one another, the attacker launching itself at its victim and instantaneously obliterating the latter from sight.

— "From Beyond," Lovecraft.

". . . I do not believe [the Hounds of Tindalos] can reach me, but I must beware of the Doels. Perhaps they can help them break through. The satyrs will help, and they can advance through the scarlet circles . . . ."

— "The Hounds of Tindalos," Long.

. . . The tiny, flesh-devouring Doels who inhabited an alien dimension shrouded in night and chaos. . . .

— "H.P. Lovecraft: Dreamer on the Nightside," Long.

In Limbo the mysterious doels are innumerable. Some scholars advance a theory that doels alone make up the Nameless Mist permeating Limbo. The truth on that subject is immaterial, since there is no way to interact with the doels in Limbo.

Steal Body

Every time a school of doels attacks a material living being — including one of their own kind — match the total POW of the doels against the target's POW on the Resistance Table. Succeeding, the doels "steal" 1D3 points from one of the target's physical characteristics (STR, CON, SIZ, or DEX), and become partly corporeal. Failing, they collectively lose 1D3 POW.

The general appearance of a materializing doel is that of a translucent grayish being, more fluid than solid. Specific details (eyes, mouths, feelers, and tentacles) are up to the keeper. As for the dissolving victim, in the first stage bodily functions slow down. In the second stage, when one characteristic is reduced to less than half its original value, the body gradually loses density to become more and more blurred and jelly-like. In the third stage, when all physical characteristics are lowered to 2 or less, the body is a mere apparition, and eventually dissolves into nothing, releasing the victim's spirit. (INT, POW, and EDU are unchanged, Move equals one-half of POW; see "Spirits," above.) The whole process — though oddly painless — is extremely debilitating, costing 0/1D6 Sanity points in the first stage and another 0/1D10 Sanity points in the second stage. The final disembodiment costs 0/1D4 Sanity points.

Note that reducing the hit points of a partly material doel to zero won't destroy it: it merely returns the doel to its original spirit form.

There is in fact only one effective defense against the doels: their "sight" is based on movement so by keeping absolutely still they cannot "see" us nor attack us.

DOELS, The Flesh Devourers

Collective INT 1

POW +1 for every doel present

Move equal to one-half of DEX (fly, minimum 1)

HP equal to (CON+SIZ)/2

Dodge equal to DEX x5

Other Names: none.

Weapon: Steal Body, damage special (see above)
Bite (DEX x5)%, damage 1D6 for every 16 in (STR+SIZ), round upwards

Armor: none, but doels are indestructible while disembodied.

Spells: none.

Sanity Loss: 1/1D3 Sanity points to witness the materialization of a single doel.

Old Ones

GREATER SERVITORS

[He felt] the rustlings of great wings, and impressions of sound like the chirpings and murmurings of objects unknown on Earth or in the solar system. Glancing backwards, he saw not one gate alone but a multiplicity of gates, at some of which clamoured Forms he strove not to remember.

—"Through the Gates of the Silver Key," Lovecraft and Price.

The Old Ones were, the Old Ones are, and the Old Ones shall be. Not in the spaces we know, but between them . . . . By Their smell can men sometimes know Them near, but of Their semblance can no man know, saving only in the features of those They have begotten on mankind; and of those are there many sorts, differing in likeness from man's truest eidolon to that shape without sight or substance which is Them. They walk unseen and foul in lonely places where the Words have been spoken and the Rites howled through at their Seasons. The wind gibbers with Their voices, and the earth mutters with Their consciousness. They bend the forest and crush the city, yet may not forest or city behold the hand that smites.

—Necronomicon.

On [the locusts'] heads were what looked like crowns of gold; their faces were like human faces, their hair like women's hair, and their teeth like lions' teeth. . . . They have as king over them the angel of the bottomless pit; his name in Hebrew is Abbadon (Destruction); and in Greek he is called Apollyon (Destroyer).

—Revelation 9:7.

The Woelcyrges have the power to choose the slain. . . . All is sinister to see, a cloud of blood moves over the sky, the air is red with the blood of men, as the battle-women chant their song.

—Njal's Saga.

Most myths of mankind mention the existence of a race of intermediary beings between men and gods. Despite the many names given to this race, most descriptions draw a disturbingly consistent image of what the *Necronomicon* calls "the Old Ones." Do not confuse them with the Great Old Ones. As the *Necronomicon* writes, "Great Cthulhu is Their cousin, yet can he spy Them only dimly."

The Old Ones are spirits serving Yog-Sothoth. They are naturally invisible but often manifest themselves by a halo of light that makes them shine like stars. In fact these beings can appear in all sorts of ominous ghostly shapes, from beautiful maidens shining with light to dreadful she-things with golden wings and bronze talons. Some accounts also allude to the smell that accompanies them. Old Ones have the gift of being able to move very quickly, and even, some say, to be everywhere at once.

The Old Ones are innumerable, they know neither good nor evil, and they walked the earth long before men did. Back then, the Old Ones used Limbo to travel through the universe, and held it in reverence. Now they wander forever "not in the spheres we know, but between them" — the Ultimate Abyss filled by Yog-Sothoth. Old Ones do meddle in human affairs from time to time. Many tales relate how they breed with the daughters of men and spawn monstrous offspring like werewolves (Dark Ages women must to cover their hair in church in order to "not tempt angels"), and also how they teach men forbidden knowledge. Yog-Sothoth the Destroyer sometimes sends the Old Ones to take part in battles, stirring up disorder, and seizing the souls of the slain.

Old One

Old Ones usually intrude into our world after sunset, under the cover of darkness, and they seem to favor deserted places.

Greek and Babylonian demons, the Arabic *shayatin* and *jinn* (made from "smokeless fire"), angels of the Old Testament, Scandinavian elves, Celtic and Germanic messengers of the Otherworld, all match the above definition of Old Ones.

Old Ones themselves are sometimes worshipped by humans but they usually possess only small cults (*e.g.*, offerings to elves). One Germanic cult of Old Ones worshippers — the *Armanen* — stands out dangerously, however, as its white-skinned members proclaim their purity and superiority above all, and use the Crux Gammata as their symbol (known nowadays as the svastika or swastika).

Old Ones have secret True Names by which they may be summoned.

OLD ONES, Choosers of the Slain

char.	rolls	averages
INT	5D6	17–18
POW	4D6+1	15

Move equal to POW (flying)

Other Names: demons, elves ("shining ones"), jinn ("hidden ones"), angels (*e.g.* seraphs—"burning ones," "fallen ones," "watchers"), woelcyrges (valkyries), bird-women, siren-birds, the Fates (fairies), furies, gorgons, harpies, drowners, etc.

Weapon: permanent Steal Life (1D3 to 1D6 POW, see Spirits).

Armor: none, but no physical weapons can harm one.

Spells: each knows at least 1D10 spells, always including Soul Singing and Fury.

Sanity Loss: 1/1D10 Sanity points to witness the insanely beautiful, dazzling radiance of an Old One, or to hear its ghastly ululation. Insanity takes the form of paralysis and catatonia.

Tomb-Herd

LESSER SERVITOR RACE

... Horrible white, gelatinous shapes flopped across the landscape toward the forefront of the scene ... and as in a dream [I] saw those frightful shapes move upon the statues nearby, and watched the outlines of those statues blur and then begin to move. Then swiftly, one of those

dreadful beings rolled and flopped toward me. I felt something cold as ice touch my ankle.

— "The Church in High Street," Campbell.

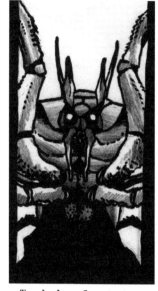

Tomb-herd statue

The tomb-herds have connections to Earth through certain tombs and crypts where they feed upon the extra-dimensional excrescences of the crypts' inhabitants, accessible to them in Limbo. Special half-humanoid, half-crustacean statues are placed within certain tombs by the followers of Yog-Sothoth, to be used as host bodies by the tomb-herd on this plane.

Tomb-herd Gates to this dimension are triggered by a living presence near the gateway to their tomb, and they immediately enter the specially prepared statues in the crypt to attack intruders and feast.

Possession: if a statue is unavailable to a member of the herd it can attempt to possess a human in the tomb by touching him and winning a POW vs. POW struggle with him on the Resistance Table. If overcome by the alien, the victim must roll his POW or less on D100 or he passes out; whether or not the victim passes out, the herd-member immediately uses the unfortunate host to feed in the tomb. A conscious host of one of these foul feasting creatures must make a Sanity roll and lose 1D3/2D4 from participating in such a ghoulish repast. The feeding complete, the herd-member leaves its temporary host, returning to Limbo and leaving its victim otherwise unharmed.

Space Folding: a unique ability of the tomb-herd is their ability to fold or disarrange space in small regions (this can be done only while the herd member is in its natural, insubstantial form). This warping of space acts as the Gate spell and drains one Sanity point and one magic point from anyone passing through the disarranged area. This unusual attack is directed at a specific individual, and can be avoided only if the target can successfully roll his POW or less on D100. It costs a herd-member one magic point for each folding of space it does; this need be done but once per victim, who continues to experience the warping until he can roll his POW or less on D100. The Gate-like disarranging usually has a range of less than five miles. The tomb-herd uses this power to repeatedly return a victim to their tomb or similar location; sometimes they merely keep a victim within the town or area in which

the aliens were encountered. Large groups of victims are usually separated so that they can be tormented individually; while some of the tomb-herd bewilder their enemies in this manner, others alert their human allies to the presence of intruders.

The Statues: when not occupied by the herd, the special statues have hit points equal to their SIZ, plus 3 points of armor; impaling weapons do only half damage to unoccupied statues. The tomb-herd automatically cross into this dimension if their statues are tampered with.

TOMB-HERD, Lurkers at the Threshold

The insubstantial herd-form has only INT and POW characteristics; the remaining values should be used in statue form only.

char.	rolls	averages
STR*	2D6+6	13
CON*	3D6	10–11
SIZ*	2D6+6	13
INT	3D6	10–11
POW	3D6+6	16–17
DEX *	2D6	7
Move 6		HP* 12

*In statue form only.

Other Names: none.

Damage Bonus: +1D4 (statue form only).

Weapons: usually none, though in statue form the herd may grapple or make other physical attacks. The herd-members' statue forms have their (STR+DEX)% chance to hit. Damage from a statue-form's attack equals the creature's damage bonus.

Armor: in natural tomb-herd form, the herd is immune to all damage inflicted by non-enchanted physical weapons. In statue form they take normal damage; however, they also have 3 points of armor.

Spells: normally none.

Sanity Loss: 0/1D6 Sanity points to see the natural form of the tomb-herd. 0/1D3 Sanity points to see the uninhabited statues used by the herd and 1/1D6 Sanity points to see a statue in use.

Deities of the Mythos

Ancient Ones

As they sat more erect, their outlines became more like those of men, though Carter knew that that they could not be men. Upon their cloaked heads there now seemed to rest tall, uncertainly coloured miters . . . while grasped in certain folds of their swathings were long sceptres

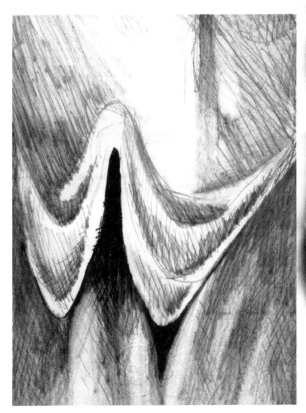

Ancient One

whose carven heads bodied forth a grotesque and archaic mystery.

— "Through the Gates of the Silver Key,"
Lovecraft and Price.

The Ancient Ones are not worshipped, although sorcerers and adventurers interested in journeying to other times and places seek them out. The Ancient Ones are the spirits of twelve creatures that were allowed to pass the Ultimate Gate guarded by Tawil at'Umr, into the Abyss, and were transfigured into godlike Old Ones (see corresponding entry). These entities dwell in a mighty temple — the "Hall of the Slain" — beyond space and time, in Limbo. The Ancient Ones are perceived as ill-defined cloaked shapes. Utter madness and destruction befall anyone who would see an Ancient One unveiled.

The Ancient Ones know all things, and communicate telepathically. They may turn people's dreams to reality, or send dreamers to other times and places.

These beings are neither good nor evil, and they would welcome and assist the worthy just as they would destroy an imprudent trespasser.

ANCIENT ONES, the Ultimate Gate

char.	rolls	averages
STR	n/a	n/a
CON	1D100+100	150–151
SIZ	3D6+9	19–20
INT	2D10+17	28
POW	5D10+20	47–48
DEX	2D10+10	21
Move 25 gliding		HP 85–86

Other Names: none.

Weapon: Touch 100%, damage transport or destruction.

Armor: none, but only magic and enchanted weapons can harm an Ancient One.

Spells: the Ancient Ones know all spells.

Sanity Loss: none while cloaked. 1D10/1D100 Sanity points if their true form is revealed.

Bugg-Shash

GREAT OLD ONE

Creeping up on all sides, to the very line of the chalked circle, the Thing came: a glistening, shuddering wall of jelly-like ooze in which many mouths gaped and just as many eyes monstrously ogled! This was Bugg-Shash the Drowner, The Black One, The Filler of Space . . . . The eyes were . . . beyond words, but worse still were those mouths.

Bugg-Shash

Sucking and whistling with thickly viscous lips, the mouths glistened and slobbered and from out of those gluttonous orifices poured the lunatic chitterings of alien song — the song of Bugg-Shash . . . .

— "The Kiss of Bugg-Shash," Lumley.

Bugg-Shash has no known organized cult. Instead it is sought out by lone sorcerers and madmen for purposes of grim vengeance and murder. Once called to earth, the Great Old One concentrates its efforts wholly upon trying to catch its victims. Reluctant to obey the commands of its summoner, Bugg-Shash immediately attacks any who call it forth unless restrained by a specially-enchanted pentagram drawn on the floor and

provided with a sacrificial victim. If either of these is lacking, the summoner suffers attack.

The Great Old One is dispelled by light; its chosen victims are relatively safe during the daylight. Any time an intended victim enters an area of darkness, however, Bugg-Shash instantly appears. Once summoned, Bugg-Shash does not return to its alien lair until it has found and killed at least one victim, either the person intended or the summoner.

Bugg-Shash has the ability to animate corpses by immersing them in its slimy secretions. Such undead are completely under the control of Bugg-Shash until the deity is permanently dispelled, or until it tires of them and allows them to die. An undead slave of Bugg-Shash appears as an animated corpse covered in viscous slime (use the zombie statistics in the core rules).

The Great Old One attacks by enveloping its victims, then bestowing its "kiss." The more victims it takes, the less its frenzy and the less effective its attack. For every victim after the first, Bugg-Shash's chance to successfully envelop is reduced by ten points. An enveloped victim may escape only by overcoming the Great Old One's STR with his own. If more than one victim is enveloped at a time Bugg-Shash must divide its STR among them. Once it has successfully enveloped a victim Bugg-Shash bestows its kiss, smothering the unfortunate with slime. Victims suffer as per the drowning rules.

Bugg-Shash appears to have some connection to the Outer God Yibb-Tstll, and both are referred to as "parasites attached to the Old Ones" in the *Cthaat Aquadingen*. Bugg-Shash may be dispelled only by reducing its hit points to zero, or with a special spell found only in the *Cthaat Aquadingen* and the *Necronomicon*. While light drives it off, it does not truly dispel Bugg-Shash.

BUGG-SHASH, He Who Comes in the Dark

STR 50	CON 45	SIZ 65	INT 15	POW 25
DEX 10	Move 6			HP 55

Other Names: The Black One, The Devourer, Drowner.

Damage Bonus: +6D6.

Weapons: Envelop 60%, damage db or hold. Kiss automatic when enveloped, damage as per drowning.

Armor: none, but only magic, enchanted weapons, fire, or lightning harm Bugg-Shash. Cold, acid, and non-enchanted weapons are useless.

Spells: Any as the keeper desires.

Sanity Loss: 1D6/1D20 Sanity to see Bugg-Shash and 1/1D6 to see its undead slaves.

Lilith

. . . He did not see IT. The open porthole, just before he turned on the lights, was clouded for a second with a certain phosphorescence, and for a moment there seemed to echo in the night outside the suggestion of a faint and hellish tittering; but no real outline met the eye.
— "The Horror at Red Hook," Lovecraft.

Wildcats shall meet with hyenas, goat-demons shall call to each other; there too Lilith shall repose, and find a place to rest.
—Isaiah 34:14.

Lilith in human form

Lilith is an Ancient One and is associated with Tawil at'Umr, the Guardian of the Ultimate Abyss. In Limbo she may be perceived as an ominous cloaked figure. She often visits sleeping men in their dreams. Victims of Lilith's spiritual "rape" are drained of magic points or POW. Those who lose all magic points are possessed until Lilith has been dispelled or until her spiritual hold is broken. Lilith may command anyone under her power to do her bidding. Victims awaken exhausted and with a successful Idea roll, may 1) perceive a vague and fleeting phosphorescence and far-sounding titters, and 2) remember a dream of being raped by a black woman of sinister beauty. Lilith can re-use drained POW to give birth to one or more Old Ones of sanity-wrecking beauty (see page 117).

In our material plane Lilith often appears as a gigantic gug (see separate statistics below). At any moment she may secrete a grayish slime onto the soil, out of which arise 1D10 she-vampires (see pages 100-101) within a few minutes. Lilith's depraved children are the lilim, the creatures of the night, and as such she has the ability to command them.

Lilith has never had any form of organized worship. She is instead sought out by sorcerers or by those interested in fertility magic.

LILITH, Queen of the Night (Ancient One)

INT 20   POW 25   Move 25 gliding

Other Names: She-devil, Darkness, The Black Moon, She-who-says-no, the Eye-Goddess.

Weapon: Touch 100%, damage instant destruction
    Permanent Steal Life, damage 1D10 POW
    Power Drain, damage 1D10 magic points

Armor: none, but only magic and enchanted weapons can harm an Ancient One.

Spells: any as desired by the keeper.

Sanity Loss: none while cloaked or in human dream-form. 1D10/1D100 Sanity points if her true form is revealed.

LILITH, The Gaping Mouth (Gug Form)

STR 30   CON 53   SIZ 72   INT 20   POW 25
DEX 20   Move 10   HP 63

Other Names: Lamia/Labia, The Great Whore.

Damage Bonus: +5D6.

Weapon: Kiss (Bite) 100%, damage 1D10
    Claw(s) 85%, damage 2D6 each
    Stomp 50%, damage 1D6+db

Armor: 10-point skin, hair, and cartilage.

Spells: any as desired by the keeper.

Sanity Loss: 0/1D10 to see Lilith in giant gug form.

Tawil at'Umr / Wotan

Tawil at'Umr

AVATAR OF YOG-SOTHOTH

There was another shape, too . . . which seemed to glide or float over the cloudy, floor-like lower level. It was not exactly permanent in outline, but held transient suggestions of something remotely preceding or paralleling the human form, though half as large again as an ordinary man. It seemed to be heavily cloaked . . . with some neutral-coloured fabric; and Carter could not detect any eyeholes through which it might gaze.

— "Through the Gates of the Silver Key," Lovecraft and Price.

All these Blacknesses are lesser than HE WHO guardeth the gateway: HE WHO will guide the rash one beyond all the worlds into the Abyss of unnamable devourers. For He

is 'UMR AT-TAWIL, the Most Ancient One, which the scribe rendereth as THE PROLONGED OF LIFE.

— *Necronomicon.*

An old man of great height, lacking one eye and clad in a hairy mantle.

— *"Gesta Danorum," II, 65.*

Tawil at'Umr, one of the forms of Yog-Sothoth, is the Most Ancient One. Tawil at'Umr is the guide of souls to Limbo and beyond the Ultimate Gate to the last void, where his dreadful other self resides. Tawil at'Umr's form in Limbo is that of a shifting heavily-cloaked dwarfed shape. In our world, Tawil at'Umr is the archetype of the accursed wanderer — a tall one-eyed old man wearing a threadbare robe of many colors. Tawil at'Umr is also worshiped from the fifth century onwards as a 24-foot-tall dog-thing, walking like a man (separate statistics are given below). The symbolism of Tawil at'Umr as a grim nomadic peddler with supernatural sight is very ancient, personified in the Norse pantheon by Odin, and having roots in the "Angel of Death" figure, known to the Arabs as Izra'il, and to Christians as Uriel, the "Fire of God."

Some cultists advance that Tawil was originally a human chosen by Yog-Sothoth to pass the Gate of the Silver Key and become an Ancient One, the Guardian of the Gate.

Tawil at'Umr is presumably the least malignant form of Yog-Sothoth. Even his most fervent worshippers nevertheless fear him for being sly and foul.

Tawil at'Umr may grant spells or open magical Gates in return for mass human sacrifices, involving simultaneous strangling and stabbing of prisoners of war after a battle. The prisoners' belongings, including horses, must be offered also, and buried in pits with the corpses.

Tawil at'Umr has many servitors, amongst which are the being Bugg-Shash, Lilith, the Ancient Ones, and the Tomb-herd. All have in common the role of "choosers of the slain," reaping the souls of the dead and guiding them to the Ultimate Gate and their ineffable Guardians.

Tawil at'Umr is sometimes confused with the Devil by Christian scholars. In fact, much stronger parallels can be drawn between Tawil at'Umr and the Destroyer of the Scriptures (Revelation 9:7): Apollyon, the avenging god who shines like the moon and kills with silver arrows (Iliad, Song 1).

Attacks: Tawil at'Umr's spear, when thrown, turns into a grim bolt of silvery fire which can reach over half a mile, and destroy all normal objects struck, slaying any humans who fail to dodge out of the way.

TAWIL AT'UMR, The Opener of the Way

The insubstantial Most Ancient One has only INT and POW characteristics; the remaining values should be used in tangible form.

STR* 51	CON* 200	SIZ* 25	INT 40	POW 100
DEX* 30	Move 25			HP* 113

*In tangible form only.

Other Names: Most Ancient One, Apollyon the Destroyer, god of wolves, Angel of Death, Wodan (meaning "furious" or "He who drives mad," also known as the "Old One"), Harlequin.

Damage Bonus: +4D6.

Weapon: Demonic spear 100%, damage instant destruction.

Armor: none, but Tawil at'Umr can only be harmed by enchanted weapons or magic.

Spells: Tawil at'Umr knows all spells.

Sanity Loss: none, unless Tawil at'Umr removes his protective cloak; 1D10/1D100 Sanity points to see him uncloaked.

TAWIL AT'UMR, The Dog

STR 51	CON 29	SIZ 51	INT 40	POW 100
DEX 19	Move 19			HP 40

Other Names: Marculfus ("Borderland Wolf"), Offero, Reprobus of the "dog-heads" tribe, Gargan, and Wepwawet ("Opener of the Way"), a dog-headed deity of ancient Egypt, guide of souls and patron of battles, worshiped in Lycopolis or "Wolf-city."

Damage Bonus: +5D6.

Weapon: Bite 40%, damage 1D10.

Armor: 3-point hide, and only magical weapons can damage the Dog.

Spells: the Dog knows all spells.

Sanity Loss: 0/1D10 Sanity points to see the Dog.

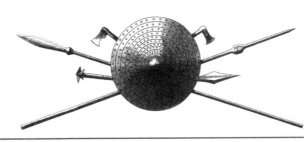

The Tomb

The living close the eyes of the dead, but it is the dead that open the eyes of the living.
—Old Slavic saying.

"The Tomb" is an initial incursion into the grim territories of *Cthulhu Dark Ages*. The scenario is historically set in 998 A.D. It transports the keeper and the players to the Eastern March of the Germanic Empire, in the thickly wooded hills to the north of Vienna.

The plot is generic enough to fit other times and places, as the keeper desires. For reasons of convenience we use the masculine gender to designate keeper and investigators.

Keeper's Information

At the settlement of Laa, German colonists and local Slavs live in uneasy partnership, brought together by their hatred of the heathen Magyars (Hungarians) of the east, once the terror of the Occident. But a more terrible foe lurks in the depths of the forest: the Dark One, a Mythos creature. For decades it hid in the dark passages of its tomb, deep in the forest. At night it prowled the region, hunting humans or buying slaves from human traders. The captives were brought back to the tomb, transformed, and handed over to mi-go who took them to one of their unearthly outposts.

The Plot

The scenario is divided into three distinct parts. In the first part, the players are confronted by a mystery involving the disappearance of their master/employer Brother Gudman, and the finding of a strange black stone. When questioning the locals they learn disturbing legends and rumors, all of which correlate too well, hinting at the cancerous influence of the Dark One. The Dark One, helped by mi-go, tries to recover the Black Stone from the investigators, and in doing so, leaves a trail of terror and destruction. In the second part of the scenario, the investigators leave the village and meet with the feared Magyars. The final part of the scenario sees the investigators descend into the Dark One's tomb to meet their fate.

Keeper's Notes: — such as this one — are italicized.

The keeper is invited to first familiarize himself with the timeline provided on the opposite page, and the maps on pages 129 and 130.

Player Information

The investigators are joining senior Brother Gudman, Brother Drogo, and five warrior monks on a two-week journey from Regensburg to Laa, an outpost on the eastern border of the Germanic Empire. The monks are missionaries sent by the Bishop of Regensburg to try to convert and pacify the heathen Magyars

Keeper Play Aids

Timeline

907 A.D. Arrival of the Dark One and the mi-go; they invade the Celtic tomb under the Black Hill. The mi-go construct a Gate to one of their otherworldly outposts, and start mining halite. The Dark One possesses the mummified body of the Celtic prince who was buried there. The local Slavs occupy the site of Laa; there is a Slavic hill fort and temple. A pagan cult soon installs a secret temple at the foot of the Black Hill, and provides the Dark One and the mi-go with the necessary human victims.

970 A.D. Arrival of the first German colonists in Laa.

975 A.D. Brant arrives in Laa, aged 22. The Slavic hill fort and temple are destroyed; the German stronghold is built.

976 A.D. Emperor Otto grants Brant authority over the pagus. The pagan cult is eradicated; its priests are arrested in the village and summarily executed. The secret temple at the foot of the Black Hill becomes history and slowly rots away.

977 A.D. Burgolf arrives in Laa, aged 16. He rapidly gets involved in slave trade with the Magyars and the Merchant (the Dark One); he shares his benefits with Lord Brant who provides some logistic support.

984 A.D. Trade embargo: Burgolf stops his slave trading activities; the Dark One and the mi-go are forced to abduct humans for their unholy schemes.

985 A.D. to present People disappear at more or less regular intervals; the Dark One needs a new host every 6 months (May and November), and the mi-go transport live human heads to otherworldly outposts.

988 A.D. Ruin of the hamlet Asparn under odd circumstances.

989 A.D. Death of the German priest and replacement by Zutto.

995 A.D. Brant donates land to the seven eremite brothers. The dispute between Bavaria and Hungary ends. Magyar rebels raid Laa and partially burn the village down. The landlord loses his wife in the attack, and a few colonists die. Construction of the hermitage house and church (this is the last time Burgolf meets with the Merchant /Dark One).

995 A.D. Two eremite brothers are sent east to Christianize the rebel Magyars; they are enslaved by the Magyars and never return.

995–997 A.D. Magyar rebels sporadically raid Laa to steal livestock.

997 A.D. Brant captures Zoltan, son of the rebel Magyar chieftain Moh-gor; Zoltan is kept in the prison pit under Brant's Tower-house. Magyar raids cease.

998 A.D. Beginning of the adventure on November first.

The Forest

The keeper should do his best to make the players nervous every time their investigators have to cross the forest, and make them fear it after dark.

Mixed forests cover the hills. In some places the tree cover is so dense as to plunge the forest into a constant twilight. Marshy oak and ash woods full of treacherous bogs cover valley bottoms and flood plains.

Note that if investigators get lost in the forest, it is theoretically possible to locate the direction of the village by listening to the hermitage bells (before it is destroyed of course). The bells are sounded five times from sunrise to sunset. This trick only works within a distance of three miles, and twice as far on a successful Listen roll.

Use the following ploys with moderation, one at a time, and avoid unnecessary repetition:

- Stress the forest's spookiness by describing the wilderness, the smells, the difficult progression, the cold and the rain, the isolation, etc.

- Encounters with wild beasts, e.g. aurochs, buffaloes, red deer, wild boars, elks, roe deer, bears, etc. Wolves in particular can display odd behavior, like following the investigators at a distance, stopping when they stop, disappearing from sight to reappear close by, etc.

- Hearing sudden sounds nearby, or seeing something suddenly move at the corner of the eyes. Whatever it is, it's gone before the investigators can react.

- Unnerving sounds of something quite heavy following the party or moving parallel to it, but never seen.

Keeper Play Aids

- Persistent feeling of being followed and observed. At times the feeling may be so strong that the "observed" may think to be able to point at where the "observer" must be. Invariably the designated area is at some distance and veiled in impenetrable shadow.

- Fleeting spooky vision of a whitish shape (mi-go) rapidly vanishing behind the trees.

- Almost imperceptible, ambient sound. The sound is difficult to describe yet ominous, a kind of distant rumbling or drumming. Over time the investigator may have the impression that the sound grows louder, and may even feel that something is coming their way.

- One investigator may suddenly get a feeling of impending doom: "there is something *wrong* here. . . . We should leave. . . . Now!" What happens if they don't is up to the keeper.

- Sudden headache and startling darkening of the daylight, making the investigators look up as if expecting to see some vast shape or cloud cast a shadow over the forest. Yet there is no such thing, only darkness.

- The ultimate threat level is a close encounter with a mi-go or the Dark One. These encounters are described elsewhere in detail and should not be randomly staged.

Manhunt

The following paragraphs provide the keeper with some optional information to realistically play a nightly manhunt in the forest:

- The keeper is advised to keep track of everybody's position on an improvised map on which basic terrain features are sketched out. Don't get bogged down in unnecessary details: absolute distances and movement rates are not critical. Secretly make Navigation rolls when appropriate. Note that the horsemen almost entirely depend on dogs to find fugitives. At close range, the fugitives need successful Hide or Sneak rolls to remain undetected. One out of three milites holds a burning torch that can be spotted from up to 100 yards away.

- There are two basic terrain types: hilltops and vales. Hilltops are mostly covered with a dense mixed forest consisting of elm, oak, and pine trees. Vales are more sparsely covered with oak woods.

- At the keeper's discretion, parties keeping to the hills can come across very dense fir woods. These woods are impenetrable to horses. They make great hiding places and force horsemen to continue on foot in order to pursue. On the other hand, facing war dogs in these dense woods is very stressful and dangerous.

- At the keeper's discretion, a brook or a river may run through terrain lows. Every brook that fugitives cross makes their track more difficult to follow. Therefore, the fugitives' best strategy is to wade the stream as far as they can to lose dogs. The river Thaya is an even better opportunity for resourceful fugitives to block their pursuers. The marshy oak and ash meadows near the river are treacherous, especially for heavy animals. Moreover, war dogs and horsemen will not venture crossing a deep river. Apply exposure rules to simulate the effects of cold water immersion (40°F) and of wearing wet clothing in the open (30°F).

to the east of Laa. The investigators can be soldiers hired to protect the monks, fellow missionaries, Slavic guides, etc. Keeper and players should agree to the investigators' relation to Brother Gudman before play begins; at least one investigator possesses a recommendation letter from the bishop.

Because of delays at the crossing of the Danube in Hainburg, the investigators end up lagging one day behind Gudman. The two parties expect to meet again in Laa.

Leaving the main south-north amber trade road the next morning, the investigators take the northeast route toward Laa.

This region has seen some serious fighting against the Magyars in the last century. There are many rumors about unholy things that haunt the forest. Needless to say, only the bravest dare spend a night outside.

November 1st, 998 A.D.

Night falls on the virgin woodlands. The investigators settle by the campfire under the cold and rainy sky, near the river Zaya. They hope to arrive in Laa the next day to catch up with Gudman. An eerie wailing can be heard far up north, followed by a distant choir of howling wolves.

Later that night, shouts and the sound of a large animal crashing through the undergrowth wake the investigators. Within seconds, a running man leaps into the camp area and in a few strides crosses the clearing. In a flash, the investigators recognize Brother Drogo, muddied and bloodied! A horseman wielding a mace then crashes into the clearing in hot pursuit. Both Drogo and the horseman disappear into the darkness of the forest, heading downhill toward the river Zaya.

When the investigators arrive at the river, they see a motionless body sprawled on a pebble beach. The horse is nowhere to be seen. The first investigator is

just in time to spot a black shape waggling into the river and disappearing into the icy waters (40º F).

The body lying on the pebbles is that of the horseman, recognized as one of Gudman's warrior monks! He is still clenching his mace in his right hand and clearly in agony (from a broken neck, **First Aid or Medicine roll** required to diagnose). Before dying, the monk utters these last words: "all dead . . . not Gudman . . ." after which he compulsively recites Greek verse: "*Kai ek tóu kápnou ex-élthon akrídes eis tén gén, kai edóthe autáis exousía, hós échousin exousían hoi skorpíoi tés gés.*" This is a rendering of the Greek *Book of Revelation*, verse 9:3, which translates: "Then out of the smoke came locusts upon the earth, and power was given them, as the scorpions of the earth have power."

In the dead monk's left hand, the investigators find a strange black stone. A description is provided in the Dark One statistics on page 162. The Dark One needs the Black Stone and will do everything to recover it.

The Slaughter

After a one-hour walk along the turbid forest trail, the investigators cross the ghost village Asparn. An unusual silence reigns amidst the ruined houses, most of which appear to have burnt down years ago. In the shadows of the first trees beyond the abandoned hamlet, the investigators find what remains of Gudman's men.

First, the investigators spot a large gray wolf nipping flesh off a headless body that lies on the trail. The wolf skulks off as the investigators approach. A quick search reveals three other decapitated monks, scattered around the trail. There is also a mysterious body that cannot be identified. It is naked, eviscerated, and in a very advanced stage of putrefaction. Sanity loss for the whole scene is 1/1D4+1.

A thorough search of the undergrowth not only reveals tracks of a human (Drogo) and a horse (the warrior monk's) heading southwest, but also the track of a heavy-footed human (the Dark One) coming from the east towards the monks' camp. This track can be traced back for some distance, but then disappears.

The mules that carried the monks' few personal effects are gone. Following their

What Happened to Gudman & His Men

Progression along the muddy forest trail was slow, so Gudman decided to set camp near the ghost village of Asparn and get to Laa the next day. While everybody was asleep — except for the warrior monk standing guard by the fire — the Dark One and seven mi-go ambushed the monks and disabled them (the pattern of the attack is very similar to the one described in the "Surprised" section later on). Only the guard managed to flee. One mi-go carried Brother Gudman back to the Dark One's lair, to be the subject of inhuman biological experiments. The Dark One then emerged from its host and passed into the body of young Drogo, leaving behind the putrefied body found by the investigators (assume for simplicity that it is the body of an anonymous traveler, unknown to the protagonists of this scenario). After its transformation the Dark One beheaded the remaining defenseless monks.

The surviving guard watched the scene in horror from a distance, hidden by the darkness of the forest. Only after the mi-go flew away with the heads did he find enough nerve to set out on his last godly mission: to track down the demon that was now Drogo and destroy it.

Before being struck down by Drogo (alias the Dark One) near the river, the warrior monk snatched the Black Stone from the Dark One. The Dark One fled when the investigators arrived, and left the Black Stone behind.

erratic spoors into the wooded hills requires endless **Track rolls** and is ultimately fruitless.

After searching the area and finding no more clues, the investigators — presumably good Christians — have little choice but to bury the bodies. It is late when this task is finished and the group, although tired, must hurry to reach Laa before nightfall.

Arrival

Twilight. The player characters know they are approaching the settlement (*civitas*) of Laa by the smell of burning wood and the distant barking of dogs.

Leaving the shadows of the trees, the party first passes through an extraordinary "forest" of tall wooden crosses (a local Slavic custom to ward off forest spirits) before crossing a half-mile wide clearing of pastures, fields, and scattered copses. Left and right they see Slavic homesteads. In front of them they see the dark outline of a fortified village, defended by a sturdy timber stockade and a water ditch fed by the river Thaya. The stockade encloses two distinct areas separated by a palisade: the village of German colonists — a compact gathering of wooden houses — and a fort that consists of low buildings hugging the outer ringworks and surrounding a wooden tower-house rising some 15 yards above ground level. On top of the tower-house, the investigators can see the black silhouette of a watch, set against the darkening skies.

A large crowd has gathered outside one of the village's gatehouses. Two guards armed with long poles are pulling a corpse out of the ditch onto the gate bridge. In the torchlight the investigators recognize Drogo's body! Everybody looks at the newcomers.

A tough looking warrior named Hunman ("Dark Man," the right hand of the local landlord) approaches and asks the investigators their names and business. Next, he invites them kindly but firmly to follow him for an audience with the landlord. Hunman orders the people to go home and to close all doors. He also yells short instructions to nearby soldiers to close all village gates and to take their posts.

The Tower-House

The investigators are escorted to the tower-house, where they meet with the local landlord. The room on the first floor is cold and dark, only lit by a fire. Lord Brant ("Flaming Sword," see pages 157) sits in a carved chair that is covered by large gray wolf skins. Two huge mastiff-

The Settlement of Laa

like war dogs are lying on each side of the seat, eyeing the investigators. Curious war trophies (Magyar shield, saber, "reflex" bow, and felt armor) are hanging on the timber wall behind Brant. Hunman and six armed retainers are present in the room, as well as the village priest Zutto. In a shadowy corner sits an old noblewoman (Brant's mother). From a roleplaying perspective, the situation is relatively simple: Brant knows nothing about the missionaries or about the investigators. The only person in Laa who was expecting them is Brother Christian from the hermitage (page 137). Brant only knows that an unidentified body has been found in the ditch before sunset: "This car-

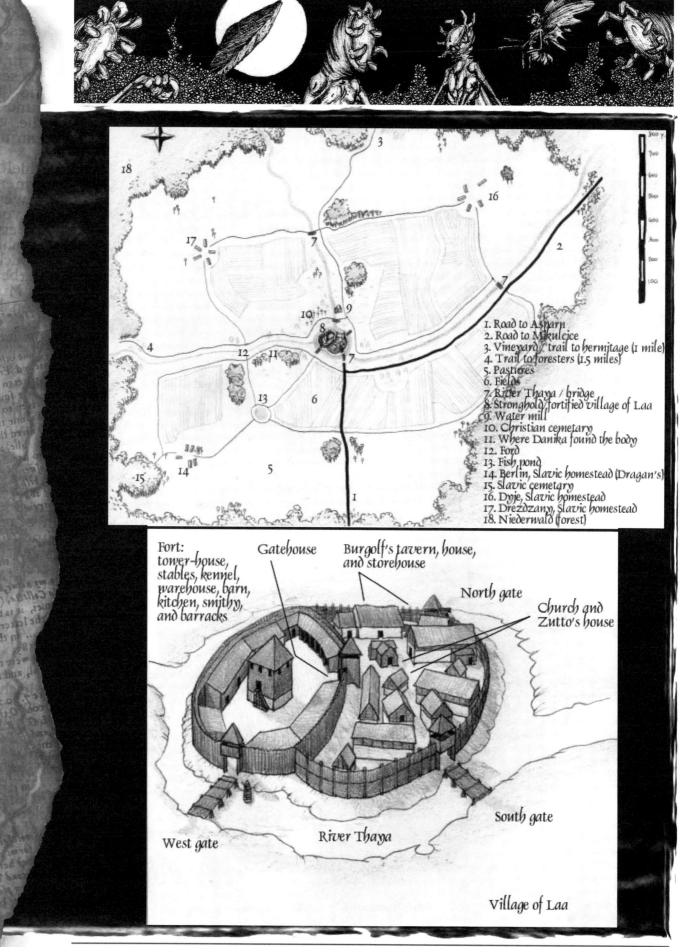

1. Road to Asparn
2. Road to Mikulcice
3. Vineyard / trail to hermitage (1 mile)
4. Trail to foresters (1.5 miles)
5. Pastures
6. Fields
7. River Thaya / bridge
8. Stronghold / fortified village of Laa
9. Water mill
10. Christian cemetary
11. Where Danika found the body
12. Ford
13. Fish pond
14. Berlin, Slavic homestead (Dragan's)
15. Slavic cemetary
16. Dyje, Slavic homestead
17. Drezdzany, Slavic homestead
18. Niederwald (forest)

Fort:
tower-house,
stables, kennel,
warehouse, barn,
kitchen, smithy,
and barracks

Gatehouse

Burgolf's tavern, house,
and storehouse

North gate

Church and
Zutto's house

West gate

River Thaya

South gate

Village of Laa

cass is a sign that I fail to comprehend. You tell me what it means!"

Eventually, Brant commands the party to stay around the village until the affair has been explained. If the investigators propose to investigate the crime, then the landlord invites them to be his guests and offers them a plain lodging in one of the fort's dependencies. The player characters may find the opportunity to ask Brant a few questions during dinner or a game of chess. At one point an inhuman ululation, muffled and seemingly originating from below the tower-house, disturbs dinner. Brant sends off one of his men, and the wail abruptly stops after a minute or two. Inquiries about the source of the disturbance are not answered (the investigators must question German colonists or military retainers in order to learn more about Brant's prisoner, Zoltan).

From now on the player characters are on their own. Possible resting-places for the night are the fort, Burgolf's place, and the priest's house. Note that the village gates are always closed at night.

Unknown to the visitors, they are already being drawn into the Dark One's machinations: the Dark One, returning to where the last warrior monk died and not finding the Black Stone, assumes that the investigators found it. Having been seen by them (in the guise of Drogo), it decided to look for a less conspicuous host. At dawn, hours before the investigators would arrive, it found a suitable host body in the settlement of Laa: that of six-year-old Dragan.

The Civitas

Investigators should first familiarize themselves with the immediate surroundings of the settlement area. Note that the hermitage bells sound five times from sunrise to sunset, and can be heard from the village. Places of interest on the map are described hereunder. The player characters can meet with important characters such as Brun and Dragan, and collect the first clues to unraveling the mystery. Generic descriptions of an anonymous German colonist and a Slav are provided on pages 158-159, and include some of the information they may know. Logical places to meet the colonists

are Burgolf's tavern and the workshops. The Slavs are best met in their homesteads or in the fields.

Burgolf's Tavern and House

Early on, the keeper should arrange for the investigators to meet a key character in the scenario, namely the girl Brun (see page 157). Brun is the 16-year-old, bright, and quite beautiful daughter of the village's richest man: the trader Burgolf ("Mountain Wolf," see page 158). The keeper should use all his art to make her as charming as possible, witty, and curious to know more about the player characters.

Although Brun can be met anywhere around Laa, the most logical place to find her at the beginning of the adventure is Burgolf's little tavern. The tavern opens in the evening. The place consists of a single room with one large table sided by two benches, and a few more

Burgolf's Daughter Brun

The keeper should role-play Brun to become the investigators' guide to Laa. Provided the investigators show enough sincerity and goodwill, Brun's father does not object to letting his daughter help the investigators. Brun knows everybody in Laa and has earned the respect of most, Germans and Slavs alike. The children especially like her a lot.

The keeper should be careful to spare Brun's life until later in the scenario, as she has a role to play—after her death!

The keeper can try to develop some intimacy between an investigator (e.g. the Black Stone bearer) and Brun (have her blush in his presence, etc.). It is not crucial for the unfolding of the plot, but adds the necessary drama.

benches along the plastered walls. There is a small fireplace in one corner. A doorway communicates with Burgolf's house.

Customers are mostly regulars, consisting of bored soldiers and two or three of the wealthiest German artisans (use the anonymous German statistics, page 158). Note that talking to Brun or to the soldiers may lead the investigators to Dragan's home (see the appropriate section below).

Burgolf and his daughter Brun serve wine from the hermitage's vineyard and food on special request. Burgolf makes little profit with this trade; Burgolf's joy is to play a game of dice or backgammon, and to keep informed about what is going on in the community. Burgolf also uses the tavern as a meeting place to discuss business matters with his guests.

Burgolf's Treasure

One of the house's dependencies serves as storage for goods. The place is locked and Burgolf keeps the only key with him at all times. On a small table near the entrance lie wax tablets and iron styli, as well as folding scales. The space is filled with merchandise: in the left corner there are Rhenish double-edged swords, knives, stirrups, spurs, bridle bits, and belt fittings. Next to it, there is a pile of baskets and barrels, containing Bavarian salt, salted white fish, and wine. Opposite the door one finds various wooden containers for honey, beeswax, and onions. Against the right wall lie staples of wolf skins and hemp fabric, as well as fine ropes, Slavic pottery and glassware.

Burgolf's dealings with the Dark One have left some traces (see pages 158ff for more details). There are a few discarded, rusty barrel-locks behind the swords, which

Burgolf used for slave trading (Idea roll required). A successful **Spot Hidden roll** comes up with a gold coin sticking out of the soil under the table. The coin is an Arabic dinar issued in Samarkand (**Other Kingdoms roll** for identification). In fact, a cylindrical basket is buried under the table, which contains 400 dinars, some 100 Frankish deniers, and silver jewelry! A large heap of thin steel bars occupies the center of the reserve. Each bar is one foot long and weighs one pound. Finally, large linen sheets (the same as used by the mi-go to protect themselves from sunlight) are piled in a shadowy corner.

The Priest's House

The priest Zutto lives in a modest house, next to the village's timber church. Zutto himself (see page 157 for his statistics) is of little help to the investigators, though he may offer them a place to sleep in his modest house. The most recent village register that Zutto is busy compiling, rests on a small table. Details are given in the section below.

The Village Charters (*Carta*)

The village charters are kept in a locked chest in the priest's house. The key is hidden in a jar. The bulk of the parchments are charters — contracts fixing the terms of transactions. The priest also keeps detailed registers of the allotment of the *civitas* (settlement area around the fortification) in terms of people, livestock, land, and goods. There are also a few imperial capitularies: administrative and religious texts.

The player characters must either persuade Zutto to let them do the research, or secretly open the chest. Uncovering the following data may require successful **Library, Read Language, or Idea rolls**. The number and the type of rolls are up to the keeper. It takes a single literate person 8 hours to complete the research. The work can be split between several persons.

Imperial Diploma (Latin): This document fixes the boundaries of the land (*pagus*) falling under the authority of the emperor's liegeman "Brantus" (Brant). It states that the river Thaya forms the northern frontier of the land, and the river Morava the eastern frontier. The diploma carries the imperial seal and monogram, and is signed: "the sign of Lord Otto, the most invincible emperor," followed by the chancellor's signature. The year is A.D. 976.

Donation Charter (Latin): "In the name of the saint and indivisible Trinity, Brantus, lord by divine favor. Let all believers of the Saint Church of God, present and future, know that I, with the benediction of the bishopric of Regensburg, have donated to the hermits of Laa some lands in my property. Given Anno Domini 995. In the name of God. Feliciter. Amen." (See ***Tomb Papers 1,*** page 164.)

Forest Laws (German): "That our woods are well watched over; where there is an area to deforest, that our foresters who live in the woods deforest it . . . . And where woods should be, that they do not permit to cut trees, and that they protect the wild beasts." (See ***Tomb Papers 2,*** page 164.)

Trade Embargo Capitulary (Latin): "About the merchants who go in the countries of the Hungarians, how far they are allowed to negotiate . . . . That they should not bring swords or armor or stirrups or Bohemian slaves to sell. That, if they are caught, all their goods be confiscated, half going to the palace and the other half being divided amongst the imperial ministers and the person who discovered the fraud." Dated 984 A.D. (See ***Tomb Papers 3,*** page 165.)

Keeper's Note: *together with the disappearance of people after 984 A.D., see below, this information is a clue to the possible involvement of Burgolf in the strange events around Laa.*

Index of Pagan Superstitions: (Opening statement to an old formulary for the conversion of pagans to Christianity, in Latin, German, and Slavonic):

- "Of sacrileges done to the deceased, *i.e.* crushing the face, driving a stake through the heart, and weighing the body down with stones.
- Of obscenities committed in May and November.
- Of the cult of the Forest and what is done upon stones.
- Of ill-famed places that are honored as being sacred.
- Of the belief in the living dead who come back to harm unbelievers, called *upir*.

Rumors

The keeper should reward good role-playing between investigators and locals with rumors and clues about the mysterious occurrences around the settlement of Laa. The first two entries are real life rituals that can be witnessed first-hand by the investigators:

1. The Slavs have disturbing burial customs. They crush the face of the defunct with hammers and pin the body down with a stake and stones, so that he *cannot come back*. Every few years the remains are disinterred, washed, wrapped in linen, and buried anew.

2. German woodcutters are in the habit of carving an occult sign on the trees they fell, in order to provide a sanctuary to the "wood-women" fleeing the "Crazy Hunter."

3. The Hungarians who live to the east of Laa are "ogres" who steal and eat children. Some say that the Magyars are not really human.

4. People shun the ghost village Asparn to the south: a sudden plague wiped out its population ten years ago. Some say that *too few bodies* were found on the site.

5. Every now and then people start to behave like strangers and vanish without a trace.

6. Rumors speak of strange whirring voices in the night and of peculiar lights above the hilltops at certain times of the year (May and November).

7. There are rumors of headless bodies of travelers found in the forest. When the Magyars or wolves are not held responsible, the Slavs blame the deaths on werewolves, vampires (*upir*), or demons (*drac*). German colonists murmur about the "Crazy Hunter."

8. Germans believe the forest to be inhabited by dwarves (*zwerc,* meaning "bent" or "twisted") who live underground and hoard huge treasures. Ghosts who come from "the land beyond the hills" haunt the forest.

9. The villager Burgolf possesses a wealth of mysterious gold coins of unknown provenance.

10. German parents threaten unruly children with the "Crazy Hunter," the local man-eating bogeyman. Opinions about the demon's appearance vary wildly.

11. The old religion of the Slavs was appalling: people were periodically sacrificed to the Black God. Sacrifices included simultaneous evisceration and decapitation.

Note that all rumors contain an element of truth, and that many refer to past or present activities of the Dark One (Crazy Hunter, vampire, demon, dwarf) and the mi-go (wood-women, ghosts).

Of the belief in wood women who can possess the heart of men, etc."

(See *Tomb Papers 4,* page 165.)

Keeper's Note: the May and November "obscenities," the "cult of the Forest," and the belief in "wood women," refer to a long forgotten secret cult around the Dark One and the mi-go.

Facts Deducible From the Documents

The keeper may tell the players any of the following facts, provided the investigators did a successful search through the village charters:

- In the 970s German colonists, benefiting from a normalization of relations with Hungarians, settle in the region. There appears to be some slave trade going on at the time, but traces of it disappear after 985 A.D.

- The German fort appears to have been built around 976 A.D., on the site of an older Slavic hillfort and pagan temple.

- In 995 A.D. the dispute between Bavaria and Hungary ends. The same year Magyar rebels raid Laa and partially burn the village. The landlord loses his wife in the attack, and a few colonists die. A few months later the fort is rebuilt and the hermitage of Laa is established, counting 7 monks plus servants.

- From 985 A.D. onward, some names of children and young adults inexplicably vanish from one register to the next. *Keeper's note: they were abducted by the mi-go and the Dark One; together with the slave trade embargo in 984 A.D. (see earlier this page), this information is a clue to the possible involvement of trader Burgolf in the strange events around Laa.*

- From 995 to 997 A.D., the Magyar rebels sporadically raid Laa to steal cattle and horses.

- In 997 A.D., Magyar attacks cease completely. *Keeper's Note: because the son of the Magyar chieftain is a prisoner of Brant.*

- Registers indicate that the population of the *civitas* (320 souls) is 50% German and 50% Slav. About a hundred Germans live in the fortified village, forty live in the foresters' camp, and twenty live at the hermitage. The Slavs live in scattered homesteads outside the stronghold. Both ethnic groups live in economic partnership, sometimes undermined by frictions between the two communities. Two-thirds of the population are farmers and craftsmen, one-fifth are artisans, and the rest military retainers and manorial servants. The Slavs seem to enjoy a more or less uniform free-farmer status. They are Christianized and their way of life seems pretty much Westernized after thirty years of German influence, at least on the surface.

- The foresters' camp is not permanent and changes location about every year.

- The *civitas* of Laa plays a dual military and merchant role. It is strategically placed at the focal point between the Germanic Empire, Moravia to the north, and Hungary to the east. It also defends the north-south amber trade route connecting the Baltic and the Mediterranean. Laa is situated at a two-day walk from the great "market of the Moravians," which is held 3 days a month in Mikulcice.

- The swamps that surround Laa are both a blessing and a curse. They provide a natural defense against potential aggressors, especially during wet seasons, but they are also a source of "swamp fever" (malaria).

The keeper is advised to put the above facts in perspective, with the timeline provided in "Play Aids" on page 125.

The Church

The mangled body of Drogo is kept for one night in the church, wrapped in a linen cloth. The next day, the priest has the body unceremoniously buried in the village cemetery, outside the fortification.

Close inspection of the body (after removing the cloth), shows that Drogo's abdomen is completely hollow.

Dragan's Home

The investigators find out about the boy Dragan (now possessed by the Dark One) by talking to the girl Brun or to the two guards who found Drogo's carcass in the ditch before sunset. The guards remember seeing the girl Danika, Dragan's sister, wandering close to the ditch in the morning. The girl Brun talked to Slavic children and heard gossip that "Dragan saw something." She plans to visit Dragan's family to inquire about the boy's condition, and she could ask the investigators to join her.

It shouldn't be difficult for the investigators to find the sunken-floor hut where the boy and his family live. It is located in the Slavic homestead of Berlin, a ten minute walk from Laa.

The boy Dragan is lying in bed. A monk from the nearby hermitage (Brother Kyril) is examining the boy in silence, and leaves quietly after having said a prayer. Dragan looks sickly pale and his head and his hands feel cold and clammy. A successful **Insight roll** reveals that the boy is in state of shock; a **First Aid or Medicine roll** reveals that Dragan's heart is weak and that he could very well be dying (in fact he is already dead). There are

no superficial clues to the presence of the Dark One inside the boy's body.

The mother Nadia tells the investigators that her little boy was home shortly before his four-year-old sister Danika, and that she was immediately very worried about him. He would not talk and was shivering terribly. She thought he might be suffering from swamp fever, and put him to bed.

When questioned, Danika tells the investigators that she and her brother saw a body (Drogo's) just before dawn on the riverbank. Danika didn't dare to approach but her brother crept into the high reeds and she heard him gasp. When Dragan called her after a minute or two to come and see she got scared and ran away. Eventually, she overcame her initial fear; she returned to the river but couldn't see the body anymore or her brother. After a while she spotted the body drifting in the river. Danika followed it until it drifted into the village's ditch. She then went back home. Danika had not told earlier about what had happened, because she thought her parents would hold her responsible for her brother's condition and punish her.

The only clue to be found at the location where Dragan discovered Drogo's body is the imprint of a large human hand, set in the mud of the riverbank (**Spot Hidden or Track roll** required).

The night after the investigators see Dragan and Brother Kyril, the keeper should stage the events described in the "Slavic Cemetery by Night" section.

Slavic Cemetery by Night

Events described in this section are triggered by the investigators' discovery of the boy Dragan, alias the Dark One.

Things take a turn on the night that the player characters first meet Dragan. The living-dead boy Dragan awakens to his next (brief) existence: inside the child, the Dark One's obscure mind is brooding. It knows that the investigators are on its track, and it is convinced that they have the Black Stone. The Dark One wants to switch to another, less vulnerable

body before it is found out. To do so, the Dark One stirs up the community, and then —

While everybody is asleep, Dragan picks up a large knife and disappears into the night, leaving the door open. Before long the freezing cold creeps into the house, waking the boy's parents. The father's shouts wake up the neighbors, starting a commotion around the Slavic homestead of Berlin. If the investigators are sleeping nearby, they hear the commotion or may even witness the scene. If not, let somebody (Brun for instance) wake them and warn: "I heard that something happened to Dragan, I think you should go and help!"

At the scene a group of Slavic men has gathered, disagreeing about what to do next. Two German soldiers are also present to help if necessary. The keeper should give the player characters an opportunity to take control by letting them organize the search for Dragan. If they don't, have Dragan's father Jan lead the search. In the fifteen minutes that follow, members of the search parties take their orders and collect torches; somebody (an investigator) is sent to the hermitage to find Brother Kyril, the only monk of Slavic origin. A few farmers fetch mastiff bloodhounds to help with the search. Roughly an hour after the search has started, Brother Kyril joins the group led by the father, Jan.

After a vain search around the settlement of Laa, Jan's group approaches the copse that conceals the Slavic row-grave cemetery. Jan, Brother Kyril, and another Slav, Kazimir, set foot under the cover of the trees with two bloodhounds.

For a few minutes, the apprehensive men waiting outside the cemetery listen to the receding barks of Kazimir's hounds. Suddenly, the barks turn into screeching yelps and die off! Shortly after, the disheveled figure of Jan emerges from the copse and collapses. He is temporarily insane and refuses to move or speak. Kazimir emerges from the tree line shortly after, without the dogs. He heard the distant sobs of a child, then Jan calling and running. He tried to follow the light of Jan's torch flickering between the trees, but lost it. Kazimir then heard two people crashing through the underbrush in the dark, running in opposite directions — the first towards the village, the second towards the hills. Kazimir tripped on a stone and fell, letting-go of the leashes: his bloodhounds ran away in the dark, barking loudly.

The different search groups gather. Two strong men drag the listless father home. If the players have not already noticed Brother Kyril's absence, let somebody else notice. The men are too tired and upset to continue the search.

The Dark One, possessing Kyril's body and carrying Dragan's corpse, met with a mi-go (#1 in the mi-go statistics on page 159) who ritualistically slaughtered the two mastiffs. They then vanished into the ancient woodlands to the south of Laa.

Hinterlands

Here are descriptions of places of interest in a wider circle around Laa. Assume that the events described under "Slavic Cemetery by Night" have taken place. Adapt the specifics if the investigators visit the Slavic cemetery, the hermitage, or the foresters' camp before the fated night.

After the nightly events in the Slavic cemetery, grant the player characters ample rest and let them wake up late. The new day is morose and rainy. Everything looks strangely different in the gray light; the Slavs seem depressed and brooding. The Germans go about their daily occupations as usual but the atmosphere is tense, as if they are weary of their Slavic neighbors' distress. The investigators quickly learn that neither Dragan nor Brother Kyril have shown up. Nobody has attempted new searches and people avoid the vicinity of the woods. Rumors prevail.

Slavic Cemetery

If the investigators return to the Slavic row-grave cemetery, allow them to find the place where Brother Kyril was "transformed." Successful **Track rolls** reveal three different trails. The small footprints of a child (Dragan) are plainly visible. Together with the heavier tracks of a man (Brother Kyril), they clearly tell the story of some kind of struggle. The stones that lined the border of a grave are displaced and dried blood can be found on some of them (successful **Spot Hidden roll** or automatically by examining a stone).

The trail of Dragan's father stops at a few yards from the place of the struggle; Jan obviously stopped there, then turned around. Both the trail of Jan and that of Dragan can be traced back to the family's home

(although the rain slowly washes away the trails in the open).

Oddly enough, the child's tracks end at the grave. In contrast, the other man's tracks continue from that point and can be followed into the wooded hills to the south. At the first failed **Track roll**, have the investigators come upon the cadavers of Kazimir's bloodhounds: one of the investigators feels large raindrops dripping on his or her forehead. Looking up, he sees the two disemboweled mastiffs hanging ten to twelve yards above ground. Their broken necks have been squeezed with great force between forking branches. How the 150-pound dogs got there is unclear (the mi-go did it). Discourage attempts to climb the trees: the climb is difficult, and a fall (3D6 maximum fall damage) can easily kill any investigator.

Finding the mangled dogs costs 0/1D2 Sanity points. On the way back the keeper can put additional pressure on the players by using one "forest" ploy (see "Play Aids," pages 125–126).

What Is Done Upon Stones

What follows is a description of what happens to the little boy, the monk, and to the boy's father in the Slavic cemetery. How closely the player characters are allowed to witness the events is up to the keeper. The trick, of course, is to find a good balance between mystery and close implication.

While the three men walk along parallel rows of graves demarcated by stones, calling for Dragan, the Dark One silently creeps closer to the monk.

Brother Kyril, hearing eerie childish whimpers a few yards away, from behind a tree, comes closer. With prodigious speed and strength the demonic boy seizes the monk and stabs him with his knife. Within seconds the boy creeps upon the writhing and croaking monk and the Dark One passes from one body to the other. Holding the leg of the inert body of the child in one hand, the monstrous monk shambles off towards the forest.

Dragan's father Jan also hears the faint whimpers and runs towards the source of the sound. He stumbles upon the nightmarish vision of his grimacing son in the torchlight, butchering Brother Kyril and then spastically gripping the monk's dying body on the ground. This proves too much for the poor man, and Jan loses his sanity on the spot. He drops his torch and flees madly in the dark.

Dragan's Home

Dragan's father Jan is temporarily insane. His wife cares for him at home, she herself on the verge of a nervous breakdown. The girl Brun and some relatives are present to comfort the mother and to help with domestic tasks. Danika is with her aunt at a nearby farm.

Jan is lying on a straw mattress in a fetal position, eyes wide open looking at the hut wall. He has not slept, eaten, or spoken since the "incident."

The man is obviously distressed and a successful Insight roll reveals that whatever he saw last night horrified him. Patient and gentle questioning should be rewarded. After a long silence, Jan starts saying things like: "No! Who, who is this? Is it—" and "Why . . . the monk . . . he . . . he isn't dead, is he? Please, tell me he isn't . . . ." After this he cries softly for a while and falls back into silence. Let the players puzzle with the apparent paradox of the tracks in the cemetery and what the father's mumbling hints at.

The Hermitage

The hermitage lies 1.5 miles to the north of Laa, in a small forest clearing. The trail to the hermitage cuts through the vineyards on the southern slope of the first hill. The five monks of the hermitage ("eremite brothers" or "eremites") own the vineyards as well as the adjoining fields.

A few simple huts are lined up near the entrance of the 200-yard-wide forest clearing. These belong to two German families who serve the eremites, working in the rye fields and in the vineyard for them. When the player characters arrive the men are busy putting wine in barrels, the women thresh corn, and children take pigs to graze in the forest. The hermitage itself consists of a modest house made out of stone — the only one in Laa — and a small stone church used by the eremites. (On Sunday the most pious Slavs attend the first and the second mass, at sunrise and at Tierce — around 9 A.M.). Wooden screens divide the hermitage house into two rooms. The entrance opens into the main room, which functions both as a small refectory and as a kitchen, with the oven in the far corner. Behind the screens is the small dormitory of the five eremite brothers. The only furniture consists of five wooden bed-frames filled with straw, and a peculiar little library (*armaria*) set against one wall.

Behind the house, the eremites keep a vegetable garden. For lack of a proper cellar, the eremites store food-

The Library

The hermitage's library contains liturgical books, two Bibles (the Greek Septuagint and the Latin Vulgate), and controversial apocryphal texts Senior Brother Christian collected during his travels. There is also a very rare profane parchment in Greek (*Hierón Aigypton*), which describes cyclopean ruins in the land where the sun rises, and the strange rites of the Dark Folk. Carefully wrapped in leather and sealed with wax, is a genuine copy of the *Kitab al-Azif* that Brother Christian acquired in Constantinople. Brother Christian, preserved by Faith and also by his imperfect knowledge of Arabic, never managed to read more than a few pages of the blasphemous tome.

stuffs in storage pits like the Slavs do. The pits are easily recognizable by their timber-and-straw caps at ground level. Opposite the garden, a long timber building houses the hermitage's primitive winepress and a storage area for wine barrels.

In the vicinity of the house all respect the rule of silence imposed by the eremites, communicating with improvised sign language when required. This gives the place a very peculiar atmosphere.

Only four of the five eremites are present. Brother Kyril has not been seen since the search for Dragan. The eremites respectfully greet their visitors by first praying with them and then prostrating their bodies to the ground. After that, senior Brother Christian signs the investigators to follow him to a remote place in the clearing and to sit down with him on cut-off trunks near the forest's tree line. There, Brother Christian engages the conversation by saying, "We have received Thy Mercy, O God, in the midst of Thy temple."

After proper introductions, the player characters may freely discuss with Brother Christian about any topic they wish. This rigorous ascetic turns out to be a remarkable scholar who has seen much of the world in his younger years, travelling as far as Baghdad, Kabul and Samarkand! Before his present mission, the man even counted amongst the close circle of advisors to King Otto.

It should be made apparent that Brother Christian is a trustworthy man, with a formidable knowledge of the world. The keeper should carefully role-play the eremite brother to actively listen to the investigators, repeating now and then what they say to invite them to tell more. Depending on how much is told and what leads are followed, here are a few things that Brother Christian may deduce or simply tell to the player characters:

Brother Christian's Digressions

- Brother Christian remembers that Brother Kyril was woken up to help search for a Slavic boy who had disappeared under curious circumstances. Brother Kyril had already visited the boy because "the mother was worried about the boy having seen a dead man." Brother Christian is only mildly concerned that Brother Kyril has not returned yet, because he had to visit the foresters and only planned to return before Vespers today (sunset). Brother Kyril of Prague is the only eremite of Slavic origin. He is described by Brother Christian as an exceptionally disciplined man with knowledge of medicine. Brother Kyril is often absent from the hermitage to care for the sick or to help the less fortunate.

- When the investigators relate the disappearance of Brother Gudman and the martyrdom of the missionaries, Brother Christian is deeply shocked and grieved. Brother Christian knew Gudman personally. He had repeatedly asked the bishopric to send someone to help re-found the mission of the hermitage to convert the rebellious Magyars to the east. Indeed, three years ago (995 A.D.), two brothers were sent east but never returned!

- Brother Christian knows that the son of the rebel Magyar headman was captured by Lord Brant one year ago and is kept in a pit under the tower-house. Brother Christian went there on several occasions to reason with the heathen but to no avail.

- In case the investigators can (partly) recall the verse uttered by the agonizing monk at the beginning of the adventure, Brother Christian says: "hmmh . . . *akris* is Greek for 'locust' . . . "He excuses himself, walks to the hermitage house, and comes back with the Septuagint Bible. Brother Christian recites verse 9:3 of the Book of Revelation: "He — the fifth angel — opened the bottomless pit, and smoke went up out of the pit, like the smoke of a great furnace; and the sun and the air were darkened by the smoke of the pit. Then out of the smoke came locusts upon the earth, and power was given them, as the scorpions of the earth have power . . . ." The keeper is free to let the players read a more substantial passage from Revelation. In the adventure, of course, the locusts refer to the mi-go seen by the warrior monk. The keeper/Brother Christian should ask aloud: "what on Earth has this martyr seen, that reminded him of this particular verse in his last moments?"

- Brother Christian has nothing valuable to say about the Black Stone.

- When asked about the survival of pagan customs, Brother Christian weakly smiles and says: "the Slavs of Laa forgot the old ways. The only real differences with us Germans are the Slavs' language, their fear of the undead, and their pottery! To find true pagans, you would have to travel north or east." Brother Christian dismisses pagan superstitions and rumors "for what they are, petty beliefs and relics from the

past." However, a successful **Insight roll** shows that Brother Christian starts at any reference to rituals taking place in May and November. When questioned further, Brother Christian recalls: "the people to the west of Kabul feared the calends of May and November . . . . At those times of the year the Scythians came down from the mountains, beyond the valley of the Giant Statues [of Buddha] . . . ." Brother Christian does not elaborate further and stares into space.

- When asked about strange disappearances, Brother Christian remembers that since he came, there may have indeed been a case or two of Slavs who seemingly vanished from the face of the earth. However, he doesn't know details, and suggests the investigators ask the Slavs about the disappearance.

- When asked about the fact that the only stone buildings in Laa are the hermitage house and the hermitage church, Brother Christian points out, "Only stone can establish a strong enough foundation for a permanent House of God in this unstable region." Brother Christian adds that Burgolf provided the building material.

Brother Christian knows much more than he cares to admit, and he is in fact very close to realizing that a Dark One is the root of all evil in the region. However, at this moment, he is primarily worried about the fate of Brother Gudman. Brother Christian asks the player characters to go to the foresters to see if Brother Kyril is there or if he has been seen: "Hurry! It is late already, you do not want to be in the forest when night falls!" If the investigators do not know the location of the foresters' camp, the monk refers them to the trader Burgolf who deals with the foresters. Brother Christian implores the group to do everything in their power to find Brother Gudman. His last words are: "I now retire to pray for Brother Gudman. There are also a few unsettling things I learned today, which I need to put into perspective."

When the conversation ends, investigators are allowed a **POW x2 roll or a Listen roll**, whichever is higher. On a successful roll, an investigator feels as if he is being observed. The investigator may hear the sound of small twigs snapping in the forest. Investigating the source of this disturbance causes an unexpected commotion nearby. Someone or something suddenly flees parallel to the tree line, moving under the one-yard-tall fern cover. Pursuing investigators eventually catch up with a frightened five-year-old boy and his pig.

Keeper's Note: unknown to the investigators, the Dark One (in the shape of Brother Kyril) and several veiled mi-go were hiding close by and reading their minds. They took advantage of the commotion caused by the child and the pig to retreat further into the forest. If the players are com-

posed enough to comfort the little boy and gently question him, he tells that he saw a "white lady" behind a tree just before the investigators started chasing him. The child is unable to describe what he saw in closer detail. Attempts at **Fast Talk, Persuade**, or anything of the kind, only upset the child more and make him cry. The crying only stops when the alarmed parents find the child and take him away.

A successful **Spot Hidden or Track roll** results in the discovery of one human track and the imprint of a large human hand on the humus, some twenty yards away from where Brother Christian and the investigators were sitting. Whoever was crouching there was observing the investigators, and eventually retreated into the woods.

The Foresters' Camp

The first things one notices when approaching the foresters' camp are Germanic runes engraved on some of the trees. Then a faint, omnipresent buzzing sound can be heard. It takes a successful **Listen roll** to locate the source of the noise. It emanates from several big hollow trees surrounding the investigators; inside the trees large honeycombs can be found. A successful **Natural World roll** tells the investigator that hibernating bees do buzz inside the comb when it is freezing outside. The foresters keep the semi-wild bees for honey and wax. In the immediate vicinity of the camp, there is a strong odor of burnt wood, related to the foresters' production of charcoal, ash, wood tar, and pitch. In a forest clearing are situated five tall conical huts, made of young beech tree trunks tightly bound together with creepers, plastered with turf, and covered with wolf hides. Felled trees lie everywhere around the clearing. Five families and their domestic animals live there, from the produce of the forest.

Unknown to all, the Dark One, helped by the mi-go, hung the little boy Dragan's body in a tree, close to the foresters' camp. The monster is eager to tell all about it to the Slavs of Laa, and thus create a major diversion before its next move (ambushing the investigators in order to recover the Black Stone, or kill the eremites who know too much). At the first opportunity — when the player characters are on their way to the hermitage — the Dark One, as Brother Kyril, walks to the nearest Slavic homestead, Drezdzany, climbs on a roof, and rallies some men. He tells that he saw the German foresters butcher the little boy Dragan and eat his entrails, before they crucified him on a tree. He tells that the Germans

and their spies (the investigators) tried to kill him (in reality his wounds were incurred in the fight with Dragan and Kazimir's bloodhounds), and that they are demons that should be sent back to the pits of hell. The Dark One then leaves as quickly as he came. Back in Laa, the investigators find themselves persona non grata around the Slavic homesteads. Some Slavs are openly aggressive towards the investigators, shouting insults like "German pigs, return to the mud you came from!" Some children throw stones at them before running away, and women make the sign of cross. All avoid coming too close to the investigators.

Vendetta

Fired up by the lies of the Dark One, a group of Slavic men organize a vendetta against the foresters. The keeper may want to time the event so that player characters headed for the foresters' camp can intervene. There are two possibilities, equally acceptable as far as the plot is concerned:

TOO LATE: If the investigators arrive too late, they only find twenty scattered corpses of the foresters killed by the vengeful Slavs. All have their throats cut. It costs 0/1D4 Sanity points to see the scene of massacre. The keeper may request **Idea rolls** to reason that about half the people probably escaped from their aggressors. The body of Dragan cannot be found, because the Slavs took it back with them.

Note that the investigators, on the way to the camp, may cross the path of the Slavic murdering party returning to their homesteads.

IN TIME: If the investigators hurry, and if a German colonist guides them (Brun, for example), they arrive at the foresters' camp before the Slavs do. What happens next is entirely up to the players and the keeper; it should be possible through good roleplaying to prevent the massacre. A number of foresters choose to avoid the confrontation anyway, and leave the camp in a hurry. Note that the body of Dragan can be found hanging from a tree less than hundred yards to the south of the camp. The configuration is the same as with the dead mastiffs in the "Slavic Cemetery" section (0/1D3 Sanity loss).

In both cases half the foresters flee from the camp and will seek refuge in the village under cover of the night.

The Ambush

This section describes an ambush, the main purpose of which is to allow the Dark One to recover the Black Stone. In it, the investigator carrying the Black Stone is separated from the others and seriously wounded. The mi-go also destroy the hermitage and kill the eremite brothers.

The keeper is free to choose the right moment and the right place to stage the ambush. In fact, the keeper can adapt the ambush or even skip it entirely, if he found other means to recover the Black Stone and to disable one investigator.

At the first opportunity, the Dark One and four mi-go (#1, #3, #5, and #7 on page 157) ambush the investigators to recover the Black Stone. The Dark One waits until the investigators are isolated and vulnerable before striking. Ten combat rounds (2 minutes) before the attack, the keeper should warn the players with some spooky precursors such as growing headaches, the sky turning black, and distant rumblings echoing in the investigators' heads — see "The Forest" on pages 125–126. The attack starts with the blinding of the party by the mi-go Black Light spell. Details are given in the appropriate section of the mi-go statistics. Blinded investigators cannot accurately recognize their attackers for the duration of the attack. To them, the Dark One (as Brother Kyril) and the veiled mi-go appear as blurred shadows, respectively dressed in blackish and grayish robes or cloaks.

Those who successfully flee recover sight half a mile away from mi-go #1. The investigators who stay behind must face the Dark One and the mi-go (see "Statistics," pages 159–162).

The attack continues until the mi-go successfully abduct one investigator and recover the Dark One's Black Stone. The Dark One then disappears into the forest.

The keeper should therefore preferably pick the player character who keeps the Black Stone. One mi-go envelops its prey with its large veil, and grapples the investigator using its ten legs (automatic success if the victim is blinded; 1D6–1D4 damage, and STR contest on the Resistance Table to immobilize target). As soon

as the grapple succeeds, the mi-go injects poison into the victim's body and clumsily flies away, carrying the half-paralyzed player character underneath its veil.

If there are non-investigators present, let the Dark One attack them first (but not Brun, who still has a role to play). If time permits, the Dark One beheads anyone it kills and takes the head with it.

Ghost Village

The following section describes what happens to the abducted player character. The keeper is advised to play the two parallel plotlines in separate sessions until the

The Ghost in the Mist

If they walk back to the hermitage within an hour of the mi-go attack, the first things the investigators notice are the eerie silence and a peculiar acrid smell floating in the air. As they approach the hermitage the smell becomes nauseating: a kind of cold mist hangs over the clearing, and vision is limited to 10 yards or less (the strange mist dissipates after an hour). The investigators cannot see the burning hermitage, though they can hear the crackling fire. Near the hermitage house the investigators first stumble across the headless cadavers of two eremite brothers and of Brother Christian (the fourth eremite lies dead inside the house, buried under the remains of the collapsed roof). A successful Spot Hidden reveals mild burn marks on the skin, and the melting of the eremites' knives! These effects are caused by the mi-go's lightning attacks.

When the investigators are close enough to discern the looming shape of the ruined house, they hear an unexpected noise coming from inside and feel a growing headache! It sounds as if somebody is rummaging loudly through the debris. At the first attempt to look inside or to enter, the noise abruptly stops. There is so much burning debris that progression inside the house is limited to MOV 1. Hidden by the unnatural mist and the smoke, a veiled mi-go is standing perfectly still next to the wreckage of the hermitage library, sensing the approaching investigators. It clumsily holds the *Kitab al-Azif* it rescued from the burning library. The first investigator to come within 5 yards of the library fleetingly sees the ghostly apparition, entirely veiled in grayish cloth and holding a 6-by-8 inch rectangular object, just before it vanishes through a part of the wall that collapsed when the roof fell. Anyone close enough to glimpse the "ghost" must make an Idea roll. A success means that the investigator got a good look at the apparition, and noted enough disturbing details to justify a Sanity roll (see "Statistics," page 159, for details). Before the investigators can react, the mi-go "flies" into the mist at great speed, and disappears from sight.

investigators meet again. The exact interpretation of the investigator's "visions" is left entirely to the player and has no further consequence on the plot.

The abducted investigator is carried to a remote location in the forest by the veiled mi-go that attacked him. Once there, the mi-go drops the investigator from a great height and flies away. In the interest of the scenario, the investigator survives the ordeal. He regains consciousness with only a few hit points left, at the keeper's discretion. He has only a few nightmarish memories. Examples are: the terrible grip of the mi-go's many legs; the sting in his backbone followed by the poison's burn; the memory of falling towards a black superstructure as large as a hill, crowned with a multitude of tall dark spires, the ground littered with dead birds, human bones, a dead horse or mule, etc. The investigator is left to wander for at least eight hours in the forest, before finding his way back to Laa.

After an indefinite span of time, the delirious investigator emerges from the forest and starts walking toward the silhouette of the fort in the distance. At first sight, the village appears deserted and there is a strange silence. The investigator realizes that he is walking on ashes, and that half the village is burned down. He then feels a presence behind the charred timbers, and hears faint whispers echoing his name — or is it the wind? Ghostly shadows become perceptible at the edge of his vision field, many shadows, and they follow him! At last, the shadows close in on the investigator, who faints.

The player character regains consciousness in a room with a slanted ceiling. There is a dark silhouette in one corner, with long black hair. When the shape suddenly shifts and comes into the pallid light of a candle, the investigator recognizes the girl Brun. She explains in soft words that the investigator was found shambling through the village, obviously disoriented and wounded. The investigator was brought to Burgolf's house, and carried upstairs to her chamber. Brun whispers: "now everything will be fine [name of the investigator]." Brun gently wipes the sweat from the investigator's forehead. "We will take care of you, you're safe with us, don't be afraid." She briefly caresses the investigator's cheek, and retreats into the shadows of the room.

Apart from the intense burning pain in his back, he notices sickening patterns of punctured skin and bruises on his upper arms and chest. These are the marks from the mi-go's legs.

The Hermitage

Three veiled mi-go raid the hermitage with their mist and lightning weapons (#2, #4, and #6 from page 159). Under the cover of their caustic mist they slaughter Brother Christian and the other eremites, and set fire to the hermitage house. It is assumed that the investigators do not witness the raid and cannot intervene.

Most servants flee from the hermitage when the mi-go raid begins. Here is an example of what a panting and terrified servant could be saying: "The monks . . . couldn't see . . . . A kind of . . . of cloud . . . came down and, and . . . . My God! Them . . . the ghosts in the mist . . . three . . . the lightning . . . . Must go, please . . . ."

A search of the area where the library originally stood comes up with two scorched bibles, and scattered pieces of charred parchment, some of which are readable:

Mythos Fragments

The source of fragment one (Revelation of Peter) can be identified with a successful **Theology or Occult roll**. The provenance of the others can be identified with a successful **Cthulhu Mythos roll**.

REVELATION OF PETER, VERSE 26 (Latin): "And other men and women were burning up to the middle and were cast into a dark place and were beaten by evil spirits, and their innards were eaten by restless worms . . . ." (See **Tomb Papers 5,** page 166.)

HIERÓN AIGYPTON **(Greek):** "The vision of Anacharsis, concerning the land where the sun rises. And in the fifth month I went between the mountains to the valley of [*illegible*] Fear the Old Evil; for it consumes your cities without fire; and it consumes your people, but they do not find death. And in the valley I saw [*illegible*] fall to earth, and it was one and a half stadia long [300 yards], and the largest part was buried underground. And it was pierced with many holes, and animals shunned the holes that led to the lairs . . . ." (See *Tomb Papers 6,* page 166.)

KITAB al-AZIF **(Arabic):** Small triangular pieces of parchment from one corner of some manuscript. The script is Arabic and written in a shaky hand. A successful **Read Arabic roll** comes up with a mention of the "forsaker" al-Khadhûlu, and a mention of a deity called Niharlat Hotep. The largest fragment reads:

"[*illegible*] say, [*illegible*] hath lain, [*illegible*] are all ashes. [*illegible*] of old rumor that [*illegible*] not from

his carnal clay, [*illegible*] instructs the very worm that gnaws; till out of corruption horrid life springs, [*illegible*] vex it and swell monstrous to plague it. [*illegible*] secretly are dug where earth's pores ought to suffice, and things have learnt to walk that ought to crawl." (See **Tomb Papers 8,** page 164.)

WRITTEN BY BROTHER CHRISTIAN (Latin): "In Constantinople I met with the men from the North (*Normanni*) who call themselves 'Rus.' Although they belong to the Eastern Church, their manners are very uncivilized. The Normanni acted with defiance and ostentation, recounting all kinds of pagan stories in an attempt to upset me. *De facto*, I was quite interested by their version of the Genesis, in particular by the part played by the so-called bent folk. It is unclear to me whether they considered these beings to have human form, because the Normanni kept on calling them maggots. Indeed, the bent folk supposedly originate in the corpses of dead gods or giants (Theodorus did not fully understand the word used). This in turn reminded me of the Book of Enoch, which mentions evil spirits proceeding from the bodies of [*illegible*] Were these the same beings that . . . ." (See also **Tomb Papers 7**, page 167.)

A successful **Other Kingdoms or Occult roll**, reveals that the text refers to Viking mythology. The "bent folk" or *dvergar* — zwerc in Old German — are a race that appeared in the corpse of the giant Ymir, from which it is believed that the earth was made. A successful **Cthulhu Mythos roll** notes that there is a Theodorus Philetas who lived in 950 A.D. in Constantinople, and who translated the *Kitab al-Azif* into Greek, and named it *Necronomicon*!

Eye of the Storm

This section closes the first part of the scenario, in which the investigators more or less freely roamed the settlement of Laa and surroundings. Incidents instigated by the Dark One converge to a dangerous dénouement, on the night after the Slavs raided the foresters' camp. It is assumed that the investigators are reunited with their abducted companion inside the stronghold.

The Dark One, taking advantage of the confused situation, wants to get rid of the meddlesome investigators for good. Since the visitors are relatively unexposed inside the stronghold, the Dark One plans to use trickery, and have them killed by the colonists themselves!

In the village of Laa, the confusion is complete. The ramblings of the abducted investigator, stories about the Slavic raid of the foresters' camp, etc., cause the wildest rumors and speculations to spread around.

The abducted investigator, still under the alienating influence of the mi-go poison, has been carried by two colonists to Burgolf's house, and brought to Brun's bed on the first floor. Brun, helped by a servant, cares for the investigator, washing him, cleaning the wounds, etc. Grant the investigator 1D3 hit points of recovery. Burgolf prepares a warm meal with some fresh bread and mead for the investigators. The keeper should create a false atmosphere of warmth and safety, in order to put the players off guard by the Dark One's next move.

At some point in the evening, everyone can hear Brant's twelve war dogs bark loudly for a few long minutes. A colonist enters the tavern to inform anyone present that twenty foresters have safely arrived at the village gates under cover of the night, and were let in. They are now sheltered in one of the stalls of the fort. Burgolf excuses himself to go and meet with the survivors. The young men and women tell anyone present that they fled when they heard that the Slavs were coming for them. For hours, they stayed hidden in the woods, at a respectful distance from the settlement, for fear of being found by the Slavs. They waited until after dark to sneak past the Slavic homesteads and reach the village.

More important for the keeper is the fact that the Dark One (Brother Kyril) joined the group of foresters in the dark, unnoticed, and entered the village! The Dark One used a moment of inattention to hide in the darkness of a narrow alley between two houses.

The Dark One was not entirely unnoticed, since Brant's war dogs sensed its presence (see the barking dogs reference two paragraphs ago). Moreover, there are only nineteen foresters in the fort, not twenty as stated by the gatekeeper, who counted the Dark One in. The keeper should be careful with releasing this disquieting clue, since what follows relies on the players being off-guard and therefore unprepared for the Dark One.

Eros et Tanatos

The investigators are exhausted and need rest. Brun advises them to stay close to their convalescent companion. Burgolf can prepare straw mattresses on the floor under Brun's bedroom for them.

That night, the Dark One kills Brun and takes her body. The exact circumstances of the crime are irrelevant for the rest of the story. The Dark One quickly hides the eremite's body somewhere in the house. The keeper may find it interesting to put the body in a place where the investigators can find it during the night — for instance in the water well, or near the latrines. If the keeper chooses this option, timing becomes critical, because Brun (the Dark One) must get a chance to molest the convalescent investigator *before* the others get a chance to stop her.

In the middle of the night, Brun walks to the bed of the sleeping investigator. She whispers in his ear, "I'm cold, can I lie next to you?" When the investigator fully awakens, the girl is cuddling him, and the investigator feels from her touch that Brun is topless! How far the contact is allowed to go is up to the keeper (and the player, of course). At a crucial moment, the investigator feels a long, warm, moist shape glide against the skin of his thighs, twisting like a snake! A sharp pain in the investigator's underside — as if something is forcing its way inside — immediately follows the repulsive sensation. As this happens, the young girl is tightening her embrace in order to immobilize the investigator, and murmurs "*consumatum est.*" It means: "it is consummated" in Latin; the investigator may or may not remember that Brun does not speak Latin (**Idea roll**).

There is a struggle as the investigator tries to free himself from the Dark One's grip. The noise wakes up anyone inside Burgolf's house. Brun relentlessly and ferociously attacks any investigator present. The keeper must leave no other option to the investigators than to strike the girl down. Eventually, Brun — alias the Dark One — lies half naked on the ground, her chest smeared with blood, feigning agony. Alarmed by the noise, Burgolf enters the scene, a punched-metal lantern in one hand and an Arabic scimitar in the other, and stares at his "agonizing" daughter in shock and disbelief: "You, you . . . YOU BEASTS! WHAT HAVE YOU DONE?" Needless to say, the poor man cannot be reasoned with in any way. Burgolf's screams of rage and despair boom through the night.

Before long, a group of German colonists (see page 158), aroused by the screams of Burgolf, converges on the tavern to see what happened. Like Burgolf, these people are on edge and cannot be brought to reason. The best strategy to deal with the angry crowd is to use verbal intimidation and threats (either by proper roleplaying or with **Fast Talk** and **Status**). However, this is not indefinitely effective, and the keeper should request **Fast Talk rolls every minute** to keep the colonists and Burgolf at bay. ("They killed my daughter! Slaughter the pigs!") At the first failed roll, or if the investigators start to run, the colonists overcome their indecision and attack them.

This is the moment that a group of seven defiant young Slavs (see pages 160), who had been fomenting a coup to avenge the murder of Dragan, choose to strike! Two of them start a fire at the foot of the palisade, while others ignite torches that they lob over the stockade onto the thatch roofs. Within minutes a few roofs catch fire. When one high-strung guard starts to shout, "The Magyars, the Magyars are here! Fire! FIRE!" panic breaks loose.

The Prisoner

Lord Brant, who believes the village to be besieged by Magyars, dispatches two soldiers to fetch his Magyar prisoner from the pit under the tower-house (see Zoltan's statistics on page 160). The Magyar is brought to the wall-walk. Holding the Magyar by the hair and waving his long sword about, Brant defiantly shouts in the dark: "you heathen bastards! I still have one of your kind, remember? Look up!"

Suddenly, the Magyar pushes Brant aside, throws himself over the palisade into the ditch, and runs away in the dark.

If the investigators do not witness this scene, let them at least hear guards shouting in alarm: "the prisoner has escaped! Shoot! Shoot!"

At the Crossroads

H ere is the climax of the scenario. It has a very open structure, and can be played in many different ways, depending on how well the players deal with the crisis situation, and of course on the keeper's decision. At the end of the day, everything should converge to an encounter between investigators and Magyars. The Magyar shaman "Taltos" then helps the investigators to find the source of evil — the Black Hill.

In order to guide the keeper through the forest of possibilities, two alternatives are sketched in broad lines. One plotline emphasizes action, the other role-playing. Many others exist, of course.

The Investigators Escape

If the investigators cannot contain the wrath of Burgolf and the colonists who came to help him, they can seek safety in flight.

There are several possibilities to escape from the stronghold. The investigators can open a village gate. Lifting the timber bar requires a successful combined **STR versus 16 roll** on the Resistance Table. The investigators can also reach the wall-walk from any of the three gatehouses (note that two soldiers defend each) and jump safely into the ditch. Alternately, they can try to climb onto the roof of a house, and by jumping from roof to roof reach the wall-walk. This last option possibly requires several **Climb and Jump rolls**. Maximum fall damage from a roof or the wall-walk is 1D6 hit points, minus 1D6 with a successful Jump roll.

Any evasive action from the investigators provokes a reaction from the guards in the gatehouses and on the wall-walk (see "Brant's Milites," page 158): the closest soldiers to the investigators try to intercept them and arrest them.

Eventually, the group reaches the cover of the trees, and can pause to recover their breath. Looking behind them, they see a roaring fire consuming half of the colonists' village in the dark, about half a mile away. In the fiery light, the investigators can make out the silhouettes of horsemen, pausing by the burning palisade. Several German families are gathering outside the gate. Next to the milites stands a footman, holding war dogs. He points in the general direction of the investigators.

Having fled, the investigators are forced to hide in the forest at night. There they meet the escaped Magyar Zoltan. See "The Magyar Speaks," pages 145.

Lord Brant's Orders

Lord Brant quickly realizes that a small group of Slavs is to blame for the attack, not the Magyars. Several problems require his immediate attention: the fire, the homeless German families, and the arrest of the Slavs who set half the village on fire. Soon enough, Brant sends out six horsemen and six war dogs to find Zoltan and the investigators. ("They can't be far! Let the dogs find them! And bring them back to me! Alive!")

The horsemen form two groups: Hunman and two milites look for the player characters, three others hunt down the Magyar. The investigators' main problem is the war dogs (see page 157): they probably have to get rid of them if they want to shake off the horsemen.

Optionally, the keeper can worsen the situation by letting Burgolf secretly bribe Hunman to kill the investigators.

Page 126 of the Play Aids sidebar provides some ideas for playing a manhunt.

The Investigators are Arrested

If investigators are arrested in Laa, captured in the forest or simply surrender, they are brought before Brant for interrogation.

The exact circumstances of the arrest should be dictated by game play. The outcome of the interrogation very much depends on the circumstances of the arrest/surrender, on the player characters' relationship with the landlord, and of course, on roleplaying. The key question is: can the investigators convince Brant of their innocence? Brant is unimpressed by **Status** or

bravado, and not easily fooled: any lie or blatant omission requires a successful **Fast Talk or Persuade roll**, and a failed **Insight roll** from Brant. When Brant detects a lie, he lets the visitors ramble on until they run out of words. After a long uncomfortable silence, he says coldly: "Strangers, the only thing you should fear is not the truth, but my wrath!"

In the best of cases, Brant asks apt investigators to find Zoltan for him (he has more urgent worries, and considering the popular anger, it may be a good idea if the investigators don't show themselves for a while). The worst-case scenario is that the investigators are found guilty and subsequently thrown into the prison pit — to be hanged in the morning!

Factors that can influence the outcome of the interrogation are: the virulence of Burgolf's testimony, the priest's position, the investigators' status, past circumstances, etc.

If the players do really badly, here is one event that will save the day: Brun is seen rising from the dead and leaving the village. This is the groups' opportunity to convince Brant that something unnatural is going on, to (re)gain his trust, and to have a free hand for what follows.

Brun Rises from the Dead

At some point, the Dark One, as Brun, decides to leave the settlement as discreetly as possible, and to return to the Black Hill. The timing of the event and its influence on the game is up to the keeper. Note that the discovery of her disappearance can clear the investigators of Brun's death.

The Magyar Speaks

The keeper can arrange the encounter with the Magyar Zoltan in two ways. If Brant gave the investigators a free hand (or if the investigators are fugitives), they can find Zoltan hiding in the forest. If the investigators are stuck in the tower-house, let Brant's men find Zoltan and bring him back before their lord.

The keeper has to choose a decisive moment to stage the encounter with Zoltan (see page 160). For instance, fleeing investigators can encounter Zoltan "by chance" in the forest, or Brant may have asked the investigators to track down the Magyar for him. The keeper should take care not to make a nightly encounter with the Magyar too stressful, for fear that panicky investigators might kill the poor man!

Note that Zoltan is too ill and too weak to survive a night outside without the investigators' help.

Zoltan turns out to be quite talkative, in spite of his limited knowledge of the German language. After proper introductions Zoltan explains: "bad things live here, in the forest. We, the Magyars, live in *Magyarorszag*, the country of the Magyars, beyond the forest, where the sun rises." He waves to the east: "a hundred years ago, our king Arpad and the *on ogur*, the ten tribes, flee from the Turks and we conquer our new land. But the Old Evil followed us at night, the *wampyr*. Thousands and thousands. Like a black cloud."

Zoltan continues: "The wampyr? They hide in swamps and in forests, in the world under the hills, everywhere." Zoltan makes a sweeping movement with his arms: "Germans call them zwerc (meaning "twisted" or "bent"). The zwerc look like you and me, but they are . . . nobody knows what the wampyr really look like. The Slavs call them devils, drac, but my people say they are . . . like worms. The wampyr hunts people, he eats the insides, and he wears the skin like . . . like clothes."

"Long, long ago, before man came, the wampyr crawl inside the body of living-dead gods, giants. Now the giants are gone, so the wampyr crawl inside men . . . . The wampyr need us, you see? That is why they follow us . . . ."

"Sometimes, in May and November, wampyr barter with evil Slavs — and sometimes Germans. The wampyr exchanges magic things, bad things, and the merchants exchange people: slaves. I believe the wampyr takes the slaves to the underworld."

When the investigators relate their experiences, Zoltan adds: "I see the wampyr in the hills, three years ago, after sunset. We hunt. It is warm. Many insects . . . . The wampyr is a dark man, without eyes, very thin, and deformed. There are three bird-women too!" If the investigators refer to the strange "living dead" they encountered, or to the veiled "ghosts" that attacked them, Zoltan confirms, "That must be the same wampyr, yes!" Zoltan laughs nervously, "the daughters of this wampyr try to catch me, but I am faster. I cannot see the women: they have a white cloak over the face. Their feet never touch the ground!"

The Magyars' Camp

Zoltan says their *taltos* (shaman) knows where the wampyr's lair (the "Black Hill") is, and that he could lead them to the Magyars' camp. There is another good reason for the investigators to stay at the

Magyars' camp for a few days: there they are safe, they can rest, and the shaman can heal them — see "Statistics," pages 161.

The Magyars' nomadic camp is spread over several hectares of pine forest, on the raised sand dunes of a braided river system (the Morava). It is located in the flood plain to the east of the wooded hills, in Magyar territory. The camp consists of two round, sunken-floored houses surrounded by ditches, and several *yurts* (circular tents made of hides stretched over wooden frames). Next to the wooden houses, one finds free-standing ovens, storage pits, small huts (smithy, wood-shop, etc.), paddocks for the horses, and cattle pens.

Seven families live in the camp. The women particularly draw the investigators' attention: they wear caftans, baggy pants, and soft leather boots, just like the men! Their hair is braided, and interlaced with decorative ribbons. Both men and women appear to be fond of glass, silver, and gold jewelry. Their clothing and their hats are also decorated with precious metals and stones.

Investigators notice that a few Magyars, including children, have malformed heads: their skulls seem much too long and their chins are underdeveloped.

The Magyars are a proud and courageous people, and they can be fierce if the situation commands them to be. On the other hand, they are very hospitable to strangers and open-minded. They certainly are not the ogres of legends. For a specific description of the warriors, see "A Band of Fierce Magyars," page 160.

At some distance from the camp lies Taltos the shaman's yurt, next to a cult place displaying heathen idols, rune stones (Turkic-Khazar runic writing), and inscribed vessels. ("Taltos" is both his name and his title.) Taltos invites the investigators to participate in a ritual trance of several hours, at night, in which Taltos' spirit — or that of the earlier abducted investigator — flies to distant places (Disembodiment spell). During the trance, the disembodied spirit finds the Black Hill ("the mountain of the wampyr and its daughters") and discovers the soul of Brother Gudman, alive, trapped in a dark place!

Taltos' single most important advice to the investigators is: "to vanquish the wampyr, find the door to the other world! Don't fear pain and death: welcome death, and you shall be saved. . . ."

The Black Hill

Accompanied by several Magyar warriors, Taltos leads the investigators to the Black Hill (though neither he nor any other Magyar dares to cross the hill's pagan wall).

The forest in the vicinity of the Black Hill is unmistakably "different," though it is difficult to say exactly why. The vegetation is certainly denser and the terrain rougher than usual. There is a strange silence all around.

The first unnatural thing the player characters spot is a white shape that moves at a distance. It turns out to be a monk's scapular (sleeveless outer cloth) hanging from a few low branches, and moving in the wind. The scapular is torn and stained with dirt and dried blood; it could very well be Brother Gudman's scapular.

From there, the investigators can make out some kind of mossy wall uphill. They also smell a foul odor nearby. In a small clearing they find the carcass of a mule in a very advanced stage of putrefaction (limbs are withered, fetid tissues are almost completely rotted away, etc.). How the animal came here and how it died is unclear. A satchel lies nearby, its contents half-spilled on the humus: a water-skin, a felt blanket, flint stones and iron, three candles, and a sopping wet letter.

Although the letter is now unreadable, the investigators recognize the personal effects of Brother Gudman!

A successful **Idea roll or Natural World roll** points out the strangeness of the find: the mule can not have been dead for more than a few days, but it looks as if it has been lying here for a full month. The Black Hill's distortion of time is caused by the Gate's warping effect (see "J. The Gate," page 154).

Walking uphill towards the mossy wall, the investigators cross a small grove littered with the 30-year-old remains of wooden fences and of a small house. The house appears to have been built around a stone platform, probably some kind of altar. Behind the platform lies the 6-foot-long rotting wooden idol of a two-faced pagan deity, covered with flaky sheets of silver. A large number of old human bones are visible, half-buried in the soil all around. Before 976 A.D., this place was a secret pagan temple of the Slavic priests, who sacrificed humans to the "Black God." When the pagan priests were executed in 976 A.D. to make room for Christianity, the location of the secret temple was unintentionally lost, and it slowly rotted away.

The Pagan Wall

The pagan wall, a few yards behind the sacral grove, extends to the left and the right of the investigators, as far as they can see. In fact, the wall completely encircles the Black hill, except for a short 15-yard-long section that is missing. The wall is of obvious antiquity (a thousand years old), weathered, and covered with moss and creepers. It varies in height from one yard to three yards, and is easy to climb over. The purpose of the wall is unclear. An investigator may note the similarity between the stones of the pagan wall, and the stones of the hermitage house and church (see "The Hermitage," pages 137). Stranger still, there are runes engraved on the wall side facing the Black Hill, as if to ward off something that is trapped inside the wall!

The climb to the top of the Black Hill takes about an hour. On their way the player characters notice dead birds scattered on the ground. At mid-slope, the temperature sharply drops below freezing for a hundred yards, before increasing back to normal. In this low-temperature belt grows a forest of dwarf mountain pines, covered in permanent frost.

At the top of the Black Hill there is a wide clearing covered with ashes and spiked with blackened stumps of pine trees. In the middle of this no man's land stands a tall black monolith. Since the Black Hill is higher than

The Pagan Wall

the surrounding hills, one can see very far. To the west rolling wooded hills extend as far as the eyes can see. To the east, across a vast plain, one can just make out hazy mountains (the White Carpathians). Clouds fly at great speed across the horizon, yet strangely enough, on top of the Black Hill, not the slightest breeze can be felt. In order to mystify the players even more, the keeper can state that night seems to be falling rapidly, no matter what the actual time of day is!

The black monolith is a natural, roughly spearhead-shaped stone nearly 10 feet tall. It leans dangerously to one side. In fact, three successful **STR versus 14** matches on the Resistance Table are enough to tip the stone over, and thus reveal the entrance to the tomb (see "The Funerary Well," page 148). A close look reveals runic inscriptions engraved on the weathered surface. The runes are Celtic, and a thousand years old; they bear enough similarity with Germanic and Nordic runes to enable decryption by investigators with Occult, German or Norse skills. However, It takes a successful **Idea roll** to realize that the language is Latin:

> This stone seals the doorway to the land
> beyond the hills.
> *On this day, the prince of the* Boii *went
> through the doorway*
> *beyond which nothing comes back.*
> *He took with him servants and beloved,*
> *and soon they shall meet with the many-faced one.*
> *Stranger or druid: kill a bull in honor of our prince,*
> *gorge on the bull's flesh, and wash the hill with its blood!*

Twelve yards to the east of the monolith, there is a SIZ 1 hole in the ground (**Spot Hidden or Luck roll** to notice). The hole reaches quite deep (seven yards actu-

ally), and reeks of urine and decay (see "Funerary Rooms," pages 149-150).

The Tomb

The lair of the Dark One is the thousand-year-old tomb of a long forgotten Celtic prince, from whom the Dark One originally borrowed the prince's mummified body. In time, the Dark One and the mi-go dug up new tunnels and extended the tomb into a large underground mining complex. The investigators find themselves in a claustrophobic space where air is scarce, where progression takes place vertically as much as horizontally, and where psychological traps and mind tricks dominate.

The keeper is referred to the schematic plan of the Dark One's tomb on this page. In order to create the proper atmosphere, the keeper must regularly remind the players of the gloominess of the tomb. In many parts of the tomb, the ceiling hangs so low that a man must walk hunched. Torchlight only reaches ten yards at best, and gives a wavering light, casting long irregular shadows on the rough stone surfaces. The confined air possesses a vaguely rancid quality, and becomes less breathable as the investigators go deeper down.

It is likely that the investigators are poorly equipped for an underground exploration of the tomb, lacking the necessary tools, light, food, and water. Some equipment can be salvaged from the well, the chamber, and the funerary rooms (see below). Exploring this first area without lantern or torch can be quite a nerve-racking experience.

One particular effect of long-lasting confinement inside the tomb is the loss of any sense of time. To simulate this, the keeper should refrain from giving any indication of the time of day to the investigators. Instead, the keeper should only state when the investigators feel tired or hungry; the timing of such warnings does not necessarily correspond to the investigators' normal patterns of sleeping and eating.

In theory, if the player characters lack food and water, they will feel the effect of dehydration on the second day of their confinement — how the investigators are penalized in practice is left to the keeper's imagination.

In the remainder of the scenario, assume for the sake of simplicity that the Dark One possesses the body of the girl Brun, and hides it in the cool lower tunnels of the tomb. Note that the mi-go and the Dark One do not use the funerary well to enter or leave the tomb (they use a secret tunnel at the foot of the Black Hill, see "K. Tunnels," page 155). Therefore the investi-

gators remain undetected and unhindered until they reach the lower level.

A. THE FUNERARY WELL

The entrance to the tomb, under the black monolith, is a cylindrical well fifty feet deep and three feet in diameter. The well is made of rough stones. At mid depth, it "traverses" a small chamber (see B. The Chamber). The lower part of the well, beneath the floor of the chamber, is entirely filled with human bones. The bones in the well are those of workers who, a thousand years ago, were sacrificed when the tomb was completed and whose bodies were thrown into the well. Three quarry hammers, one pickax, and one shovel (all in fair condition despite their age), can be found in the well among human bones and other scraps.

It is possible to descend the well without ropes, using the so-called "opposition" technique. Because of the slippery moss and fungus in the top ten feet of the well, the keeper should require a **Climb roll** to reach the top of the chamber. If the investigator jumps or falls, he must attempt a **Jump roll**. Failing the roll, the investigator's leg, arm, or head hits the edge of the well in the chamber and he incurs 1D6 damage for every 10 feet of fall (maximum 3D6). If the falling investigator succeeds the Jump roll, he falls straight onto the piles of bone in the lower half of the well, below the chamber. In that case, consider 1D6 potential damage for every 10 feet fallen (maximum 30 feet), minus 1D6. With a bit of luck, the falling investigator may come out unharmed.

Note that the investigators can tie a rope (as found for instance in the funerary rooms) to a pine tree stump close to the mouth of the funerary well, to provide them an easy way in and out.

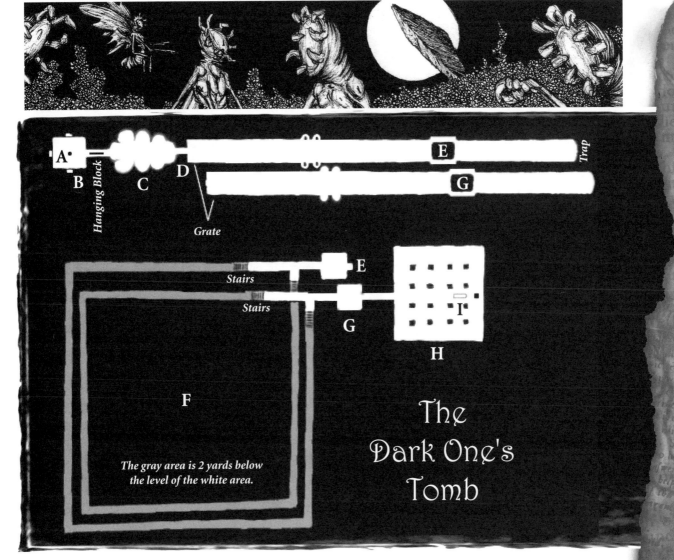

Hanging Block

A
B
C
D

Grate

E

Trap

G

Stairs

E

Stairs

G

H

I

F

The gray area is 2 yards below the level of the white area.

The Dark One's Tomb

B. THE CHAMBER

The chamber is an empty quadrangular space, seventeen feet wide and ten feet high. The walls are made of squared off blocks of limestone. In the center of each wall, there is one doorway five feet wide and seven feet tall. Four fitting slabs of stone block these doorways. Hitting the doors with a hard object reveals that only the eastern door sounds hollow. There are two techniques to open the door. The fastest technique (30 to 60 minutes of work) is to dislodge a few stones framing the door slab, and remove some rubble. Then insert a long solid object to act as a lever and pull the door open (watch out when the limestone slab falls to the ground). Breaking down the door with a quarry hammer or a pickax requires eight hours of work. Reduce this to four hours of intensive work if two persons work together. These times assume at least a 25% skill with the tool.

Beyond the east door lies a short corridor. A huge block of limestone blocks the corridor. It is quite apparent that the block fell through an opening in the ceiling, and that it was supposed to reach down to the floor. However, for some reason the block stopped one and a half feet above the ground. By looking underneath the

block one can see that it is about ten feet long. The floor appears to continue into the darkness beyond.

Note that this is as far as daylight falling through the well, can reach. Beyond that point, and without (improvised) torches, candles, or oil lamps, the investigators set forth in total darkness!

In fact, the limestone block hangs between the corridor walls through friction. Although the investigators can safely crawl to the other side, the keeper should make the experience as stressful as possible. Let crawling investigators notice that the block above them is not rigidly set, but shifts a little!

C. FUNERARY ROOMS

This area consists of a very crude, thirty-foot-long corridor. A ceiling of megalithic stone slabs covers the corridor. There are three shadowy alcoves on each side of the corridor. This area appears to be distorted, because the far end of the corridor is twisted and has subsided. A lot of muddy soil has leaked through disjointed slabs of stones, and partly filled up the far end of the corridor. Because of this, the height of the corridor drops from

seven feet down to four feet at the far end. One seven-foot beam and two thirteen-foot beams are buried in the mud. The short beam weighs 130 pounds, and the long ones 240 pounds each. It takes at least ten minutes to dig up and dislodge each beam.

The two half-sunken alcoves at the end of the corridor give off a very strong smell of urine and decay. Close inspection reveals that their ceiling is covered with a writhing mass of large bats. Any sudden movement disrupts the bats and sends the swarm flying about.

The alcoves are filled with funerary furniture. Only the objects in the first two alcoves are relatively undamaged. A thorough search through the dirt and the debris comes up with the following items:

- Empty cauldrons, embossed with pagan motifs of half-human half-beast creatures battling.
- An ancient bronze calendar, and engraved tablets. Successful **Read Latin and Other Kingdoms rolls** show that the tomb is at least a thousand years old.
- A chest containing a bronze mirror, moldy garments, and jewelry (ivory, coral, and glass).
- Amphorae filled with vinegar.
- Many sealed urns, containing salt and whale oil.
- Rusty swords, javelins, battle-axes, helmets, and shields of unknown make.

- One long metal box containing iron utensils as well as four strong ropes about twelve yards long.

Resourceful investigators can devise torches and oil lamps using the above material. If they do not think of it themselves, the keeper may help them on the right track with **Idea rolls and Repair/Devise rolls**.

At the other end of the corridor, one must crawl into a cramped mud-filled gap, under a ceiling slab that collapsed to one side. A small draft of cold air can be felt halfway. There is a narrow, near-vertical shaft (SIZ 1) through which bats come and go, and through which muddy rainwater can flow into the tomb. This shaft corresponds to a hole at the surface of the Black Hill, twelve yards to the east of the funerary well (see "A. The Funerary Well," page 148).

D. THE ROOFED ALLEY

The gap under the stone slab leads to a twelve-foot-wide passageway. Both the floor and the ceiling are made of megalithic stone slabs. The walls are made of stacks of flat stones. The floor of the alley appears to be subtly slanting upwards. The roofed alley is about forty yards long.

Rusted iron gratings span the first eight feet of floor, and bridge a deep abyss. Investigators hear the hint of an underground river far below, and feel a rising draft of cold air. It is impossible to jump over this section of the floor, because there is no way to get a running start. Only one investigator at a time can safely cross the grate. Match the **combined SIZ of investigators standing on the grate, versus the grate's strength of 21** on the Resistance Table. If the roll fails, parts of the grate start to break — reduce the grate strength by 1D6. At zero strength, the grate is completely destroyed. A fall into the abyss underneath is a certain death.

As the investigators reach the middle of the alley, they notice two dark silhouettes on each side of the alley, half-embedded into niches in the walls.

These are stone statues representing warriors holding round shields. The heads are missing and the feet are planted into the stone floor.

E. THE PIT

The roofed alley stops at a 12-foot square pit, plunging into darkness. The pit walls are cut directly into the limestone.

To the left and to the right of the pit are aborted alleys about three feet deep. The alley continues into darkness on the other side of the pit (this part is twenty yards

long). At the end of the alley there is a door similar to the one in the access chamber. It is possible to cross the pit by jumping two corners. It takes a **Jump roll every time at triple normal skill rating**. A direct long jump can be attempted on a regular **Jump roll**. Another way to cross the pit is to let a rough-hewn beam — as found in the funerary rooms — rest upon opposite ledges, and use it as a bridge. A rope tied to the middle of the beam can be used to climb down the pit.

The door at the end of the alley is a trap! There is no corridor behind it, just an alcove. Note: stone rubble litters this part of the alley. The stones make great weapons when thrown or pushed into the pit. On a hit, count 1D6 damage for every pound of stone.

The pit is eighteen yards deep, enough to kill any investigator unlucky enough to fall into it (6D6 falling damage). If an investigator fails a **Jump roll**, the keeper should allow a **Dexterity roll** (DEX x5) for the investigator to grab the edge of the pit, of a beam, or a dangling rope.

At the bottom of the pit, in the middle of the west wall, there is a narrow two-foot-wide and six-foot-high shaft. The shaft is forty feet long, and makes a "T" junction with the labyrinth, see the plan on page 149.

Lower Level

There is no trace of mi-go or Dark One activity, until the investigators' first "night" in the tomb. After the investigators reach the bottom of the pit, the keeper should regularly remind the players that their characters are fatigued and that they need some rest. If necessary, apply fatigue rules.

F. THE LABYRINTH

The labyrinth is a very simple but deceptive construction. It basically consists of two linked square corridors (see page 149). The corridors are only three feet wide and six feet tall. The sides of the square corridors are 35 – 40 yards long. Someone or something has dug the corridors directly into the limestone.

Going full circle, an investigator is likely to think that he has returned to his starting point, but in reality he is at the corresponding point of the second corridor. An investigator needs to walk around twice to come back to his starting point.

The most mystifying aspect of the labyrinth is that there is a second pit. The builders of the tomb certainly did their best to make the two square corridors and the

two pits as similar as possible. The keeper should anticipate the players' confusion.

G. THE SECOND PIT

The geometry of the second pit is the same as that of the first one, except for a narrow six yard long shaft opposite the entrance to the pit. Squeezing through the shaft, the investigators can reach the sanctuary, which leads to the deeper parts of the tomb.

Close examination or a **Spot Hidden roll** reveals dark stains on the pit's floor. The vaguely sweet metallic smell that oozes from the stains is unmistakably that of blood.

Nightmares

Sleeping investigators are plagued by nightmares. The keeper is advised to play the nightmare scenes with the players as if they were "real." For instance, one investigator dreams that he wakes up, and keeper and player role-play the nightmare until the player is told that the investigator (really) awakens. If the keeper wishes, some nightmares can be collective, i.e. shared by all investigators. In that case, role-playing proceeds as usual, as if the nightmare was "real" to all.

NIGHTMARE 1: faint sounds lure one investigator into the labyrinth (see below). The investigator turns at least 3 corners, before seeing greenish phosphorescence just around the next corner, 40 yards away! The sounds are quite clear now (shuffling and scraping). Now and then an aberrant shadow (of a mi-go or of the girl Brun) is cast against a wall. At the first noise the investigator makes, all lights die out, and there is a scurrying noise. Invisible hunters stalk the investigator in the dark. One of the stalkers chuckles like a young girl. Then the labyrinth's exit passageway inexplicably vanishes, and the investigator finds himself trapped in a square corridor with his pursuers!

NIGHTMARE 2: lured as previously, one investigator enters a muddy tunnel he hadn't noticed before. The tunnel goes on and on, endlessly. Turning back, the investigator cannot find the entrance to the tunnel anymore. All of a sudden, the floor gives way and the investigator falls into a very deep, grimy hole. He is gradually buried under masses of putrid mud. A green glow appears far, far above, and the investigator distinguishes a dark silhouette with long black hair peering into the hole.

NIGHTMARE 3: one investigator wakes up in the absolute darkness of a cramped stone sarcophagus, next to some dead body (the girl Brun). After a while, when panic starts to creep in, the body comes to "life," and tries to have intercourse with the investigator! Details of the rotting cadaver (the stench, the feel of the withering flesh, the maggots, the long greasy hair, etc.) are left to the keeper.

If the investigators stand long enough near the stains they will see, hear, or feel drops of fluid falling from the darkness of the pit above them, onto the floor. On a successful **Listen roll**, investigators can also hear a very faint, recurrent squeaking sound coming from up there.

If the investigators throw up their torches high enough, the keeper should let them catch a glimpse of the horror dangling thirteen yards above their heads.

Vivisection

A seven-foot cubic frame made of two-inch-thick bone-gray bars is floating in mid-air, and rotating very slowly about its center. Large spans of wrinkled, glistening, grayish-green skins and other organic filaments are stretched across the cubic frame. The organic stuff is made of the same matter as mi-go bio-webs. Caught inside the web is the naked, pulled-apart, and headless body of a human being. The skin of the thorax and abdomen has been incised and delicately peeled off, revealing fat and muscle. The skin is somehow attached to, or extends into, the strange organic matter, stretching out from the flanks of the body like two disgusting wings. The soft abdominal organs are held in place by a web of gray strings.

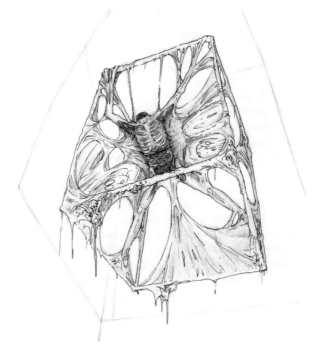

By looking closely, it is possible to see that the body is alive! Indeed, from time to time, it appears to shift and twitch, as if making weak attempts to free itself.

Note that after several exposures to strong light, the mi-go webs start to glow in the dark with greenish phosphorescence. This in turn reveals countless pulsating veins embedded in the membranes and the strings, connecting the wretched body to the cubic frame.

Seeing the undead horror costs 0/1D4 to 0/1D6 Sanity points, depending on how hard an investigator is trying to understand what he sees.

The body is Brother Gudman's. The mi-go are testing the limits of their knowledge of human biology, and how far they can deconstruct a living body. The head of Brother Gudman is kept inside a mi-go "head box" in the well of heads. The levitating cube is made of hollow bars filled with alien machinery, fluid sacks, power cells, and so forth.

The players can try to figure a way to climb up the second pit. If they come up with a no-nonsense solution, the keeper should give them the benefit of the doubt, and a good chance to succeed.

If the investigators succeed in climbing up the second pit, they find a (second) roofed alley. This alley lacks the four statues of the first alley — eight holes in the ground mark the positions where the statues should be. This second alley is a dead end.

H. THE SANCTUARY

The sanctuary is a 15-yard-square Celtic temple. Sixteen limestone pillars support the ceiling. A large area of the floor is covered with a thick layer of human bones, rising gradually towards the sanctuary walls. The sanctuary pillars are crude quadrangular blocks, with niches holding human skulls. A number of crude stone tablets inscribed with Celtic runes line the pillars. The script is an unknown language, hence attempts to decrypt the tablets are bound to fail.

At the far end of the sanctuary stands a five-foot-tall limestone statue, which represents some kind of two-faced god. The god crosses his arms, and his two faces (one looking toward the entrance to the sanctuary, the other toward the wall) have an enigmatic expression. The god's head exhibits two horns or ears pointing upward, which gives a lupine appearance to the whole. A successful **Occult roll** reveals that the statue probably represents the Roman god of gates, Janus. A successful **Cthulhu Mythos roll** interprets the two masks of the statue as a possible symbol of Nyarlathotep.

Not far from the statue lies the mummy of the Celtic prince that the Dark One had originally possessed for 70 years. The body is naked, smells bad, and its leathery skin is strangely shriveled and blackened.

On the floor at the foot of the statue, one can see the outline of a 4-foot-square carved stone, chiseled with the following Latin sentence: "anima deorum sum," which means "I am the soul of the gods." There is a small finger-sized hole in the middle of the slab.

The investigators have no obvious means to haul the slab (mi-go can introduce the long tip of one articulated limb into the hole, and pull the slab up — **STR versus 12** on the Resistance Table). The investigators can relatively easily break the slab (3 inches thick) with a quarry hammer. But before they do, they hear faint whisperings close by! The investigators quickly realize that the voice comes from underneath the slab! The only way to understand what is said is to put one's ear against the hole in the slab.

Brother Gudman

A whirring whisper can be heard through the hole in the sanctuary floor. It is impossible to measure how far away the speaker is:

"Who, who is there? I . . . uh, I cannot see, ehrrr. The pain . . . please untie me, arhhhh. Don't hurt me anymore . . . ."

In fact the investigators hear Brother Gudman — although his voice is unrecognizable. The head of Brother Gudman has been put in a mi-go "head box"

(the precursor of the infamous brain cylinder). The steel box sits in one of the many small niches lining the sides of the well underneath the stone slab. Brother Gudman's ears and larynx are interfaced with primitive resonance boxes that allow him to speak and hear. Horribly enough, Brother Gudman can *feel* his body hanging in the second pit, via some sinister "wireless" technology the mi-go are experimenting with. The first player to actually realize this must make a **Sanity roll** (0/1D6). Because of the physical torture, the alien drugs, and the sensory deprivation, Gudman is well on his way to insanity. Nevertheless, he can answer simple questions about who he is and what happened:

- "Attacked by, by white demons. One devil takes me to the sky . . . . God have mercy! Hear the distress of your servants! What . . . what is done to them?"

- "Darkness, always darkness . . . . The echo! The devil takes me to hell, what else . . . . God, what have I done to . . ." [Strange sob-like sounds.]

- "Oh no! I can see them floating in the green light! They bind me inside a . . . a cage? They torture me . . . . Long needles pierce my eyes, my ears! The pain, the endless pain . . ." [Long silence.]

- "This must be hell . . . . What sins? I'm . . . I'm blind, I'm tied to the, the cage . . . . My body is burning, burning like a thousand furnaces . . . ." [Unearthly moanings.] "I can hear the demons clicking now . . . ."

Investigators inside the sanctuary feel a growing headache, as a mi-go (telepathically attuned to Brother Gudman's head), noiselessly approaches the stone slab from below. The mi-go is wearing glowing green web armor. Anyone looking into the hole first sees the green light bathing one side of the well of heads, and a misshapen glowing shape hovering from a side tunnel into the well (Sanity loss 0/1D4). The mi-go then shoots up in the blink of an eye and attempts to pierce the head of the investigator through the hole, with the serrated tip of one limb. If the attack succeeds and the player fails the **Dodge roll**, the investigator loses one eye and 2D6 hit points. If the Dodge succeeds, the investigators hear a loud thud, and a six-inch long pointy object darts through the hole. The stone slab cracks in two pieces under the shock.

If nobody is looking into the hole, the investigators can see a pencil of green light swaying above it. Then something slowly pushes the stone slab upwards. The investigators see several huge spidery limbs lift the slab for a few seconds, then place the slab back (Sanity loss 0/1D4).

The mi-go retreats a few yards into the tunnel it came from, ready to attack any investigator who descends into the well of heads.

I. THE WELL OF HEADS

The well of heads is a few hundred yards deep. As far as the eye can see, tunnel openings, roughly four to five feet in diameter, pierce the well walls at more or less regular intervals of ten feet.

There are many small niches dug into the first twelve yards of the well. Each niche contains a head box (similar to the future brain cylinder, but simpler, with only two tiny holes for speech, and two more for hearing). Most head boxes are empty; the keeper is free to imagine who else might be trapped in the ones that are not. The first head box within reach contains the head of Brother Gudman.

The safest technique to descend into the well of heads, and to reach the first tunnel, is to climb down a rope tied around the feet of the statue in the sanctuary. The tunnel is guarded by a single mi-go — the only one in the tomb at that time (mi-go #2 in the "Statistics" section, page 159). The other mi-go are beyond the Gate, on their otherworldly outpost. The mi-go guard keeps the controller to the Gate in the tunnel. Defeating the mi-go, the investigators can take the controller box, and operate the Gate (see "J. The Gate," below). A successful **Repair/Devise or Luck roll** is sufficient to open the Gate with the controller. How the investigators can close the Gate once it is open, or whether the Gate can be closed at all, is up to the keeper.

J. THE GATE

The mi-go created a Gate inside the well of heads, at about 15 feet under the floor level of the sanctuary.

Once activated, the Gate appears as a pitch-black horizontal surface spanning the whole section of the well of heads. When the Gate is open, a gale-force wind blows through the well towards the Gate, as the air of the tomb is sucked into it.

Mi-go Hell

Any investigator descending (or falling) into the well while the Gate is open, continues to the other side, and after another five feet hits the ground of an alien world! The investigator sees a vast windswept plain of red gravel, under a gigantic red sun. The low-pressure gaseous atmosphere is not breathable for humans. However, as long as the investigator stays under the Gate (a black square floating five feet above the gravel), he can breathe the earthly air gushing through it. The keeper should make clear that moving away from the Gate is deadly: suffocation/drowning rules apply immediately.

The other world's horizon is unnaturally close by, a mile at most, and, like the gravel plain itself, seems to be strongly curved. In the distance, one can see a procession of hundreds of mi-go pulling floating platforms that carry unidentifiable cargo. Everything from the reddish dust clouds overhead to the mi-go appears to move at a ridiculously accelerated speed, as if time flows faster here than elsewhere. Immediately, dozens of mi-go break away from the procession and converge on the Gate. It takes them about four minutes to cover the distance.

The investigator suffers a loss of 0/1D10 Sanity points because of the outlandish experience. The only way to be rescued is to be hauled back through the Gate. Note that an investigator can in theory stick his head through the mi-go Gate and call for help on the other side.

Each trip through the Gate costs 3 magic points and 1 Sanity point.

Mi-go Swarm

Once the Gate is open, the investigators only have a few minutes to consider their options. If they do not quickly close the open Gate, twenty-one mi-go swarm the tomb through the Gate. For the sake of simplicity, use the same mi-go statistics for every group of seven mi-go (see page 104).

The investigators' best chance to survive the mi-go swarm is: 1) to keep to narrow corridors and take their enemies out one by one (the mi-go cannot fly in narrow corridors); and 2) escape from the tomb as soon as possible. The mi-go are cruel, but not stupid. For instance, they never go into a narrow passageway or tunnel if a human is waiting to ambush them at the other side.

The keeper should improvise the mi-go onslaught in such a way as to put maximum psychological pressure on the players. At the same time, the keeper must take care not to overwhelm the investigators. If necessary, have the mi-go hesitate or make mistakes. The mi-go abandon the tomb if more than half of them are killed, or if the player characters

somehow succeed in resisting them for a long period of time (how long is left to the keeper).

In case the group ends up in a hopeless situation, shortcut the mi-go attack with the arrival of the Dark One. Tell the players that the mi-go suddenly back away for no apparent reason, and play the final confrontation below.

K. TUNNELS

The tunnels below the sanctuary are part of a large mining complex crisscrossing the depths of the Black Hill. The mi-go and the Dark One built most of the complex starting from thousand-year-old Celtic salt mines. The mines are dug into a vitreous, colorless mineral that seems to catch torchlight, and tastes like salt (halite). The longest tunnels are found near the bottom of the Black Hill.

The Dark One and the mi-go have closed all the Celtic tunnels except for one tunnel that they use to go in and out of the salt mines. The entrance to the muddy exit tunnel lies at the foot of the Black Hill. It is well hidden in the shadowy hollow under a shale outcrop, at some distance above the pagan wall.

The exact layout of the tunnel complex is not relevant. The keeper should improvise the tunnel layout as required. All tunnels are straight, narrow, and are connected to each other by slanting side tunnels.

Investigators who search long enough in the tunnel complex should always find what they are looking for. The well of heads, for instance, is easily found, since most tunnels originate from it. When the Gate is open, the investigators can easily find the secret exit at the foot of the Black Hill, by progressing against the air current that flows towards the Gate.

Finale

The location and the exact timing of the final confrontation with the Dark One is left to the keeper's discretion. The party could be in the upper level of the tomb, in the tunnels around the well of heads, or even in the forest outside the tomb. Using a variant of the Soul Singing spell, the Dark One stages the confrontation largely in the investigators' minds! They can only escape the sanity-wrecking nightmare by "dreaming" or by willing themselves awake. As long as they try to survive and have hit points left, investigators keep on losing Sanity!

Dark One Hell

The first task of the keeper is to separate players whose investigators are within range of the Dark One's spell from the ones who aren't. The keeper then alters the bewitched player chracters' surroundings into a hellish nightmare: the Soul Pit! See the Dark One's statistics for details. The alteration must be progressive and subtle so as to mystify the players. The overall atmosphere should be gloomy and threatening.

Remember that a half-hour spent in the Soul Pit corresponds to a single combat round in the waking world!

Common features of the Soul Pit are:

- A bottomless pit or well (the Abyss) that spills out an obnoxious freezing smoke. Distant echoes of things moving in the Abyss' depths can be overheard.

- A darkening of the light. The surroundings are only lit by the strange gray glow that the smoke from the Abyss diffuses. The investigators are able to see, but vision is limited to 10–20 yards.

- The ground is covered in a kind of cold muddy clay. The whole area has turned into a mass grave, and countless decayed corpses are found half-buried in the clay. The stench is overpowering. Every now and then, two- to three-foot long worm-like creatures (dark ones) can be felt or glimpsed, restlessly wriggling through the rotting muck.

- The geometry of this hell is warped like the interior of a sphere. An investigator moving away from the Abyss invariably returns to it after 600 yards of walking "around." Despite this oddity, the ground feels flat, not curved.

- Close to the Abyss (less than 20 yards), the corpse-packed mud slides into the bottomless pit at a slow but inexorable rate (MOV 2). The mudslide drags everything towards the Abyss.

Sanity loss is caused by:

- Just being there (Sanity loss 0/1D4)!

- Out of the smoke come swarms of mi-go that try to grapple the investigators (Grapple 30%, Sanity loss 0/1D6). Alternately, living dead corpses rising from the muck try to grab the investigators (Grapple 30%, Sanity loss 1/1D10). The keeper should continuously harass the investigators: if they rest for longer than one combat round, they are attacked. After a while, fatigue kicks in.

- An investigator caught by mi-go or by the living dead, is subjected to mind-bend-

ing physical torture. The victim is immobilized and held against the ground. Within seconds the victim sees or feels a dozen two-foot-long flattish worm-like creatures converging towards him in the clay. The flatworms burrow themselves into the victim's abdomen. They then slowly suck in and dissolve the victim's intestines. The pain is excruciating. Every 10 minutes of torture, the keeper should ask the player if the investigator tries to resist the torture and the pain, or gives in to it. If the investigator resists, the torture costs only 1 hit point of damage but 1/1D10 Sanity points! If the investigator gives in to the pain, the cost is 1D10 hit points and only 1 Sanity point.

- An investigator falling into the Abyss disappears for good (or for as long as the keeper judges necessary). Both his physical body and his dream-self simply vanish.

The keeper is free to heighten the horror with nightmare effects of his own devising. If you know the players, exploit their personal weaknesses and phobias! Inspiring ideas can also be gleaned from the *H. P. Lovecraft's Dreamlands* supplement.

The only two ways for a player character to break away from the Soul Pit are: 1) to "die" there, or 2) to will himself awake. The keeper is referred to the "Soul Pit" section in the Dark One statistics for details.

Investigators who escape from the Dark One's nightmarish Soul Pit can try to destroy the Dark One/Brun. While the Dark One is controlling the investigators' minds, the girl's corpse stands immobile and it cannot actively defend itself. At the first hit, the spell is broken, releasing the dreaming investigators. The players now have a few decisive combat rounds to destroy the Dark One for good.

Conclusion

The keeper can greet investigators who exit the tomb with a clear blue sky and a landscape covered in snow. This should nicely contrast with recent experiences and maybe mystify the players about how long exactly the investigators did stay in the underworld.

If the investigators survive the tomb, the mi-go definitely close the Gate and abandon the region. Grant 1D10 Sanity points to the investigators for foiling the Dark One and the mi-go. Killing seven or more mi-go nets each investigator 6 additional Sanity points. At the keeper's discretion, any laudable action (saving the foresters, helping Zoltan) could be worth 1D3 Sanity points. Conversely, the keeper may want to penalize players who behaved poorly (having intercourse with the Dark One/Brun, being responsible for the death of innocent villagers).

The investigators' troubles do not end with the destruction of the Dark One. They are many loose ends: can they prove themselves innocent of Brun's ruin? Can they possibly return to their former life? How does the *Al-Azif* end up a thousand years later in some obscure Hungarian catalogue? And above all, what do they do with poor Brother Gudman?

Statistics

Brant, Age 45, Local Landlord (German)

STR 13	CON 08	SIZ 16	INT 16	POW 09
DEX 17	APP 09	EDU 12	SAN 45	HP 12

Damage Bonus: +1D4.

Weapons: Frankish Long Sword 55%, damage 1D8+1+db
 Grapple 45%, damage special

Armor: chainmail 7 points, medium shield 70% (25 HP)

Skills: Insight 55%, Own Kingdom 40%, Ride 35%, Status 45%, Track 40%.

Brant is a nobleman, a scion of a branch of the Babenberg family of Bavaria. The man is bald and exceptionally tall. Brant must have been handsome in the past, but the skin of his face and cranium bears terrible burn scars.

Brant arrived in Laa in 975 A.D., aged 22, a naïve and ambitious young lord. Brant and his priest, the predecessor of Zutto, destroyed the Slavic hill fort and temple, and built their stronghold. Brant vividly remembers the rites of some pagans, which involved human sacrifices. He also remembers that the pagan priests brought victims to a secret place somewhere in the forest, but he never bothered to find out where. The cult was swiftly eradicated in 976 A.D., when the pagan priests were arrested in the village and executed in public. Brant's initial dreams of grandeur died a slow death in Laa, and gave way to resignation. Brant lost his wife in the 995 A.D. Magyar raid, when she burned alive in the tower-house. She could never give him the children he wanted (in fact he is sterile).

Brant avoids talking about the Magyar he captured during a patrol in October 997 A.D. The prisoner is now kept in the prison pit under the tower-house. Brant's companions, on the other hand, are not so close-mouthed — especially after a few strong drinks.

Brant does not refrain from exerting quick justice, but his justice is never arbitrary. He is too intelligent for that, and he cares for his people.

Brant is well aware of the sporadic disappearances of people in the region, and believes the Magyars of the east to be responsible. He periodically sends patrols to watch over the trading routes of the region.

Before the 984 A.D. trade embargo, Brant had a shared interest in Burgolf's Bohemian slave trade. He provided some logistic support (military escort, temporary shelter inside the stronghold, etc.), in exchange for half of Burgolf's profits. Brant is unaware of Burgolf's connection with the "Merchant" (the Dark One).

Brant has 21 military retainers and 12 war dogs. The table on page 158 lists the statistics of Brant's servant Hunman and 6 milites. War dog average statistics are shown below.

TWELVE WAR DOGS

STR 12	CON 08	SIZ 10	INT 05	POW 12
DEX 09	MOV 12	–	–	HP 09

Damage Bonus: none.

Weapons: Bite 30%, damage 1D6

Armor: none, no Dodge either.

Skills: Spot Hidden 60%, Track by Smell 70%.

Brant's war dogs are of a giant mastiff breed, closely resembling modern-day Great Danes. They have a brindle-colored coat and black mask and ears. They stand 30 inches at the shoulder, and weigh 160–170 pounds on average. They always accompany their master in battle, and are not afraid to attack bears and other big game.

Zutto, Age 32, Lame Priest (German)

STR 12	CON 09	SIZ 12	INT 10	POW 12
DEX 14	APP 08	EDU 12	SAN 60	HP 11

Damage Bonus: none.

Weapons: none.

Skills: Latin 40%, Sermon (Persuade) 25%, Write Latin 40%.

The priest is narrow-minded, lazy, and cowardly. He keeps an underage concubine (a 15-year-old orphan he calls a "servant"). Ironically, he despises the Slavs and their way of life. Zutto resents the eremite brothers because they see him for what he is — an opportunist — though he would never admit that.

Put under stress, Zutto can become unreasonable. For instance, in "The Eye of the Storm," he might very well turn the popular anger against the investigators.

("Burn the sorcerers, and our sins will be washed away!")

His sermons, delivered in German, are rather long and uninspiring.

The priest is in charge of compiling the yearly registers. His Latin is fit for the purpose. He doesn't know much more information than what is contained in the registers. He has no opinion about the periodic disappearances of Slavs. His predecessor (a very capable priest in fact) died of swamp fever in 989 A.D.

Brun, Age 16, Lovable Maiden (German)

STR 08	CON 07	SIZ 08	INT 11	POW 11
DEX 10	APP 15	EDU 12	SAN 55	HP 08

Damage Bonus: –1D4.

Weapons: Embrace (Grapple) 25%, damage special

Skills: Accounting 30%, Insight 35%, Own Kingdom 25%, Slav 40%, Write German 55%.

Brun is the 16-year-old, bright, and quite beautiful daughter of the village's richest man: the trader Burgolf. She owes her name to her lovely long brown hair ("brun" is Germanic for brown). Brun has a good knowledge of people, and shows great kindness. If this scenario did not predestine her to prematurely "die," she could have become a person of (good) influence in the region. But greater and darker forces are at play, and her fate is sealed.

Information

- Brun can describe the settlement's organization and main personalities to the investigators. She is not very superstitious: she does not indulge in any of the village rumors, except to refute them.

- If the investigators need to go some place, she can explain how to get there, and may even accompany them. For instance, Brun knows the location of the foresters' camp. The keeper should take care not to put her in a life-threatening situation.

- Brun may introduce the players to almost all settlers, Germans and Slavs, including the foresters and the eremites. One thing she cannot do is to get the investigators inside the lord's tower-house.

- Brun is always one of the first to learn village news.

- Brun is fluent in German and Slavic, and may thus be the investigators' translator if required. She is also literate, and may help the investigators read simple German or Slavonic texts. She doesn't know Latin!

- Brun is a good Christian. She will try to help a person in need, as long as it does not endanger her own life.

- Most significant maybe is that Brun stays faithful to the investigators until the end — her end.

Burgolf, Age 37, Trader with a Bad Conscience (German)

STR 10	CON 13	SIZ 16	INT 12	POW 14
DEX 11	APP 10	EDU 12	SAN 70	HP 15

Damage Bonus: +1D4.

Weapons: Scimitar 15%, damage 1D8+db
Dagger 30%, damage 1D4+db

Skills: Accounting 15%, Arabic 10%, Bargain 70%, Drive Horses 50%, Fast Talk 40%, Insight 35%, Magyar 10%, Other Kingdoms 30%, Own Kingdom 55%, Slav 35%, Status 45%.

Burgolf means "Mountain Wolf" in Germanic. Burgolf is a big man, and always wears expensive shirts, cloaks, and furs. He lost his wife while she was giving birth to his daughter Brun, whom he loves above everything.

Burgolf came to Laa in 977 A.D., at the age of 16. Over the years, Brun's father became a central figure in the village: he controls the trade and acts as a mediator to the local landlord. Despite his bullish appearance, he is more open-minded than his fellow colonists, and certainly better informed. He deals both with the German colonists and the Slavs, selling their products to Polish, Jewish, and Arab merchants.

Information

- Burgolf knows all the information found under the "anonymous German colonist" entry. He knows in particular the location of the foresters' camp, in the forest.

- Burgolf indulged in occasional slave trade before the trade embargo in 984 A.D. Most slaves were pagan Slavs captured in Bohemia, transiting through Laa, before being sold to Jewish and Arab merchants, and sometimes even Magyar warlords. These prisoners were usually kept in the stronghold, and half of the revenue went to Brant.

- If Burgolf is shown the Black Stone he distinctly shudders, but eludes questions about it or about his reaction.

- When put under pressure (through forceful questioning or threats of eternal damnation) Burgolf tells his secret. The Dark One, presenting himself as "the Merchant," approached Burgolf on several occasions before 985 A.D., always at night. The Merchant bought human slaves, steel bars, and linen sheets, and paid Burgolf in solid gold. On several occasions, Burgolf saw the Merchant's Black Stone. The Merchant's last nightly visit was in 995 A.D., when he gave Burgolf stones from the Black Hill's pagan wall for the construction of the hermitage house and church, in exchange for goods. Burgolf never saw the Merchant's face, but acutely remembers the inhuman quality of his voice, and the nauseating smell of carrion that he always brought with him. Now Burgolf is terrified about the Merchant's true nature, and about the salvation of his own soul.

Anonymous German Colonist

STR 10	CON 11	SIZ 11	INT 10	POW 10
DEX 10	APP 10	EDU 10	SAN 50	HP 11

Damage Bonus: none.

Weapons: Improvised Weapon (small club, sling, small knife) 25%, damage 1D4+db

Skills: Bargain 25%, Craft (see below) 45%, Fast Talk 30%, Insight 20%, Own Kingdom 50%, Slav 20%.

Craft: blacksmith, iron founder, carpenter, cooper, tanner, wheelwright, or wood turner. Manorial servants know specific crafts; choose baker, cook, miller, washer folk, vintner (at the hermitage), fisherman, or herdsman/keeper.

The large majority of German colonists display a subtle "master-servant" attitude towards the Slavs. Even after 30 years of living together, the Germans still consider the Slavs to be obtuse and potentially dangerous half-pagans.

Brant's Milites

char.	Hunman	#1	#2	#3	#4	#5	#6
STR	12	14	14	8	10	10	14
CON	7	13	12	10	13	7	11
SIZ	13	11	10	12	14	9	15
INT	15	13	12	8	10	12	10
POW	9	10	6	11	13	7	12
DEX	10	12	9	11	9	16	6
APP	10	14	9	9	12	8	11
HP	10	12	11	11	14	8	13
DB	+1D4	+1D4	–	–	–	–	+1D4

Weapons: Long Sword 45%, damage 1D8+db
Large Knife 40%, damage 1D6+db
Bow (base range 60 y.) 35%, damage 1D8

Armor: 2-point soft leather in general, 5-point leather and rings for Hunman

Skills: Ride 30% (MOV 12), Track 35%

Information

- Since early 998 A.D., Magyars haven't stolen cattle or attacked the settlement of Laa. The reason is that the son of the rebel chieftain was captured by Brant and is now kept in a bleak prison pit under the tower.

- Most Germans — especially the foresters — believe in the Crazy Hunter and the Wood Women. The Wood Women are insanely beautiful woodland spirits. At day, they hide under waterbed rocks or in trees. The Crazy Hunter is a night demon (zwerc) whose only purpose seems to be hunting down the Wood Women. This legend probably has its source in the ancient Greek myth of satyrs and nymphs. Some foresters even witnessed manifestations of the Wood Women (strange green lights in the forest, eerie whispers, ghostly apparitions). Some tales mention that long ago, the Crazy Hunter sometimes prowled the fortified village.

char.	#1[1]	#2	#3	#4	#5	#6	#7
STR	15	12	7	13	5	7	9
CON	10	11	14	16	10	11	11
SIZ	7	10	17	9	9	14	10
INT	16	13	14	6	9	13	14
POW	14	12	12	11	12	14	10
DEX	16	17	17	17	16	12	14
HP	9	11	16	13	10	13	11
Weapon[2]	Limb	Gun	Limb	Limb	Limb	Limb	Limb
	30%	25%	30%	30%	30%	30%	30%
	1D6	1D10	1D6	1D6	1D6–1D4	1D6	1D6
Armor[3]	–	5-pt bioweb	–	–	–	–	–

The Mi-Go

MOV 7/9 flying.

[1]Mi-go #1 is the leader. It avoids physical combat, preferring the Black Light magical attack instead (see below). Mi-go #2 is a guard, armed with a lightning weapon and a mist projector.

[2]The lightning gun immobilizes the target for as many rounds as damage points inflicted. Humans cannot operate the gun.

[3]Impaling weapons do minimum damage.

Sanity Loss: 0/1D3 if veiled, 0/1D6 if not.

- He or she knows a forester who, in recent years, changed behavior and then vanished without a trace. The truth is that the forester was either possessed by the Dark One for six months, or beheaded by the mi-go; in any case the body was never found. The keeper is invited to come up with an exciting tale around the incident, possibly involving Wood Women, the Crazy Hunter, the People from the Hills, etc.

- The Germans respect Burgolf at least as much as Brant. Nevertheless, his few enemies circulate the rumor that Burgolf hoards a treasure of Jewish gold gained with the slave trade.

A Few Armed Colonists

Re-use the anonymous German statistics to create a group of upset Germans.

Foresters

Use the same statistics, except for the crafts that are very specific to the foresters.

Anonymous Slavic Local

STR 10	**CON** 11	**SIZ** 10	**INT** 11	**POW** 10
DEX 10	**APP** 11	**EDU** 08	**SAN** 50	**HP** 11

Damage Bonus: none.

Weapons: Improvised Weapon (club, wooden spear, large knife, ax) 30%, damage 1D6

Skills: Bargain 20%, Craft (see below) 40%, Drive Horses 30%, German 20%, Listen 45%, Natural World 30%, Occult 25%, Track 25%.

Craft: jeweler, blacksmith, carpenter, cooper, antler-worker, or farmer.

The Slavs of Laa call themselves *Drevani*, "people of the woodlands," and are part of the larger tribe of the *Moravani*, the Moravians. Their economic relationship with the German masters, however unconstrained (relatively speaking), is tainted by reciprocal mistrust. Some young Slavs in particular adopt a clearly hostile attitude towards the Germans' authority (the milites and the priest are the focus of many frustrations). In contrast, the eremites are rather well liked.

Information

- Knows a family member who, in recent years, changed behavior and then vanished without a trace. The truth is that the Slav was either possessed by the Dark One, or decapitated by the mi-go; in any case the body was never found. The keeper is invited to come up with an exciting tale around the incident, possibly involving vampires, dragons, or ogres (Magyars).

As the Slavs' burial rites attest, all believe in the existence of ogres, vampires, and werewolves. The most superstitious confuse the ogres with the Magyars, and the word ogre may be derived from a deformation of *on ongur* ("Hungarian") and Orcus, a dreadful god of the old Romans. The eldest Slavs in particular tell the tale of a vampire-like demon (drac) that lives beneath a Black Hill somewhere in the forest, and is served by his three daughters who are "bird-women." This folk tale has many similarities with the German foresters' stories about the Crazy Hunter and the Wood Women, but comes closer to the hidden truth about the Dark One and its (veiled) mi-go associates.

Before the Germans came, the Slavs believed in the old gods, even sacrificing human lives to appease the most terrible gods such as Czerneboch, the Black God. Besides the official temple next to the Slavic hillfort, the priests of the cult kept a secret temple hidden in the forest, where sacrificial victims were offered. The secret of the temple's location (the Black Hill) was unintentionally lost in 976 A.D., when Brant arrested the pagan priests in the village and had them summarily executed. The Black God is a nomadic peddler who takes a different form every night. It may even come in the form of a person you know. The Black God buys people who are going to die from their families, and takes them to the "land beyond the hills." (**Keeper's Note:** *this old belief possibly draws on the evildoings of the Dark One.*)

A Group of Belligerent Slavs

Re-use the anonymous Slavs' statistics to create a group of defiant young Slavs.

Zoltan, Age 19, Magyar Rebel and Prisoner

STR 11*	CON 09*	SIZ 09*	INT 11	POW 15
DEX 13	APP 08	EDU 13	SAN 75	HP 09

Note that Zoltan's STR, CON, SIZ, and HP are 2 points below their normal maximum level, because of his one-year imprisonment.

Damage Bonus: none.

Weapons: Magyar Saber 50%, damage 1D8+db
Reflex Bow (base range 100 y.) 70%, damage 1D8+1

Armor: none or 2-point felt armor

Skills: German 20%, Natural World 30%, Navigate 35%, Slavic 20%, Sneak 65%, Spot Hidden 85%, Status 75%, Throw 70%, Track 80%.

Zoltan is the son of a Magyar headman. His father Mohgor is still alive, but incapacitated by serious wounds sustained in the clan's battle against the Christian mercenaries of Istvan, the would-be king of Hungary. As Zoltan would say: "my clan must hide, because King Istvan, the Christian dog, is at war with his own people,

his own blood. Praise Koppany, keeper of the old ways, because this year — with our help — he will oust Istvan!"

Zoltan is a proud and fierce fighter, and rejects the Christian god. He is not intolerant though, and values honor, courage, and friendship above everything.

Zoltan was captured by Brant's men during a patrol along the Amber Road in 997 A.D. Zoltan has been terribly weakened by his one-year imprisonment in the dire prison under Brant's tower-house. His will to survive and avenge himself is strong however, even helping him to survive spotted fever (typhus).

Zoltan wears the dirty rags he wore in prison (his battle gear hangs as trophies in Brant's tower-house). He is filthy and shaggy, a shadow of his former self. Despite the unkempt hair and his beard, one can see that his skull at the back of his head is unnaturally long, and that his chin is underdeveloped. Ordinary people could easily think that Zoltan is not quite human, and be frightened by his appearance. If questioned about this, Zoltan proudly explains that skull deformation is a common custom amongst highborn boys and girls of his race. Deformation is carried out with two bandages tightly bound around the children's skull!

Zoltan remembers that when he was five or six years old, a huge German called "Mountain Wolf" (Burgolf) came to his father's village to sell Bohemian Slavs. Zoltan's knowledge of the Dark One is worked into the plot; see "The Magyar Speaks" on pages 145.

A Band of Fierce Magyars

char.	#1	#2	#3	#4	#5	#6
STR	13	10	09	15	12	13
CON	10	18	12	12	10	06
SIZ	10	13	10	08	18	14
INT	12	11	13	08	13	13
POW	08	11	12	10	12	11
DEX	11	08	09	10	13	11
APP	08	08	14	09	05	08
HP	10	16	11	10	14	10
DB	–	–	–	–	+1D4	+1D4

Weapons: Saber 45%, damage 1D8+db
Two-handed Ax 45%, damage 2D6+db
Reflex Bow (base range 100 y.) 45%, damage 1D8

Armor: 3-point heavy felt and skin armor (as boiled leather)

Skills: Listen 55%, Natural World 40%, Navigate 40%, Sneak 40%, Track 40%.

The Magyar warriors wear the customary clothes of their race (caftans, baggy pants, and leather boots), and a lot of jewelry. Some of them have long deformed skulls and small chins. The warriors protect their chest and their heads with felt armor and animal skins. A few carry small shields and some even wear tree-bark armor. It is easy to mistake the Magyars for swamp-forest spirits or werewolves! Their principal weapons are the saber and the reflex bow made of maple wood strengthened with bone plates. The bow and the arrows are kept in a rigid quiver.

One of the Magyars is an eremitic brother from the priory of Laa. He was enslaved together with another eremite — who has disappeared since then — in 995 A.D., during a mission to convert the Magyars. Two other Magyar warriors are the sons of non-Christian slaves sold by Christians to the Hungarians long ago. Amongst the warriors there is also a Moslem of Pecheneg origin whose native language is Turkic. This mixed bunch has sworn allegiance to the rebel Magyar chieftain Koppany.

"Taltos," Age 51, Magyar Shaman

| STR 08 | CON 12 | SIZ 08 | INT 09 | POW 15 |
| DEX 10 | APP 07 | EDU 14 | SAN 75 | HP 10 |

Damage Bonus: –1D4.

Weapons: none.

Armor: none.

Skills: First Aid 65%, Insight 40%, Listen 60%, Occult 50%, Potions 35%.

Spells: Disembodiment, Heal (3 magic points heal 3 HP per investigator per week, and 6 HP with a successful Potions roll)

"Taltos" means shaman in Hungarian. Taltos is the soul of the Magyar clan, and well versed in the world of the spirits. According to his belief, the world is split into three levels: the upper world of spirits and gods, the median world of humans, and the underworld of evil spirits. These levels are spanned by the cosmic Tree of Life.

Taltos' single most important advice to the investigators is: "to vanquish the wampyr, find the door to the otherworld! Don't fear pain and death: welcome death, and you shall be saved. . . ."

Mi-go, Otherworldly Locusts

The mi-go in this scenario are associates of the Dark One. Their primary object on earth is salt (halite) min-ing under the Black Hill. They are also interested in studying the cerebral functions of humans and in collecting living human heads (with a clear preference for learned humans, especially monks). The mi-go transport the salt and the heads through their Gate, to one of their outposts outside the solar system. What they do with the living human heads remains a mystery. The mi-go have a special interest in Brother Gudman's body, which they keep alive in the Dark One's tomb to carry out macabre experiments and thus advance their knowledge of human biology.

The mi-go breed in this scenario differs somewhat from the rules book creature. First of all, they are even more extra-terrene than their distant cousins. Looking at one of them and failing the Sanity roll reveals something more than just an alien appearance: the entity is difficult to look at, because parts of its body and its movements shift in and out of our space-time. The best description of this phenomenon is that the creature vibrates, and flickers in and out of sight very rapidly. Looking at the creature for some time, one registers a remotely insect-like outline, resembling a giant locust. The vaguely egg-shaped head is always blurred, with hairs or filaments extending from it. Two rows of fuzzy shadows in the mi-go's back suggest wings fluttering at an impossible speed (though no wind can be felt).

From a few yards' distance, not only a strong smell of ozone can be noticed, but also an ill-defined noise: a kind of humming or buzzing. The mi-go's monstrous intrusion into our reality can be felt by all sentient animals from a distance of 20 yards, and manifests itself as a headache. The nearer the creature, the stronger the headache. The mi-go have a natural ability to read minds up to a distance of 20 yards.

The mi-go wear large ragged veils to protect their sensitive bodies from sunlight. They do not need eyes or vision to see anyway, though it is anybody's guess what senses they do use. They only remove the veils in the darkness of the tomb. Superficially, a veiled mi-go looks like a ghost. If the witness fails his Sanity roll however, he may glimpse a mi-go limb sticking out of the veil, or notice the abnormal bulges and vibrations of the veil, etc.

When a mi-go loses all hit points, it dies in a characteristic way: its image flickers for a few seconds, then the mi-go implodes with a sound like the cracking of a whip, splattering a few pints of residual viscous fluids all around.

BLACK LIGHT: The mi-go leader knows a "Black Light" spell that interferes with the brain processes of

most animals, including humans. For game purposes, consider the Black Light as a variant of the Old Grimoire's Blind spell. The Black Light affects all within half a mile of the caster, and costs 12 magic points. The only chance to resist the spell's effects is to move out of range. Investigators within range of the mi-go immediately lose their central vision field: whatever they look at is obliterated by pure blackness. Cut all skills (including combat skills) and movement rates by half, because of the sensory impairment. Since peripheral vision only renders a blurred image of reality, victims have trouble distinguishing who is who. Fellow investigators, as well as the Dark One in human guise, appear as vague silhouettes, and a veiled mi-go is a mere ghostly shape.

Those who flee fully recover their senses half a mile away from the mi-go.

MI-GO POISON: The mi-go leader (mi-go #1) has a long articulated tail extending into a sharp one-foot-long grayish dart. If it succeeds in grappling a victim (STR match on the Resistance table), the mi-go uses the dart to inject a paralyzing poison into the victim's spinal cord. The sting costs only 1 hit point of damage, but is very painful and causes a burning sensation. The poison upsets the nervous system of an average human for about 2 hours. Poisoned victims are paralyzed. Moreover, victims are unable to remember anything that happens in the first 8 hours after the sting.

MIST PROJECTOR: The mi-go guard #2 possesses a primitive mist projector. Unlike later versions of the mist projector, this one does not cause any cold damage. The projector is a gleaming metallic sphere, 4 inches in diameter, and punched with many small holes. Once per day, it can generate a nauseating cold mist, which slowly dissipates in about an hour. In the mist, human vision is limited to 10 yards or less. The area covered by the mist is left to the keeper's discretion. Investigators who manipulate the artifact are allowed an Idea roll or a Luck roll to release the mist.

The Dark One, Maggot of the Great Old Ones

The statistics below are incremental, to be added to the statistics of the host, (the girl Brun). (Remember that the host's INT and POW are reduced to 0.) Hit points and damage bonus must be recomputed as usual, based on (CON+SIZ)/2 and STR+SIZ.

STR +6	CON +12	SIZ +4	INT +7	POW +0
DEX +1	APP −3	HP +8		

DB as per host's modified STR and SIZ.
MOV +2

Weapons: large knife or short sword 30%, damage 1D6+db
Grapple 25%, damage 1D3 hit points per round.

Armor: none

Spells: Soul pit (Soul Singing)

Skills: Sneak 90%, Ride 75%, plus skills of the host.

Sanity Loss: 0/1D2 to see the Dark One.

The ways of the Dark One (wampyr according to the Magyars, drac for the Slavs, and zwerc to Germans) are mysterious. It came 90 years ago to the Black Hill. Is he an agent of the mi-go, or are the mi-go his servants? Impossible to say.

Generalities about the Dark Folk can be found in the Bestiary chapter on page 101. In this particular scenario, we suggest that the Dark One's true nature is as some kind of parasite of the Great Old Ones, and that it now preys on humans. It is a particularly strong and large member of its species, thus its exceptional STR and SIZ statistics. The parasite looks like a giant flatworm, twenty feet long, with one head at each extremity. ("Regular" Dark One maggots are 1–3 feet long; see page 101 and "Dark One Hell," page 155.) The creature is blind. Its mouth is a hole in the middle of the body; out of the hole it can extend a kind of long wrinkled tube — the pharynx — that can suck out a human's intestines in less than a minute.

The *modus operandi* of the parasite is as follows: it first catches a human being, penetrates the abdomen via the rectum, and digests the intestines with its pharynx. In principle the parasite does not damage the body during penetration, and there are no superficial traces of its presence. Then the parasite takes control of the dead brain and body of the host and animates the corpse into a parody of the living — a "Dark One." Gaining control of the host takes time, from a few minutes to a day at the keeper's discretion. During that period, the Dark One is clumsy and vulnerable, and therefore avoids direct confrontation.

The Dark One progressively loses its human qualities as time goes by. The body slowly rots, forcing the Dark One to find a new host within six months, usually around the calends of May and November. Before 976 A.D., the Dark One relied on the Slavic priests of the cult of Czerneboch to provide him and his mi-go associates with the required human victims. After the cult was eradicated, the Dark One bought human slaves from the German trader Burgolf. In 984 A.D., when Burgolf got nervous and the trade embargo was implemented, the Dark One and the mi-go resorted to abducting villagers or travelers.

The Dark One is psychopathic by nature, though evil seems a more appropriate adjective for the Dark Ages. The Dark One is indeed obsessed with power and control. It takes pleasure in tormenting earthly life forms, and it pursues a state of perpetual stress. Recent events (the loss of the Black Stone, the intrusion of the investigators) have made the Dark One particularly unpredictable!

Note that the Dark One does not necessarily depend on human vision to function. Therefore it can operate quite effectively in darkness, compensating with any other senses available.

To destroy the Dark One, one must first incapacitate the host, and then kill the parasite lodged inside the host's abdomen.

THE BLACK STONE: the Dark One owns a magical artifact that superficially looks like a smooth, sullen night-black stone, the size of a large egg, with seven cryptic characters carved upon its surface. The Black Stone has a pool of 120 magic points, which it can regenerate entirely every 24 hours. Only the Dark One can operate the artifact, and needs it to power the Soul Pit spell.

SOUL PIT: The Soul Pit spell is a powerful variant of the Soul Singing spell in the Old Grimoire (see page 91).

Because the Dark One has no POW or magic points of its own, it needs the Black Stone to power the spell. The main difference with Soul Singing is that the Soul Pit is a collective "nightmare" that can affect all sentient beings within earshot. The spell costs 8 magic points per target per round (with the Black Stone the Dark One can control the minds of 5 persons for 3 consecutive rounds). There are no means to resist the spell at first, though there are means to escape from the Soul Pit (see below). All spell targets are cast into the Dark One's mindscape. One possible description of the Soul Pit is provided in the finale of the scenario. We advise the keeper to only use the Soul Pit spell once during the game.

Note that nightmare time flows roughly 150 times faster than real time: 30 minutes in the Soul Pit correspond to 1 combat round in the waking world. Any hit points lost in the Soul Pit are restored upon waking. On the other hand, sanity loss and its effects are real.

The only two ways for a target of the spell to break away from the Soul Pit are: 1) to "die" in the Soul Pit (reach zero hit points), or 2) to will himself awake. In order to do the latter, the target must first explicitly state that the whole experience is "not real," and that he tries to will himself awake. The target must make a successful POW x5 roll. Only one attempt per target is allowed.

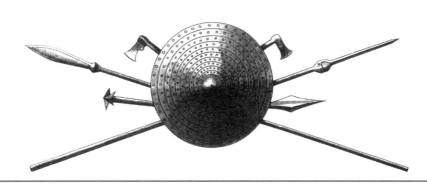

Player Handouts

In the name of the saint and indivisible trinity, brantus, lord by divine favor. let all believers of the saint church of god, present and future, know that I, with the benediction of the bishopric of regensburg, have donated to the hermits of laa some lands in my property.

given anno domini 995.

in the name of god.

feliciter. amen.

that our woods are we ll watched over; wh ere there is an area to deforest, that our foresters who live in the woods deforest it

and where woods sh ould be, that they do not permit to cut tr ees, and that they pr otect the wild beasts.

nd in

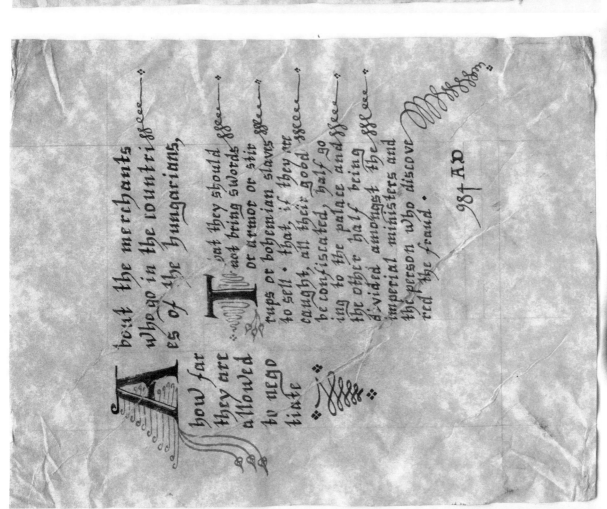

Tomb Papers 4: Index of Pagan Superstitions

Of sacrileges done to the deceased, i.e. crushing the face, driving a stake trough the heart and washing the body down with stones.

Of obscenities committed in may and november.

Of the cult of the forest and what is done upon stones.

Of ill-famed places that are honored as being sacred.

Of the belief in the living dead who come back to harm unbelievers, called upir.

Of the belief in wood women who can possess the heart of men, etc.

Tomb Papers 3: Trade Embargo Capitulary

About the merchants who go in the countriss...es of the Hungarians, how far they are allowed to negotiate

That they should not bring swords or armor or stirrups or bohemian slaves to sell. that, if they are caught, all their good be confiscated, half going to the palace and the other half being divided amongst the imperial ministers and the person who discovered the fraud.

987 AD

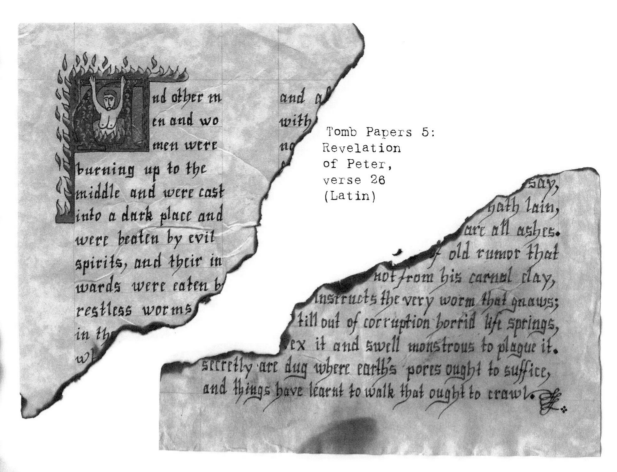

nd other m
en and wo
men were
burning up to the
middle and were cast
into a dark place and
were beaten by evil
spirits, and their in
wards were eaten b
restless worms

and a
with
no

say,
hath lain,
are all ashes.
f old rumor that
not from his carnal clay,
instructs the very worm that gnaws;
till out of corruption horrid life springs,
ex it and swell monstrous to plague it.
secretly are dug where earth's pores ought to suffice,
and things have learnt to walk that ought to crawl.

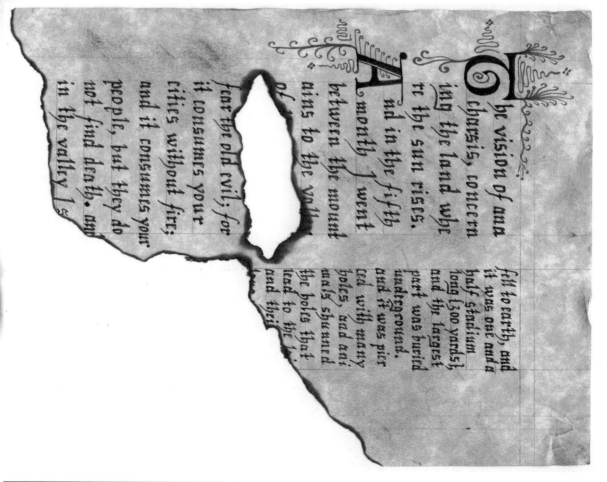

he vision of ana
charsis, concern
ing the land whe
re the sun rises.
nd in the fifth
month I went
between the mount
ains to the vall
of t

fell to earth, and
it was one and a
half stadium
long (300 yards),
and the largest
part was buried
underground,
and it was pier
ced with many
holes, and ani
mals shunned
the holes that
lead to the
and their

fear the old evil; for
it consumes your
cities without fire;
and it consumes your
people, but they do
not find death. and
in the valley is

CTHULHU DARK AGES

In constantinople I met with the men from the north · normanni · who call themselves rus. although they belong to the eastern church, their manners are very uncivilized. the normanni acted with defiance and ostentation, recounting all kinds of pagan stories in an attempt to up set me.

De facto, I was quite interested by their versi on of the genesis, in particular by the part played by the so-called bent folk. it is unclear to me whether they considered these beings to have human form, because the normanni kept on calling them maggots. indeed, the bent folk su pposedly originate in the corpses of dead gods or giants. · theodorus did not fully understand the word used. · this in turn reminded me of the book of enoch, which mentions evil spirits proceeding from the bodies of were these the same beings th

Tomb Papers 7: written by Brother Christian (Latin)

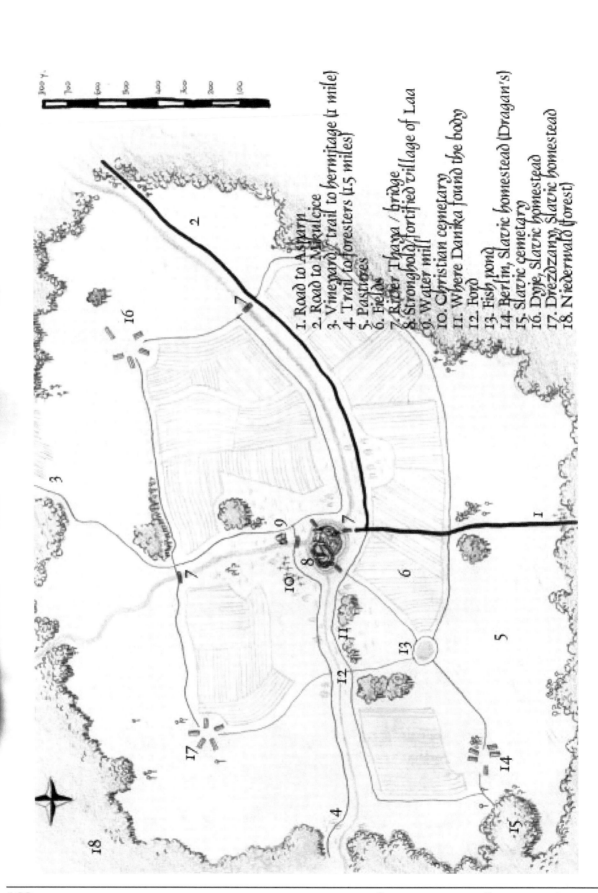

1. Road to Asparn
2. Road to Mikulcice
3. Vineyard / trail to hermitage (1 mile)
4. Trail to foresters (1.5 miles)
5. Pastures
6. Fields
7. River Thaya / bridge
8. Stronghold/fortified village of Laa
9. Water mill
10. Christian cemetary
11. Where Danika found the body
12. Ford
13. Fish pond
14. Berlin, Slavic homestead
15. Slavic cemetary
16. Doje, Slavic homestead
17. Drezdzany, Slavic homestead (Dragan's)
18. Niederwald (forest)

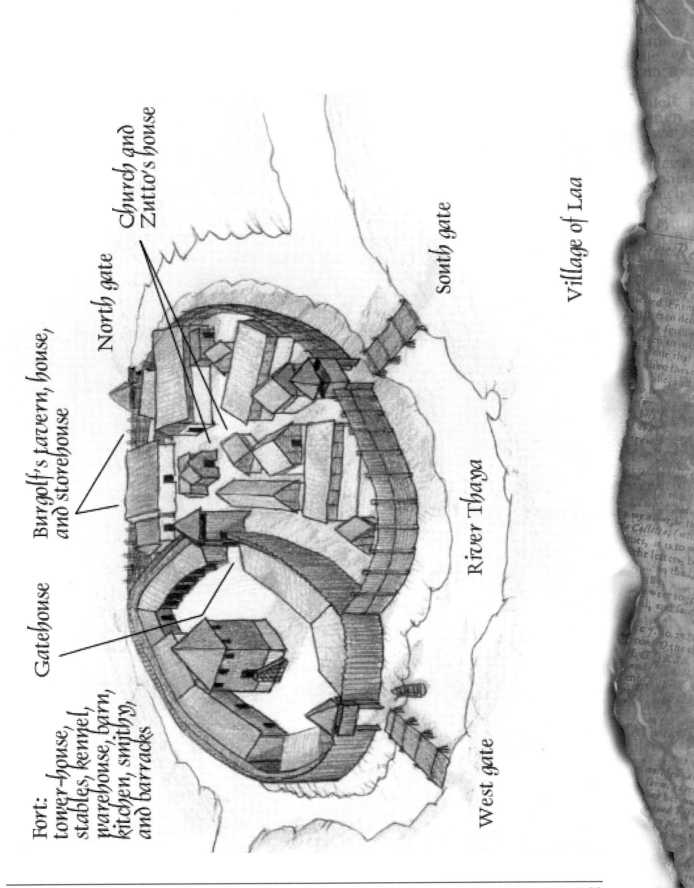

Fort:
tower-house,
stables, kennel,
warehouse, barn,
kitchen, smithy,
and barracks

Gatehouse

Burgolf's tavern, house,
and storehouse

North gate

Church and
Zutto's house

South gate

River Thaya

West gate

Village of Laa

Dark Ages

Investigator Name _____
Birthplace _____
Language _____
Lord/Order _____
Afflictions _____
Sex _____ **Age** _____

Characteristics & Rolls

STR ____	DEX ____	INT ____	Idea ____
CON ____	APP ____	POW ____	Luck ____
SIZ ____	SAN ____	EDU ____	Know ____

99-Cthulhu Mythos ____   Damage Bonus ____

Sanity Points

Insane 0	1	2	3	4	5	6	7	8	9	10	11	12	13	14
15	16	17	18	19	20	21	22	23	24	25	26	27	28	29	30	31
32	33	34	35	36	37	38	39	40	41	42	43	44	45	46	47	48
49	50	51	52	53	54	55	56	57	58	59	60	61	62	63	64	65
66	67	68	69	70	71	72	73	74	75	76	77	78	79	80	81	82
83	84	85	86	87	88	89	90	91	92	93	94	95	96	97	98	99

Magic Points

Unconscious 0	1	2	3
4	5	6	7	8	9	10	11
12	13	14	15	16	17	18	19
20	21	22	23	24	25	26	27
28	29	30	31	32	33	34	35
36	37	38	39	40	41	42	43

Hit Points

Dead	-2	-1	0	1	2	3
4	5	6	7	8	9	10	11
12	13	14	15	16	17	18	19
20	21	22	23	24	25	26	27
28	29	30	31	32	33	34	35
36	37	38	39	40	41	42	43

CTHULHU DARK AGES

Investigator Skills

☐ Accounting (10%) _____
  Art (05%):
☐ _____ _____
☐ _____ _____
☐ _____ _____
☐ Bargain (05%) _____
☐ Climb (DEX+STR%) _____
☐ Conceal (15%) _____
  Craft (05%):
☐ _____ _____
☐ _____ _____
☐ _____ _____
  Cthulhu Mythos (00) _____
☐ Dodge (DEX x2) _____
☐ Drive Horses (20%) _____
☐ Fast Talk (05%) _____
☐ First Aid (30%) _____
☐ Hide (10%) _____
☐ Insight (05%) _____
☐ Jump (25%) _____
☐ Library Use (25%) _____

☐ Listen (25%) _____
☐ Medicine (05%) _____
☐ Natural World (10%) _____
☐ Navigate (10%) _____
☐ Occult (05%) _____
☐ Other Kingdoms (01%) _____
  Other Language (01%):
☐ _____ _____
☐ _____ _____
☐ _____ _____
☐ Own Kingdom (20%) _____
  Own Language (EDUx5%):
☐ _____ _____
☐ Persuade (15%) _____
☐ Pilot Boat (01%) _____
☐ Potions (01%) _____
☐ Repair/Devise (20%) _____
☐ Ride Horse (05%) _____
  Science (01%):
☐ _____ _____
☐ _____ _____

☐ Sneak (10%) _____
☐ Spot Hidden (25%) _____
☐ Status (15%) _____
☐ Swim (25%) _____
☐ Throw (25%) _____
☐ Track (10%) _____
  Write Language (01%):
☐ _____ _____
☐ _____ _____
  Other Skills
☐ _____ _____
☐ _____ _____

Weapons

	melee	%	damage	hand	range	#att	hp
☐	Fist (50%)	____	1D3+db	1	touch	1	n/a
☐	Grapple (25%)	____	special	2	touch	1	n/a
☐	Head (10%)	____	1D4+db	0	touch	1	n/a
☐	Kick (25%)	____	1D6+db	0	touch	1	n/a
☐	_____	____	_____	__	_____	__	___
☐	_____	____	_____	__	_____	__	___
☐	_____	____	_____	__	_____	__	___
☐	_____	____	_____	__	_____	__	___
☐	_____	____	_____	__	_____	__	___

	missile	%	damage	range	#att	shots	hp
☐	_____	____	_____	_____	___	____	___
☐	_____	____	_____	_____	___	____	___
☐	_____	____	_____	_____	___	____	___
☐	_____	____	_____	_____	___	____	___
☐	_____	____	_____	_____	___	____	___
☐	_____	____	_____	_____	___	____	___
☐	_____	____	_____	_____	___	____	___
☐	_____	____	_____	_____	___	____	___

Player Name: _____

Personal Data

Investigator Name _____

Residence _____

Personal Description _____

_____

Family & Friends _____

_____

_____

_____

Episodes of Insanity

_____

Wounds & Injuries _____

_____

Marks & Scars _____

_____

Investigator History

_____

_____

_____

_____

_____

_____

_____

_____

_____

_____

_____

_____

_____

_____

Income & Savings

Income _____

Deniers on Hand _____

Savings (where) _____

Inheritable Property _____

_____

_____

Favors Owed _____

_____

Adventuring Gear & Possessions

_____ _____ _____

_____ _____ _____

_____ _____ _____

_____ _____ _____

_____ _____ _____

_____ _____ _____

_____ _____ _____

_____ _____ _____

_____ _____ _____

_____ _____ _____

Mythos Tomes Read

_____ _____

_____ _____

_____ _____

_____ _____

Investigator History

_____ _____

_____ _____

_____ _____

_____ _____

_____ _____

_____ _____

_____ _____

Magical Artifacts/Spells Known

Artifacts _____ Spells _____

_____ _____

_____ _____

_____ _____

_____ _____

Index

(to all excepting the scenario "The Tomb")

90% skills 34
accounting skill 23
acid .36
actions 32
adventure 15
age & aging 18
Al-Azif
(see also *Necronomicon*) 93
Ancient Ones 119
angels 97
animals 98
APP (appearance) 11
Arab World 61
armor 40, 45
artifacts 81
art skill 23
Attraction roll 11
Augur spell 82
automatic actions 32
Baghdad 62
bargain skill 23
base chance 14
basilisks 98
Beatus Methodivo 96
Become Spectral spell 82
big targets 47
Bind Soul spell 82
birthplace & language 18
Black Rites 93
Black Tome 94
Bless Blade spell 83
Bless (Characteristic) spell 83
Bless (Skill Class) spell 83
Blindness spell 83
blunt weapons 43
boats .51
Body Warping spell 83
books of the mythos 93
Bugg-Shash 120
Burgundy 63
Byzantium 62
Cabala of Saboth 94
calendar 56
Cast Out the Devil spell 83
castle .59
cathedral cities 60
Canon Episcopi 96
characteristics 11, 12
Charisma roll 11
chases & fatigue 29
check 14, 34
cities .59

climb skill 24
Cloud Memory spell 83
clubs and blunt weapons 43
combat 39
combat round 14, 39
Compel (Creature) spell 84
CON (constitution) 11
conceal skill 24
concealment, partial 41
*Confessions of the
Mad Monk Clithanus* 94
Contact (Creature) spell 84
Constantinople 62
Cordoba 62
costs, equipment,
& services table 52
craft skill 24
Create Limbo Gate spell 84
Create Mystic Portal spell 85
Cthaat Aquadingen 94
Cthulhu 14, 75
Cthulhu Mythos 14
cthulhu mythos skill 24
Curse (Characteristic) spell . . .85
Curse (Skill Class) spell 85
D100 rolls 32
Daemonolorum 94
Dagon 97
damage 14, 35
damage bonus 14, 16
damage bonus table 16
dark ones 101, 162
darkness 41
Deafness spell 85
death (of investigators) 38
    back from 39
Death's Breath spell 85
deep ones 102
Demon Hearing spell 86
Demon Sight spell 86
deniers 19
DEX (dexterity) 11
    order of attack 43
Dexterity roll 11
dice, types and rolling 9–10
    D100 rolls 32
    resistance table 34
digging/quarrying table 31
dimensional shamblers 103
disease 37
    disease table 38
Disembodiment spell 86

Dismiss Spirit spell 86
distances & movement table . . .29
dodge skill 24, 40
doels 116
dragons 103
drive horses/oxen skill 24
drowning & suffocation 36
EDU (education) 11
elder gods 74
encounter tables 99
England 63
Enthrall spell 86
Exaltation spell 87
exorcists 55
experience check 14, 34
explosion 36
exposure table 30
extended range 47
fainting 14
falling .36
farmers 19, 57
    costume 58
    diet 58
fast talk skill 24
fatigue 29
Fear spell 87
Find (Substance) spell 87
fire and light 30, 36
first aid 14, 24, 39
fist/punch skill 24
Flesh Ward spell 87
France 60, 63
Frankish weapons 44
fumble 14
Fury spell 87
game time 31
German Empire 62
ghouls 104
giants 105
glossary 66–68
goblins 105
God 73
goroda 60
grapple skill 25
Gray Binding spell 88
great old ones 75
group ritual 81
gugs .106
hand-to-hand 14, 39, 43
halflings 105
head butt skill 25
Heal spell 88

healing 14, 39, 88
heresies 55
hermits 55
hide skill 25
Hierón Aigypton 94
hit points 14, 16, 34, 39
    hit point loss table 39
    hit point, what is? 39
horror 14
hounds of Tindalos 107
Hundred Years and More . .69–71
Idea roll 12
independent races 76
impale 14, 40
insanity 49
    cthulhu mythos skill 49
    indefinite 14, 50
    mythos causes 48
    permanent 14, 50
    playing insanity 50
    quality of insanity 51
    results (table) 48
    temporary 14, 49
insight skill 25
INT (intelligence) 12
investigator 17
    names 17–18
    sex 18
investigator creation summary
(table) 17
invisibility 41
Italy 63
jump skill 25
keeper 14
keeper's dilemma 77
kick skill 25
Kiev .64
kings & emperors (list) 73
Kitab al-Kimya 96
knives 43
knock-out attack 41
Know roll 12
languages 19, 54
Leviathan 105
Levitate spell 88
Liber Ivonis 94
library use skill 25
Lilith 121
Limbo 91–93
listen skill 25
Loki .105
Lovecraft, H. P. 2, 74

CTHULHU DARK AGES

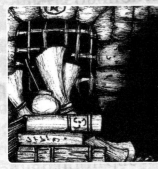

Index

(to all excepting the scenario "The Tomb")

Luck roll 12
magi 77, 78
magic 19, 77-91
magic points 12, 14, 93
magical artifacts 81
man-made obstacles table . . .31
medicine skill 14, 26, 39
mi-go 108
missile weapons 45, 46
money & equipment 19, 53
monks 21, 55, 73
  costume 56
  meals 57
Moonlight spell 88
motte-and-bailey 57
movement 29
  handling movement 29
  chases & fatigue 29
  table 29
names 17-18
Nameless Mist 109
Natural Disasters
& Occult Events 71-72
natural healing 39
natural obstacles 31
natural world skill 26
navigate skill 26
Necronomicon 94-95
nobles 58
Nyhargo Dirge spell 89
occult skill 26, 78
occupations 15, 18-22
  beggar 19
  cleric 19
  craftsman/shopkeeper 19
  farmer 19
  guard 19
  healer 20
  hermit/heretic 20, 55
  household officer 20
  juggler/minstrel 20
  mercenary/brigand 20
  merchant 20
  monk/nun 21
  pilgrim 21, 55
  priest 21
  sailor 21
  scholar 21
  sergeant/mayor 22
  small trader 22
  warrior 22
  woodsman/fisherman . . .22

Old Ones 116, 117-118
order of attack 43
other kingdoms skill 26
other langauge skill 26
other gods 74
outer gods 74
own kingdom skill 26
own language skill 26
Pact of Quachil Uttaus spell . . .89
Papal States 63
parry 15, 40-41
percentage 15
percentile 15
personal attack 15, 43
personal interest 15
persuade skill 27
physical injury 34ff
pilgrims 55
pilot boat skill 27
players 15
Pnakotica 95
point-blank fire 47
poison 35, 37
  poison table 35
Poison Blood spell 89
potions skill 27
POW (power) 12
Power Drain spell 89
Power Source spell 89
Praesidia Finium 95
Prague 64
precision aim 47
prince 58
  portrait 59
  palace 59
  castle 59
ranks, social 54
Rasul al-Albarin 95
Reflections 95
religion 54
  conversions 55
  heresies 55
repair/devise skill 27
resistance table 15
  Resistance Table 33
resistance table rolls 34
*Return Follower of
Mad Cthulhu* spell 89
ride horse skill 27
ritual magic 81
Rome 63
round 14, 39

Russia 64
Sapienta Maglorum 95
SAN (sanity) 12, 15, 16
  maximum 16
  points 15
  roll 15
  sanity point costs table 49
  using 49
sanity & insanity 47
  temp. insanity table 48
Satan 108-109
Scandinavia 64
scenario 15
science skill 27
Scrying Window spell 89
Seal of Nephren-Ka spell 90
serpent people 109
servitor races 76
Shield spell 90
shields 45
shock 38
shoggoths 110
Shrivelling spell 90
Sibylline Books 96
sixth sense 91
SIZ (size) 16
skill classes 22
  communication 22
  manipulation 23
  perception 23
  physical movement 23
  thought 23
skills 15, 22-28
  90% 34
  base chance (table) 23
  definitions 23-28
  time 32
skill check 14, 34
skill roll 15
Slavonic states 64
sneak skill 27
social pyramid 56
solitary ritual 81
Song of Yste 95
sorcerers 79
Soul Singing spell 91
Spain 64
spells 78-91
  casting spells 79
  descriptions 79
  learning 78
spirits 114-115

spirit attacks & possession . . .92
spot hidden skill 27
spot rule 15, 36-37, 40-42
star-spawn of cthulhu 111
status skill 28
stun .35
STR (strength) 16
success 15
suffocation 36
surprise attack 41
swim skill 28
swords and scimitars 46
Tabula Smaragdina 96
Tawil at'Umr 122-123
technology 60-61
Testament of Carnamagos 95
The Three Codices 95
throw skill 28
thrown object 42
time 31-32, 53
  game time 31
  skill time 32
tomb-herd 118-119
track skill 28
trade 59
travel 31
Tupsimati 95-96
Tuscan Rituals 96
two weapons 42
ultimate abyss 92
unconscious 15, 38
unicorns 100
Venice 63
vampires 100-101
war engines 46
warlords 58
  portrait 58
  diet 58
weapons tables 44-45
weapon length 42
werewolves 112
wilderness survival 29-30
Winds of Desolation spell 91
world, the 53
world map 65
worms of the earth 112-114
write language 28

"All Rumors Are True!"

Chaosium Gazette

2004 EDITION, VOL. 1

RECOMMENDED TITLES
CALL OF CTHULHU

H. P. Lovecraft's Arkham
#8803 $28.95   ISBN 1-56882-165-4

"Behind everything crouched the brooding, festering horror of the ancient town . . . the changeless, legend-haunted city of Arkham, with its clustering gambrel roofs that sway and sag over attics where witches hid from the King's men in the dark, olden days of the Province.

It was always a very bad time in Arkham . . . ."

—H. P. Lovecraft

Arkham is a small town along the Massachusetts coast-the setting favored by author Howard Phillips Lovecraft in his tales of monstrous horror. All in all a quiet place, Arkham is best-known as the home of Miskatonic University, an excellent school becoming known for its esoteric and disturbing volumes residing in its library's Restricted Collection. These tomes form the foundation of all current efforts to thwart the dire desires of the Mythos legion.

H. P. Lovecraft's Arkham contains extensive background information about this haunted New England town-written to be used by serious investigators as a base from which to further explore the mysteries of the Cthulhu Mythos. Pertinent buildings, useful people, and important locations are described in depth. A 17x22" players' map of Arkham is bound into the back, and four thrilling adventures complete the package.

Includes the H.P. Lovecraft short story "The Dreams in the Witchhouse" (1933).

H. P. Lovecraft's Dunwich
#8802 $25.95   ISBN 1-56882-164-6

Dunwich is a small village located along the Miskatonic, upriver from Arkham. Until 1806, Dunwich was a thriving community, boasting many mills and the powerful Whateley family.

Those among the Whateleys came to know dark secrets about the world, and they fell into the worship of unwholesome creatures from other times and places. Retreating to the hills and forests surrounding the town, they betrayed their uncorrupted kin.

Prosperity fled, and a dark despair seized the people. What remains is a skeleton town, mills closed, its citizens without hope or future. However, secrets of the Mythos survive, to be discovered by brave and enterprising investigators.

H.P. Lovecraft's Dunwich begins with "The Dunwich Horror," Lovecraft's masterful tale of life in the town and its surrounds. It expands upon the story with extensive

information about the town: pertinent buildings, useful people, and important locations are described in detail. A 17x22" map depicts the area for miles around, and two scenarios are included. All statistics and gameplay notes for d20 Cthulhu are also provided.

H. P. Lovecraft's Kingsport
#8804 $25.95   ISBN 1-56882-167-0

"In the morning, mist comes up from the sea by the cliffs beyond Kingsport. White and feathery it comes from the deep to its brothers the clouds, full of dreams of dank pastures and caves of leviathan. And later, in the still summer rains on the steep roofs of poets, the clouds scatter bits of those dreams, that men shall not live without rumor of old strange secrets, and wonders that planets tell planets alone in the night."

— H. P. Lovecraft

Kingsport is a coastal town located a morning's stroll from Arkham. Draped in mists and fog, it is home to artists and fishermen, sailors and dreamers. Here dreams and reality mingle to an unsettling degree.

Some find solace in such dreams; others find only terror and death. Charles Baxter's dreams drove him to despair. He took his own life, throwing himself into the sea. The only clues to his demise: a water-soaked collection of poems.

Horrors exist in the real world of Kingsport as well, remnants of an ancient witch-cult that once infested the town. Unspeakable things crawl through their burrows beneath Central Hill and lurk in the fog off Jersey Reef, preying on fishermen and unsuspecting tourists alike.

Kingsport's soothing atmosphere and beautiful setting beckons to vacationers. Its perch on the brink of the dream-world inspires artists. Investigators come to Kingsport to find understanding of the dark realms of the Cthulhu Mythos.

H. P. Lovecraft's Kingsport describes this fabled Massachusetts town in meticulous detail-its important personalities, buildings, history, and its weird people and places. This book also features a foldout players' map of the town, a tourist brochure describing places of interest, and three adventures with player aids for added realism and enjoyment.

Includes the H.P. Lovecraft short story "The Strange High House In The Mist" (1931) and "The Festival"

Keeper's Companion II
#2395 $23.95   ISBN 1-56882-186-7

A CORE BOOK FOR KEEPERS, VOL. 2—New to Call of Cthulhu? A battle-scarred veteran of many campaigns? Here are essential background articles useful to most keepers.

"The History Behind Prohibition" - A lengthy article bringing anti-alcohol advocates, law enforcement, gangsters, rum-runners, and consumers into focus. Lots of good stories.

"The Keeper's Master List of Call of Cthulhu Scenarios" - Lists are alphabetical by the following topics: scenario era; creature / maniacs / great old ones; legendary heroes and villains; cults / sects / secret societies; Mythos tomes; fictitious locations; and Mythos books from publishers other than Chaosium.

"Iron: a Survey of Civilian Small Arms Used in the 1890's, 1920's, and the Present". Practicalities of firearms; common malfunctions; new skills Handloading and Gunsmithing. Firearms considered are likely to be encountered or thought specially useful by investigators. Insightful discussions of nine specific rifles, five shotguns, ten handguns, a sniper rifle, and the Thompson submachine gun. Hot load damage values for most weapons, along with comparative ratings for noise, maintenance, powder, reloading per round, more, plus standard stats.

"Medical Examiner's Report" discusses the unusual corpse recovered by the Essex County Sheriff's Department, as does "Dr. Lippincot's Diary" from another point of view. Also a short article on deep one / human reproduction.

Brian Sammon's "Mythos Collector" submits write-ups for the *Book of Iod, Chronike von Nath, Confessions of the Mad Monk Clinthanus, Letters of Nestar, The Nyhargo Codex, Soul of Chaos, Testament of Carnamago, The Tunneler Below, Visions From Yaddith, Von denen Verdammten,* as well as for more than a dozen new spells.

And More: "Mythos ex Machina" gathers about forty examples of alien technology from Cthulhu supplements. Gordon Olmstead-Dean outlines the odd connections between H. P. Lovecraft and the Satanists HPL never knew, in "LaVey, Satanism, and the Big Squid". Indexed.

COMING SOON FOR
CALL OF CTHULHU

Shadows of Yog-Sothoth
#2397 $23.95   ISBN 1-56882-174-3

The Silver Twilight is a secretive, international order dedicated to the destruction of the human race. As brave investigators, you must piece together passages from esoteric books, shards of strange artifacts and puzzling letters to discover the Silver Twilight's loathsome goals.

Shadows of Yog-Sothoth is a modestly-sized campaign of seven scenarios. During the course of play the investigators penetrate the outer layers of a secret sinister occult organization led by the lords of the Silver Twilight. Beginning in Boston they investigate an organization in New York, run afoul of a coven in Scotland, roam the desert of the American southwest, vacation off the coast of Maine, and explore the mysteries of the South Pacific.

In addition to the campaign, this book includes two bonus scenarios. *The People of the Monolith* introduces the mysteries of the Cthulhu Mythos, and no harm

can come to the investigators except through insanity. As such, is perfect for introducing new players to the wonders of *Call of Cthulhu*.

The other bonus scenario, *The Warren*, presents and unsettling challenge for even experienced players.

Originally published in 1982, this new edition includes modified episode scene changes, player-handouts guide for the keeper, and new illustrations and diagrams. It is 160 pages, perfect-bound, illustrated with an index.

H.P. Lovecraft's Dreamlands
#2394 $34.95   ISBN 1-56882-157-3

We all dream. For some, dreams can become reality. H.P. Lovecraft's Dreamlands provides everything needed for Call of Cthulhu investigators to travel down the seven hundred steps, through the Gates of Deeper Slumber, and into the realm of dreams. Includes a travelogue of the dreamlands, a huge gazetteer, dreamlands character creation rules, over thirty prominent NPC's, over 60 monsters who dwell within the dreamlands, descriptions of the dreamlands gods and their cults, six adventures to help jump start a dreamlands campaign, and a new full-color fold out map of the Dreamlands by Andy Hopp. 256 pages; Hardcover.

H. P. Lovecraft's Miskatonic University™
#2389 $39.95   ISBN 1-56882-140-9

A 1920's HARDBACK GUIDE—A sourcebook detailing the campus, courses, students and personnel of one of the world's most prestigious institutions of deeper learning. Filled with data on various University departments and professors, this book weaves the details drawn from Lovecraft's Mythos tales with the Call of Cthulhu game background to create an indispensible sourcebook.

Secrets of San Francisco
#2378 $16.95   ISBN 1-56882-136-0

For some, San Francisco is the Paris of the West, where immigrants and outcasts reinvent themselves to make a cosmopolitan haven for refugees of every nation—and all their gods. For others, it is the golden gateway to the inscrutable Orient, and the unwitting heir to many of its darkest mysteries. For those who know where to look, The City is a house of doorways, leading to secrets beneath the Earth and sea, and outside time and space.

This book will give you all the background essential for a 1920's Bay Area campaign, including history, maps, research venues, scenario hooks, and the outlandish urban legends that make San Francisco unique among all the cities of the world.

Secrets of Japan
#2392 $36.95   ISBN 1-56882-156-5

MODERN-DAY EXPLORATION OF THE LAND OF THE RISING SUN—As we start the twenty-first century few corners of the world remain unexplored and unilluminated by the lamp of reason in this scientific age. The fewer places there are to hide, the more bewildering and shocking the experience when we suddenly face cosmic terror.

In this meticulously-researched sourcebook you will find a comprehensive portrayal of the culture, history, and people of Japan presented in a Lovecraftian setting. SECRETS FOF JAPAN presents a new world of possibilities for keepers and investigators wishing to take their adventures East.

Encyclopedia Cthulhiana
#6022 $17.95   ISBN 1-56882-119-0

The Cthulhu Mythos was created by H.P. Lovecraft (1890-1937), a Providence author considered by many to be the finest American horror story writer of the twentieth century. Lovecraft's tales are a blend of fantasy, science fiction, and horror, with the latter being especially prominent. His tales describe a pantheon of powerful beings known as the Great Old Ones.

Since Lovecraft's time the Cthulhu Mythos has grown exponentially, until it has become increasingly difficult to keep track of, even for devoted fans. Many writers have contributed to it, including Robert E. Howard, Robert Bloch, Brian Lumley, and Stephen King. This book is the first major attempt in many years to provide a comprehensive guide to H.P. Lovecraft's Cthulhu Mythos.

This second edition of *Encyclopedia Cthulhiana* has been extensively revised and contains over a hundred and fifty additional pages and scores of new entries. New features include thumbnail illustrations of the most important signs and symbols and a timeline of the Cthulhu Mythos spanning billions of years. Many entries have been revised to reflect our latest understanding of the Mythos, and the infamous *Necronomicon* appendix has been greatly expanded. Also present for the first time is "A Brief History of the Cthulhu Mythos", which examines the evolution of the genre from the 1920's to today.

Disciples of Cthulhu II
#6033 $13.95   ISBN 1-56882-143-3

Bad things tend happen to people who go where they are not wanted, or who over-stay their welcome once they reach their destination. This book contains thirteen new personal explorations of the Cthulhu Mythos. As its title suggests, this is a companion volume to Edward P. Berglund's earlier classic Mythos collection, *The Disciples of Cthulhu*. Both books are published by Chaosium, but their contents are entirely different. All of the stories in Cthulhu II are original and have never been published before. All the stories record the dire fates of people whose destinies intertwine with the Mythos.

The Necronomicon
#6034 $19.95   ISBN 1-56882-162-X

EXPANDED AND CORRECTED—Although skeptics claim that the *Necronomicon* is a fantastic tome created by H. P. Lovecraft, true seekers into the esoteric mysteries of the world know the truth: the *Necronomicon* is the blasphemous tome of forbidden knowledge written by the mad Arab, Abdul Alhazred. Even today, after attempts over the centuries to destroy any and all copies in any language, some few copies still exist, secreted away.

Within this book you will find stories about the *Necronomicon*, different versions of the *Necronomicon*, and two essays on this blasphemous tome. Nearly 600 pages.

The Book of Eibon
#6026 $17.95   ISBN 1-56882-129-8

Tales of lore tell of the *Book of Eibon*, a tome so ancient that it was originally written in the Hyperborean language of Tsath-Yo, long before Atlantis was born from the sea. It goes by dozens of names and predates even the *Necronomicon* and *Unaussprechlichen Kulten*. Now, Chaosium reveals the true secrets of the *Book of Eibon* for the first time.

The contents of the *Book of Eibon* are primarily the work of Clark Ashton Smith, one of the most famous authors of *Weird Tales* and the inventor of the *Book of Eibon*, as well as Lin Carter, esteemed fantasy and horror editor Robert Price, Richard Tierney, Joseph Pulver, and a number of other authors have helped complete the text, resulting in a tome that reveals all the secrets of the Cthulhu Mythos, from the history of the first alien races to come to Earth, to the histories of the Elder Magi of Hyperborea, and the story of Eibon's life and death.

The White People & Other Tales
#6035 $14.95   ISBN 1-56882-147-6

THE BEST WEIRD TALES OF ARTHUR MACHEN, VOL 2.—Born in Wales in 1863, Machen was a London journalist for much of his life. Among his fiction, he may be best known for the allusive, haunting title story of this book, "The White People", which H. P. Lovecraft thought to be the second greatest horror story ever written (after Blackwood's "The Willows"). This wide ranging collection also includes the crystalline novelette "A Fragment of Life", the "Angel of Mons" (a story so coolly reported that it was imagined true by millions in the grim initial days of the Great War), and "The Great Return", telling of the stately visions which graced the Welsh village of Llantristant for a time. Four more tales and the poetical "Ornaments in Jade" are all finely told. This is the second of three Machen volumes edited by S. T. Joshi and published by Chaosium; the first volume is *The Three Impostors*. 312 pages.

WWW.CHAOSIUM.COM